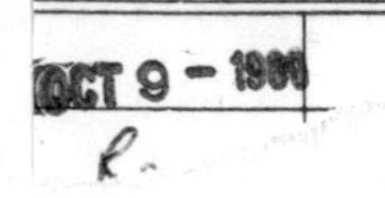

ROBESON: LABOR'S FORGOTTEN CHAMPION

CHARLES H. WRIGHT
Founder and Chairman of the Board of Trustees, The Afro-American Museum of Detroit, Michigan

Balamp Publishing

Library of Congress Cataloging in Publication Data

Wright, Charles H. 1918–
Robeson, labor's forgotten champion.
Bibliography: p. 153
Includes index.
1. Robeson, Paul, 1898– 2. Labor and laboring classes – History. 3. Race discrimination. I. Title.
HD8073.R57W74 331.88'092'4 [B] 74-79061
ISBN 0-913642-06-1

Library of Congress Catalog Card Number: 74-79061.

ISBN: 0-913642-06-1
Printed in the United States of America.
10 9 8 7 6 5 4 3 2 1

BALAMP PUBLISHING
7430 Second Boulevard
Detroit, Mich. 48202

CONTENTS

(Photo of portrait taken by Richard Jaynes, M.D.)

This book is dedicated to
FREEDOM
that essential quality of
life for which real men
are willing to fight,
unto death.

The painting of Robeson on the opposite page is by *Leroy Foster* of Detroit, and it hangs in Detroit's Afro-American Museum. Photo of the author on dust jacket is by *J. Edward Bailey* of Detroit.

PREFACE

This book is not offered as a biography of Robeson or as a history of the labor movement. Its purpose is to hold up to public view some aspects of Robeson's career as a labor activist, a subject about which very little has been written.

Any effort to overcome years of deliberate historical neglect is frought with great difficulty. Such has been the case in trying to reconstruct Robeson's role in the trade union movement. Leads that began as rumors had to be checked through records that were frequently inadequate, unavailable, or destroyed. Lips sealed by soaring fears of past intimidations added to the problems of getting at the facts. With only a few exceptions, however, help came when it was needed; and the story continued to unravel.

A suggestion for chronological order could not be honored. Robeson's complicated and prolonged labor involvements do not lend themselves to such treatment. One of his earliest American labor affiliations (ILWU, 1942) was also his last (1958). Some readers felt that the introductory parts of some chapters were too long. For example, the chapters on the Spanish Civil War, the Welsh Miners, and the United Automobile Workers. In each instance, extenuating circumstances appeared to justify the additional information. The Spanish Civil War, for instance, was Robeson's second direct confrontation with Fascism. The scars from this encounter would show for many years. In order to appreciate the value of Robeson's invitation to the Welsh's Eisteddfod, one must know something of the historical background of that event.

The one aspect of this effort that caused greatest concern is what various readers referred to as its "political overtones." This is both understandable and unavoidable. Robeson was a political animal who struggled to change this Republic so that black men could survive in it as first-class citizens. He hoped that organized labor would be an instrument for such change. While the disquiet of some readers has been great, it is small when compared to the fears of the guardians of status quo when Robeson was storming their bastions.

I am grateful to many individuals for assisting me in the unraveling of the facts as they are presented herein.

A report on the British sources has already been given. They provided valuable help in the construction of the chapters on Wales, Manchester, Scotland, and India. National Maritime officials, along with the editorial staff of the *Pilot,* gave freely of information concerning their union. Such was the case, also, with the International Longshoremen's and Warehousemen's Union, the staff of the "Dispatcher," and the union librarian. Harvey Murphy opened files of the Mine, Mill and Smelter Workers' Union. His advice and assistance have been consistent and priceless.

Thomas Coleman brought a bag full of newspaper clippings and sat for hours of taping to support his charges of mistreatment by the city of Detroit. Additional corroborative data came from Ernest Goodman, George Crockett, and Mel Ravitz.

Winston-Salem's tobacco workers almost suffered in silence. Thanks to Dr. William Bruce, Velma Hopkins, and Marilyn Robbins of Winston-Salem's *Journal and Sentinel,* some of the facts emerged. A later chat with Winston Salem's Mayor Franklin R. Shirley provided an interesting updating of the tobacco story.

Although not the longest, the most difficult chapter to write was that on the United Public Workers. It hung in the balance until a trip to Harvard University enabled me to examine the files of Ewart Guinier. Personal communications from Abram Flaxer expanded Robeson's role in their union. Testimony and data from Panama were provided by Jilma Urban and Griselda Bethanourt.

A rich source of information, especially about the Automobile Workers, is the Labor Archives of Detroit's Wayne State University. Roberta McBride and her staff were unstinting in their support of this project. Additional contributors to the UAW segment were Sheldon Tappes, Christopher Alston, Ed Lock, and Percy Llewellyn. The richest vein of all was the Detroit Public Library. When Helen Sisson heard of the project, she volunteered to help and help she did, well beyond the call of duty. Equally productive was the library staff in the General Information section, especially Marjorie Leftwich.

In a variety of ways, many other people helped to produce this product. Julia Cunningham comes to mind first. She read my first product with a critical eye and handed it back with an exasperating regularity, scarred with three red words – Revise! Revise! Revise! Verona Morton spent hours indexing names and subject titles. Richard Jaynes assumed the photographic responsibility without persuasion or pay. It is not possible to recall all of those who have played supportive roles in this literary production. Representatives of a larger group are Katherine Atkins; Carol Brooks; Joseph and Minnie Carter; Vikky Carter; Yvonne Green; Joe, Mavis and Maxine Johnson; Anita Smoot (who refined the title); and Bedia Thomas. This is but a partial list of the willing hands and minds that helped to make it possible.

Lastly, permission was requested and received to quote from newspapers, books, and other sources, and I thank each source for granting me this privilege.

Charles H. Wright
Detroit, Michigan
April, 1974

INTRODUCTION

Professor Harold D. Weaver summoned a group of Robeson Scholars to Rutgers University in April, 1973 to give progress reports on their common project – Paul Robeson. Among those answering the summons were Lofton Mitchell, the State University of New York; Edward Scobie, Harold Weaver, Robert Smith, Eugene Robinson and Willie Ellison, all of Rutgers University; Thomas Cripps, Morgan State College; Lamont Yeakey, Black Economic Research Center; Claude "Buddy" Young, National Football League; Anatol Schlosser, York University, Canada; John Henrik Clarke, *Freedomways* magazine; Ewart Guinier, Director of Afro-American Studies, Harvard College; Sterling Stuckey, Northwestern University; and James Jackson, the Communist Party of the USA. Speakers and audience were enriched by the experience.

While the place was appropriate (Robeson's alma mater) and the time was opportune (his 75th birthmonth), the response of the Rutgers faculty and students, both black and white, left much to be desired. Such disinterest may reflect the success of the national effort to destroy and bury Robeson during the 1940s and 1950s. It should serve also as a challenge to scholars to recover Robeson from obscurity and force an objective re-evaluation of him. With a subject so complicated and controversial, this is not easy. Few people, if any, were indifferent to Robeson. He was admired or abused, respected or feared, loved or hated, by his public.

Most foreigners appear to have only a positive reaction to Robeson, and they find it difficult to understand or appreciate the violent hatred to which he was (and is) subjected at home. Thus, the problem before the scholars is, for the most part, a domestic one. Some idea of the magnitude of Robeson's recovery operation was suggested by an article in *The Dispatcher*, published by the International Longshoremen's and Warehousemen's Union (ILWU), on June 8, 1973:

> When a union back in New York decided three years ago to stage a tribute to Paul Robeson, *The New York Times*, in announcing the event, referred to him as "the late" Paul Robeson.
> The mistake by such a prestigious newspaper indicated how completely the once-celebrated singer-actor-activist had been swept under the rug of history – partly by the calculated design of his enemies.

Marie Seton's *Paul Robeson* (1958) was the last major publication on Robeson's life until the publication of Edwin Hoyt's *Paul Robeson, An American Othello* (1967). While Seton's book has withstood the test of time for reliability and accuracy, Hoyt's work has come under heavy fire from Robeson admirers. Another literary offering that has caused dissent in the Robeson camp is Harold Cruse's *The Crisis of the Black Intellectual* (1967). Cruse makes many critical references to Robeson throughout his book.

The 1970s have brought a few shafts of light at the end of the dark tunnel where Robeson "lies buried." The Afro-American Museum (AAM) of Detroit produced an hour-long radio special on Robeson's birthday in 1970. The Canadian Broadcasting Corporation did a two-hour broadcast on the life of Robeson in March, 1971 (according to *Variety,* the program outdrew television programs in the areas where it was heard). *Freedomways* magazine was dedicated to Robeson for the first quarter of 1971 under the title, "The Great Forerunner." In 1972, AAM produced a record album, "An Evening with Paul Robeson," which, unlike other Robeson records, allowed Robeson to speak his mind about the challenges of his day.

A rash of events helped to celebrate Robeson's 75th year during 1973. Reference has already been made to the conference at Rutgers University. This was followed by a "Salute to Paul Robeson" at Carnegie Hall on April 15, 1973. AAM's Board of Trustees designated 1973 as "The Robeson Year." The 1970 documentary, "The Voice of the Century," was repeated over a local radio station. As a joint venture with Gil Maddox, special program director of WWJ-TV, Detroit, AAM produced a half-hour television special on the life of Robeson on April 8, 1973. The Museum was commissioned by Edward Simpkins, then Director of The Institute for Black Studies at Wayne State University, to build an exhibit of Robeson as a freedom fighter. This exhibit is called, "The Making of a Militant." AAM's research assistant, Verona Morton, completed the project in time for the African-American Week Program of 1973. AAM's final offering for The Robeson Year was the album "Robeson at the Peace Arch Park, 1953." This disc presents a recording of a concert that was held at the international border (Blaine, Washington) when Robeson was not allowed to enter Canada.

A sign of the future, we hope, was an hour-long auditorium program at Detroit's McFarland Junior High School on the life of Robeson. The program coincided with the birthday of Robeson and was the brainchild of Richard James, teacher at McFarland.

This must be only a beginning. If the Robeson Scholars rise to meet the challenge of the "conspirators of silence," we shall see a series of publications that explore the many sides of Robeson's activities and careers.

My original goal in writing about Robeson as a labor activist was to produce a "scientific" paper that would cover the essential facts of his trade union efforts. One research finding led to another, and it soon became apparent that a fuller treatment was necessary.

Following in Robeson's wake has not been easy. The trail led to the British Museum's reading room. My chances of drinking from that great fountain of knowledge looked dim until I mentioned that the subject was Robeson. Hesitation gave way to encouragement and helpful suggestions. No less gracious and helpful were the people at the London headquarters of the Miner's Union and the Transport Worker's Union. The former provided long distance telephone service to Wales and information on Welsh miners. The latter put at my disposal all of their files relating to Robeson's labor activities in the British Isles.

My longest journey was to the Hawaiian Islands to talk with Eddie Tangen, International Representative of the Longshoremen's and Warehousemen's Union (ILWU). Tangen was helpful in uncovering Robeson's activities on the West Coast and in Hawaii. Back home, cooperative people were found – ILWU, UAW, NMU, Harvard College, Winston-Salem, N.C., and the Detroit Public Library, to name just a few. On the other hand, many pepole who have first-hand information about Robeson would not talk. A fever of fear still afflicts many who knew and worked with Robeson. The tincture of time has not been sufficient to heal the hurts of the past.

This effort was designed to study, in depth, Robeson's wide-ranging support for the trade union movement, at home and abroad. Of all the works in print, Marie Seton's gives the fullest account of his labor activities. Her emphasis, however, was clearly in the area of his artistry. It was not easy to avoid the surge of three "Othellos," Robeson's effort on behalf of the Progressive Party in 1948, the Council of African Affairs, and his film activities. Such events as the passport fight and the government's charges of Communism would not be denied a role as the drama unfolded; they were too close to the main theme. In order to make Robeson's role in the labor movement plausible and understandable, I have attempted to focus some light on those events leading up to and surrounding his involvement with labor. Despite these efforts by a non-historian, the question may still remain, "Why did he do it?"

The segment on Tom Coleman may require some explanation; for Robeson's role may, at first glance, appear to be a minor one. While Coleman was being harrassed on the local scene for his affiliation with a Local of the United Public Workers' (UPW) Union, Robeson and the national officers of UPW were under attack by federal officials. Coleman's experiences are offered as an example of the misfortunes of many such citizens, throughout the United States, who followed Robeson's leadership. The price that Coleman paid for his labor leadership was quite small when compared to Robeson's whose citations before Congressional Committees on Subversion exceeded 200, many of them because of his labor activities.

What started out as a paper grew into a book – but not the definitive book on Robeson in the labor movement. Not until those tortured victims of unspeakable assaults feel free to tell it like it was can the full story be told.

PAUL WHO?

At the outset of this project, a group of young black adults was asked to identify Paul Robeson. Not a single one of them could do so. Their guesses ranged from prize fighter to blues singer. One young man finally remembered that he had heard the name, but his parents had advised him never to mention it in public.

Patriotism flowed into Robeson's veins from both sides of his family. Cyrus Bustill, his great-great-grandfather, joined the Revolutionary Army hoping that a victory over the British would mean a better life for black Americans. Benjamin Franklin reported in his "Journal" that Cyrus Bustill baked bread and carried it to George Washington's forces at Valley Forge. When the new republic failed to keep its promises to its black citizens, Bustill, anticipating his great-great-grandson by 170 years, acted on his own. He was one of the founders of the Free Africa Society, the first self-help black organization in Philadelphia. Risking the enmity of the white establishment, Bustill led one of the first abolition movements in his area. Joseph Bustill, Cyrus' son, was equally interested in the freedom of his black brothers and sisters. He taught school at the Colored Presbyterian Church and, also, became an agent in the Underground Railroad. In his book, *The Underground Railroad,* William Still reproduced a letter that Joseph Bustill wrote to him early in his career as a conductor of the enslaved to freedom:

> Friend Still:
> I suppose that ere this you have seen, those five large and three small packages I sent by way of Reading, consisting of three men, women and children. They arrived here this morning at 8½ o'clock and left 30 minutes past three. You will be pleased to send me any information likely to prove interesting in relation to them.
> Lately we formed a society, here, called the Fugitives Aid Society. This is our first case: I hope it will prove successful.
> When you wrote, please inform us what signs and symbols you make use of in your dispatches and any other information in relation to operation of the Underground Railroad.
> Our reason for sending by Reading Road was to gain time. It is expected the owners will be in town this afternoon, and by this road we gained five hours time, which is a matter of much importance. And we may have occasion to use it some time in the future.
> Yours with great respect, Jos. C. Bustill.

The call to freedom was equally strong from the paternal side. Reverend William Drew Robeson, Paul's father, was born a slave in Martin County, N.C. At the age of fifteen, he fled north via the Underground Railroad. The year after his escape, at the age of sixteen, William Drew Robeson joined 200,000 other blacks in helping the Union Army defeat the Confederate Forces. As a young man, he studied at Lincoln University (Pa.) to become a minister. While at Lincoln, he met Maria Louisa Bustill, a Philadelphia school teacher. They were married on July 11, 1878. Six children were born to this union, but only five survived. The youngest, Paul Leroy Robeson, was born on April 9, 1898. The family was subjected to the severest of poverty and rank discrimination as they struggled to survive, at the turn of the century.

Tragedy struck the family on January 19, 1904 when Maria Robeson, Paul's mother, was burned to death in a home accident. Reverend Robeson assumed the responsibility of rearing the family. Although assisted by an assortment of aunts and cousins, the major force in the lives of the Robeson children was their father. By example as well as with words, he taught them honesty, loyalty, and the value of freedom at any price.

Princeton, New Jersey, where the Robeson children spent their early years, was called a "northern town with a southern persuasion," thanks to the domineering influence of the sons of southern bourbons who attended the famous University in sufficient numbers to set the social tone of the town. The Robesons attended segregated grade schools in Princeton and the university's doors were locked to them.

Robeson's brilliant high school record at Somerville (N.J.) High School earned him a scholarship to Rutgers University at New Brunswick, New Jersey. He arrived there in 1915 with his father's advice incorporated as a way of life – "strive for excellence at all times. Compete against yourself for improvement, no matter what others do." Robeson, already a giant when he arrived on the campus, left an indelible impression on the university that is still visible. While four other seniors earned four varsity letters at Rutgers, Robeson was the only one with a Phi Beta Kappa key, earned his junior year. He won many other honors during his four years as a Rutger's student, including Cap and Gown Honor Society, and honors on the debating team.

Despite the destructiveness of racism in the classroom and on the athletic field, Robeson read the valedictory address for his class. His subject was "The Fourteenth Amendment, The Sleeping Giant of the American Constitution." The theme was developed to justify the claim of black Americans for equal rights on constitutional grounds. He gave a learned analysis of the potential of this statute as a vehicle for justice. It anticipated the NAACP's civil rights activities by more than thirty years. This provocative, stirring presentation was a fitting climax to a brilliant college career and gave a clear indication of Robeson's future course.

Even before graduation from college, he had manifested a profound interest in people by becoming involved in the issues that affected the black citizens of New Brunswick. He stated that the local YMCA gave him the opportunity to work with youth in the community. Just before graduation, the black members of the community gave a banquet in Robeson's honor, in appreciation of his work with them. He gave a speech at the affair: ". . . I hope that my life's work will be a memorial to my father's training. My work is not for myself; it is to help my race to a higher life."

Occasionally Robeson returned to address his friends in New Brunswick. On one such visit his topic was "The Future of the Negro in America and What Shall Be His Place In American Life?" He suggested a closer cooperation between the races for their mutual benefit. One of his listeners later reported, "He often came and sang for us. He was always the same Paul. Learning didn't go to his head."

Robeson married Eslanda (Essie) Goode on August 17, 1921. She was a brilliant woman whose contributions were a match for those of her illustrious husband. In 1927, she bore him a son, Paul Jr., who went on to a fine career in engineering. The three of them formed a tightly knit family group that stood up to what may be some of the worst defamation and abuse in the history of this republic. Essie Robeson died in 1965, but father and son closed ranks to maintain their bulwark of strength.

Robeson graduated from law school in 1922, but he never entered the private practice of law. The legal training was very useful during his many court battles of the 1940s and 1950s.

Starting his stage career as a concert artist in 1924, Robeson saw himself as a teacher, with the auditorium as his classroom. Songs, as well as parts in dramatic plays, were vehicles for teaching as well as for entertainment. Robeson's stage and screen careers, exciting and memorable, are described in considerable detail elsewhere. Suffice it to say that by 1934 he was at the peak of international fame. Having lived in London for seven years where his blackness was not a millstone, as in America, the British aristocracy claimed him as its own. Already, an outstanding performance as Shakespeare's Othello was behind him. He was listed in The British *Who's Who.* He and Essie were often invited to Embassy functions of various countries, except that of the United States.

Thus, Robeson's self-esteem was at its crest when he, Essie, and Marie Seton (his British biographer) set out on his first trip to Russia, in December of 1934. The purpose of the visit was to discuss the possibility of making a film with Sergei Eisenstein, the great Russian filmdirector. In a personal interview, Marie Seton described the events of December 20, 1934, a date that she believes was one of the turning points in Robeson's life.

> We had a lay-over in Berlin while waiting for the train to Moscow. Paul was uncomfortable around all of those stormtroopers; they stared at him with hatred and contempt. We left our hotel and arrived at the station in time to gather our luggage and find our train. I saw Paul grow very tense. When I looked around, there was a semi-circle of stormtroopers forming near Paul. They were hurling racial epithets at him in German. Paul was fluent in German; so he understood everything that they said.
>
> Paul advised me to run. I couldn't move. Essie joined us without realizing what was happening. At first, I think Paul was afraid; but his fear turned to a blazing fury. He told us to stand still and show no fear, "If they think that we are afraid, they will have the courage to attack." He told us that the Germans thought that Essie and I were German women. Although fully armed, the soldiers did not move within arms reach of Robeson. Providentially, the train came and we backed into it and got away. Paul was very quiet on the train to Moscow. Essie and I knew better than to bother him at a time like that.

Just the year before, Robeson had reluctantly given a benefit performance of his play, "All God's Chilun," for Jewish refugees from Germany. Certainly at that time, Hitler's fascist Germany seemed far away. The Berlin encounter was something real, personal, and dangerous. There is every reason to believe that from that moment onward, Robeson became anti-fascist, at times even a rabid anti-fascist.

Sharply contrasting his reception in Germany was his reception in Russia, some hours later. His color did not matter to the Russians and they accepted him with warmth and genuine friendship. Just as he had become an eternal foe of Fascism in Berlin, he and the Russian people forged a bond of friendship in Moscow that would endure for many years. He was to pay a dear price for both!

Marie Seton reports that Robeson was never the same after his trip to the east. Shortly after his return, he walked out of the premiere of his latest film, "Sanders of the River," in protest of the white supremacist slant the directors had given the final version of the film. His son told me that his father tried to buy up all prints of the film. These, and other related experiences, forced Robeson to reappraise his views of and his position in the white world. His quest for new ideas brought him into contact with Kingsley Martin, editor of the *New Statesman and Nation.* George Padmore, Maurice Hindus, and other left-wing Socialist thinkers of the period.

Robeson's move toward an identification with the laboring classes took a giant step in 1935 with the London production of the play "Stevedore." He starred as Lonnie Thompson, a stevedore who is trying to organize his fellow black laborers to improve their working conditions. Framed by the white boss, he dies attempting to defend them. Finally, the black workers are joined by white workers to drive off the oppressors. The play brought Robeson into contact with a large body of blacks, African and West Indian, in a common endeavor. In preparing for the role Robeson spent time on the London docks setting the stage for his work with seamen in the United States a few years later. Marie Seton (1958, p. 103) wrote the following summation of Robeson's appearance in "Stevedore": "'Stevedore' opened at the Embassy Theatre on May 6, 1935. In the role of Lonnie Thompson, Paul Robeson gave expression to feelings and thoughts taking shape within him. He was consciously using his ability to act in a play which accorded with his newly developing ideas. His views and his role had fused as never before." A year later, Robeson appeared in, "The Song of Freedom." The film opens with him working as a longshoreman on the London docks.

Robeson's popularity with the working classes of the British Islands increased in 1937 when he gave up his celebrity concerts that attracted the middle class and aristocracy. He began to sing in the large music halls for six-pence and up, despite censure from some of the top guest artists and their agents. On some occasions the overflow crowds demanded, and got, three concerts in one day.

As a champion of the common man, Robeson's evolution was further advanced in 1938 by the Spanish Civil War. On December 20, 1937, exactly three years from the date of his Berlin confrontation, Robeson listened along with 9,000 others to Clement Attlee's personal account of fascist atrocities from the Spanish front. After the report, Robeson sang. Marie Seton (1958, p. 112) was there: "At last, Robeson appeared. For the first time, he transformed the song which had made him famous from a lament at fate to a song of protest. He altered 'Ol' Man River,' changing the line 'I'm tired of livin' and feared of dyin' to 'I must keep fighting' until I'm dyin'—and the people roared applause. A new Robeson stood before them." In less than five weeks, Robeson and his wife entered Spain to entertain and encourage the Loyalist troops and their allies. Among the foreigners who made up the International and Abraham Lincoln brigades were men who were destined to become prominent in the trade union movement around the world. When they returned home to do battle with the industrial barons, they would seek the support of this courageous black giant with the golden voice.

For the next two and one-half years of his London exile, Robeson became increasingly identified with the workers of Wales, Scotland, and Manchester as well as London. It was during this period that he made the film, "Proud Valley," with a supporting cast of Welsh miners. Robeson assisted a group of London trade unionists to form the Unity theatre where they would develop their own creative talents. One of their early productions was, "Plant in the Sun." This was an American Labor production in which Robeson volunteered to play the role of the union organizer. Increasingly, Robeson began to equate the plight of the working classes, in general, with that of the black man in America. On several occasions, he said that the future of the Negro is within the ranks of labor.

ROBESON AND THE SPANISH CIVIL WAR

The Spanish Civil War erupted in June, 1936 and was less than a year old when the destruction of Guernica was ordered. This tragic event brought that war to the attention of the world when on the morning of April 26 ,1937, the unfortunate people of Guernica, Spain were startled to hear the thunderous noises of war planes approaching from the south. Without warning, the bombers unloaded their death-dealing cargo on the Basque village and fled. When the German flight commander placed his pointer on the map at the morning briefing, Guernica was no more than a dot on the northeastern coast of Spain. When the Nazi pilots returned for the debriefing, they were able to report that more than 80 percent of the dot had been destroyed. The air arm of Hitler's famed and feared Condor Legions had written the first chapter in a new book, *Terror From the Skies.*

The remoteness of this tiny village and the Basque inclination to go their own way had isolated them from the Civil War to the south. Certainly, they had priorities that did not include a war that they could neither understand nor appreciate. Yet, the war had come to them. When the fires had burned themselves out and the survivors had reassembled their dead and injured, the toll was 1,654 and 889, respectively – out of a population of less than 4,000. Not so easily measured was the misery of hundreds of children who miraculously escaped the hail of fire and steel that had rendered them instant orphans.

Paul Robeson could never deny children anymore than they could deny him. When he heard of the gutting of Guernica, he became involved in a fund-raising drive to assist the orphaned children. In support of the effort, he said:

> I am deeply happy to contribute to this cause of Spanish Culture and to the Basque children in particular, a cause that must concern everyone who stands for freedom, progressive democracy and for all humanity.
>
> Today, the artist cannot hold himself aloof. The scientist, the artist, the writer is challenged. The children must be taken up. The forces of reaction have made no distinction between combatant and non-combatant.
>
> The beautiful village of Guernica, nestled up the Basque hills with

its blood-soaked streets, is proof that these victims must be given every possible aid. This, common humanity demands.

Pablo Picasso, the great Spanish painter, was so moved as to paint one of his greatest works entitled, "Guernica," a disturbing denunciation of war. The original masterpiece hangs in New York's Museum of Modern Art. Many of the survivors of Guernica display prints of the painting in their homes as a reminder of their day of infamy. Picasso's disillusionment with the indifference of the west toward Fascism caused him to drift toward Communism.

The Spanish people were not allowed to settle their differences among themselves. In addition to the German Condors, Generalissimo Franco's Nationalist forces were supported by 200,000 of Mussolini's Black Arrow troops. The Russians provided men and material to the loyalists. Among the Russian officers who fought on the Spanish front was Alexander Rodimstev, who later distinguished himself in the Russian defeat of the German juggernaught at Stalingrad.

Volunteers joined the Loyalists from Poland, Czechoslovakia, Hungary, and anti-Fascists from Italy, Germany, and America, in an ill-fated struggle to stop Fascism before it spread over all of Europe. This group of volunteers included, for the most part, working-class liberals, leftists, socialists, and communists, black and white.

The 3,200 Americans who fought in Spain formed a part of the front-line shock troops of the Fifteenth International Brigade of the Spanish Republican (Loyalist) Army. Most of them fought together in what came to be known as the Abraham Lincoln Brigade. Their heroism at Quinto, Teruel, and Brunete cost them nearly half of the Brigade. When their cause was all but lost, the brigade's survivors were pulled out to find their way home by the best routes possible. Arriving home, these veterans found themselves re-united on the Attorney General's list of subversives.

Another national leader who shared Picasso's horror of the Fascist adventure in Spain was Jawaharal Nehru, President of the Indian Congress. He made a trip to the west in 1938 and one of the first countries visited was Spain. Accompanied by Krishna Menon, head of the India League of London, Nehru spent five days in Barcelona and in the front lines on the outskirts of the city. After a careful review of his findings, Nehru stated that the future of European civilization was at stake in the Spanish Civil War. When the Republican Army was defeated Nehru said: "The Republic was killed by Britain and France; history, long ages hence, will remember this infamy and will not forgive them."

On December 20, 1937, Robeson participated in a meeting on the Spanish Civil War, at London's Albert Hall. Nine thousand people were present. Among them were members of Britain's Labour Party who demanded arms, food, and justice for democratic Spain. Chief speaker for the occasion was the Labour Party leader, Clement

Attlee. Having just returned from the Spanish front, he was able to give a first-hand account of the plight of the Republican army.

Robeson lost little time in going to Spain to see for himself. He and Eslanda his wife, entered Spain from France on January 23, 1938. Their immediate destinations were Teruel and Madrid. Plans had already been made for Robeson to sing to the troops in the International and Abraham Lincoln Brigades. He sang Negro Spirituals and folk songs of the many nationalities making up the Brigades, many times in the original languages. The Republic War Ministry made special arrangements for Robeson to visit the front lines of the battle zones. Loudspeakers were set up so that his voice could be heard by the Fascist as well as the Loyalist soldiers. He included the all-time Spanish favorite, "The Four Star General." Robeson's commanding voice stilled the guns on both sides of the battle line. Both friend and foe cheered as the concert ended, and death's respite ended, also.

Robeson saw the struggles of the working classes of Spain in the same terms that he saw the struggles of the black man in the United States. He made this clear after he left Spain and embarked on a series of public appreances on behalf of the Republicans, both on the continent and in England. It was from the continent, probably the Spanish Embassy in Paris, that he issued what became known as his Manifesto against Fascism.

> Every artist, every scientist must decide, now, where he stands. He has no alternative. There are no impartial observers.
> Through the destruction, in certain countries, of man's literary heritage, through the propagation of false ideas of national and racial superiority, the artist, the scientist, the writer is challenged. This struggle invades the former cloistered halls of our universities and all her seats of learning.
> The battlefront is everywhere. There is no sheltered rear. The artist elects to fight for freedom or slavery.
> I have made my choice! I had no alternative!
> The history of the era is characterized by the degradation of my people. Despoiled of their lands, their culture destroyed, they are denied equal opportunity of the law and deprived of their rightful place in the respect of their fellows.
> Not through blind faith or through coercion, but conscious of my course, I take my place with you. I stand with you in unalterable support of the lawful government of Spain, duly and regularly chosen by its sons and daughters.

This proclamation created a sensation in the United States. Opinion among American Catholics heavily favored the Franco forces in Spain. Many people took exception to Robeson's statements and accused him of meddling in the foreign affairs of the government, a charge that would cost him his passport twelve years later.

The Department of State was particularly disenchanted with Robeson's anti-fascist activities. The official U. S. policy toward the Spanish Civil War was one of "moral aloofness." Secretary of State Cordell Hull had already made this clear to the Spanish Ambassador to the U. S., Fernando-de La Rosa, in denying his plea for military aid.

The American foreign policy on Robeson was one of ignoring him whenever possible. The American Embassy in London had already assumed the "proper" posture on Robeson for all of the twelve years that he lived in London by never inviting him to any of its functions, even when he was the toast of London and a frequent visitor to select functions of the aristocracy. William Patterson, long time friend of Robeson, recalled an incident that occurred in Moscow about the time of the Spanish Civil War that illustrated the State Department's attitude toward Robeson:

> . . . As usual, the American Ambassador to the Soviet Union gave a Fourth-of-July affair and invited all of the prominent Americans throughout the Soviet Union, except Paul and Eslanda Robeson. The reaction of the Soviet public was very interesting, especially the notables in the theater, arts and sciences. They were amazed that this man should be affronted in this way by the leaders of the American Embassy.
>
> The theater and movie artists of the Soviet Union decided to throw a big party for Robeson on the same day as the American affair. It was an outstanding success. Most all of the celebrated people in Moscow came to Paul's party.

These were but the opening salvos of a twenty-year battle between Robeson and the U. S. government. Abrasive confrontations would occur at the Canadian border, in a New York court house, before Congressional Committees, and before President Truman.

Robeson gathered his wife and son and ended his twelve-year exile to London on May 15, 1939. The superior forces of Fascism had overrun Spain and were poised to lay waste to the rest of Europe. After briefly considering permanent residence abroad, he had decided to return and continue his vendetta against Fascism on his home ground.

Robeson's reception was mixed. Veteran organizations objected to his declarations of friendship for the Chinese and Russian people. The Catholics would not soon forget his interference in the Spanish Civil War on the wrong side. The federal government resented being put on the defensive by Robeson's public denunciations of its racist practices. They were biding their time. Many black leaders were embarrassed and frightened by Robeson's apparent contempt for the seats of power.

For many ordinary people, Robeson was friend and supporter. Among these were the labor organizers in the infantile industrial unions, some of whom Robeson had met in the trenches around Barcelona and in the outskirts of Madrid. At the moment of his return, many labor unions were locked in a life-and-death struggle for survival with the industrial barons of America. Organized labor needed all of the support it could muster, and Robeson needed an arena to continue his unending battle against racism. Robeson's rapid entry into the national struggle, on the side of labor, brought cheers from the workers but netted him the everlasting enmity of the industrialists.

Robeson continued to support the half million Spanish Loyalists who fled across the Pyreness into southern France, when the fascists overran their country in 1939.

Their respite was very brief. The Germans soon followed and killed thousands of them in combat and in the concentration camps of Dachau, Buchenwald, and Mauthausen.

Robeson gave his endorsement and pledged his support when the Spanish Refugee Aid, Inc. was established in May, 1953. Pablo Casals and Mexican ex-President Lazaro Cardenas were chosen as honorary co-chairmen. Despite more than twenty years of aid, nearly 50,000 of these victims remain unwelcome "guests" in a foreign land.

ROBESON IN WALES AND SCOTLAND

Wales

One of the highest compliments that the Welsh can pay a performing artist is to invite him to participate in the annual Eisteddfod. The South Wales Miners' Union invited Paul Robeson to sing at their Eisteddfod in 1953 and 1957.

The Eisteddfod is the highlight of the cultural season for Welshmen everywhere. Starting about the 7th century, the Eisteddfod continued as a national celebration until about 1568. Lax rules and general confusion became so rampant during the Elizabethan period that even Elizabeth ("Whereas it has come to the knowledge of the Lord President . . . that vagrant and idle persons, naming themselves mynstrells ritmors and bards are lately grown in such intolerable multitude . . .") could not bring order out of the chaos. The celebration gradually died out. Early in the 19th century, the feeling of nationalism that swept over Europe washed ashore in Wales, and the Eisteddfod was revived in its present form. The national Welsh costume of tall hat and long gown was introduced by Lady Llanover in 1834. Chief of the festival is the Archdruid (Chief Bard) who presides for three years. The chairing, or enthroning of the victorious bard of the year is the highest ceremony of this national musical, literary, and artistic festival. Although the competitions do include literature, poetry, and the arts in general, the interest is highest and the competition is keenest in music, especially singing. The highest honor known is the winning of the Chair. The winner is known as the Chair Eisteddfod.

Eisteddfodau are usually held in Wales but may be held elsewhere by large Welsh populations. The first Eisteddfod to be held in the United States took place in Carbondale, Pa. in 1890.

A report of the 1953 Eisteddfod, found in the British Museum's reading room, reflects the international character of the festival. It was held in Measteg, Wales. Over 150 choirs and dance groups from 23 countries participated. Fifteen thousand persons attended the performances. It was no accident that Robeson was invited as a guest artist on this momentous occasion. His friendship with the coal miners of South Wales began during the 1930s while he was living in London. Over the next quarter century he shared many of the joys and hardships of his friends in the Rhondda Valley. He dined at their tables and fed a prodigious appetite under the incredulous eyes of his gracious hosts.

The miners told him about the history of their hardships and the constant dangers of their occupation. Despite their concern for his safety, Robeson rode with them into the "black holes," sharing their total experience. Explosions and other mining accidents sometimes caused as many as a thousand deaths per year. Absentee mine owners appeared to be insensitive to the inhuman and degrading conditions under which the miners lived and worked.

A satirical and anonymous report, "What's Wrong With South Wales?", published in 1935, provided at least one man's view of the situation about the time Robeson arrived in the Valley:

> The miners worked like blacks and on their bellies, if this is how blacks work, in the bowels of the earth: and the puddlers swilled down barrels of beer at the furnaces and sweated them out again for the sake of progress of the Imports and Exports.
>
> Coal miners and iron owners practically risked all they possessed and all they could borrow in order to extend the frontiers of the British Commonwealth and the range of profitable business, whichever was the wider. And on balance and in the long run, if not the short, they were repaid, both for their self-denying abstinence in postponing the enjoyment of their capital and their courage in taking sides.
>
> In due course, they were honored by a great country and a discerning sovereign with invitations to Buckingham Palace and to some were given monument in the top hats and frock coats of the period of the adornment of the National Park at Cardiff. That the industry of these pioneers was justified has been amply demonstrated by the careers of their descendents, unto the third and fourth generations.
>
> Many of them have escaped the primal curse; but, if they have not needed to work, they have not been inactive or indifferent to the higher interests of mankind. There are polo ponies on Long Island, palatial stables at Manton, pedigreed bulls outside Hereford, yachts on the Solent, gardens on the Riviera, tapestries in many mansions, Altars in Westminster Cathedral, all of which owe their beautiful being, in part, to the subterranean and superheated sweat of the toiling miners. So long as any of these survive, it cannot be said that they sweat to no purpose.
>
> Nor is it uninspiring though it may be slightly paradoxical to observe that the grandchildren of the rugged pioneers, when they have not been hunting the fox or the otter, have labored directly or by deputy to amass the products of the pre-revolutionary era: old masters, old furniture, old silver, each work of art stamped with the genius of some individual craftsman who had no need to prostrate himself, front nor back, to execute it. The possessions are not only the object of pride on the part of the owners and evidence of an enviable country status and culture, but they have the advantage of holding wealth in cold storage, so to speak, and in a form less amenable, if not accessable to taxation. Nowhere does one see suspended in the hall of billiard rooms, a miner's pick and

> shovel or a puddler's tongs but only the heads of foxes, the antlers of deer and other trophies of the chase.
> It cannot be that the scions of the rude forefathers' desire to forget the rock from which they were hewn or the hole of the pit whence they were digged. But some color is given to the uncharitable vies by their remoteness from the valleys by their present and pleasant dwelling places, their houses full of good things, which they fill not, their cisterns and cellars which they hewed not, filled with fruit of the vineyard which they planted not as told in the 5th book of Moses, commonly called Deuteronomy. Thus, in the course of time, creative activity is transferred into contemplative possessions and progress is stabilized.

Robeson arrived in the Rhondda Valley between the Great Wars when rising prices, runaway inflation, and the disclosure of unshared war profits brought on more than the usual labor unrest. Fortunately for the miners, the period produced its own daring union leadership in such men as William Paynter, D. D. Evans, and Dia Francis. They have followed in the wake of such giants of the past as Frank Hodges, Tommy Hepburn, and others who withstood the mounting pressures of mine owners and government in their quest for better working conditions for the men they represented.

Robeson's close relationship with the Welsh miners was reflected in the film "Proud Valley." The movie was shot in the Rhondda Valley in 1938-39. During the shooting, Robeson lived with the miners, many of whom appeared in the film. Scenes in the movie show miners in their homes, stores, and the mines. Marie Seton, having a special interest in films, reviewed "Proud Valley" in her biography of Robeson (1958, p. 120):

> The story of "Proud Valley" concerned a group of miners in Rhondda Valley where mining towns were decaying under the blight of unemployment. It was typical of the life in any Rhondda Village where the people struggled to survive. The people work, love and sing. The continuity and self expression is the Eisteddfod, where the choirs from the villages compete for the prize.
> The role which Robeson played was based on life. An American Negro miner, from the coal fields of West Virginia, a member of John L. Lewis' union, had come to England and found his way to Wales where he had carried on as a miner along with the Welshmen with whom he had become as one. Playing the part of this man, Robeson formed the hub of the action. He was the fellow who helped the lovers, joined the choir and aided his village to win the coveted prize at the Eisteddfod. Finally, in a mine disaster, he was the comrade whose strength saved his fellow workers.
> The character was that of a typical worker; and prototype in life was to be found not only in the Welsh mines, but in New Orleans, New York, Cardiff, London, and Liverpool. Yet, this character, based upon an actual man was revolutionary in the history of the screen. Never before in either America or England had a typical Negro worker figured as a hero or as a supporting character in a film, although just such a character represented the majority of Negroes all over the world.
> In all the years of Robeson's life, and he was now forty years old, but a very small fraction of Negroes, anywhere, had ever passed out of the working class. Of that fraction, only an insignificant percentage had been permitted to reach the apex of their professions and become known to the general public either in their own

nations or the world. Of those who had, Robeson, alone, at that time was identified in the minds of the people of the world with the cause of liberation of his own people.

"Proud Valley" was completed in mid-September and Robeson sailed for America in mid-May of 1939, ending his twelve-year exile in London.

Marie Seton felt that Robeson's close relationship with the Welsh miners influenced his decision to return home in 1939. The poor working conditions in the mines reminded him of the intolerable conditions of his relatives on the tobacco plantations in North Carolina and the mine fields in West Virginia. He saw here again the ruthless exploitation of the working class that makes the problems of the poor all over the world difficult, if not insoluble. Robeson cast his lot with the miners, championing their causes whenever and wherever the opportunity arose. Such behavior alienated the mine owners but insured a life-long friendship between Robeson and the people of the Valley.

As early as 1953, The Miner's Union of South Wales joined with many other groups from many parts of the world, to register their outrage at the way Robeson was "persecuted" by the United States' Government and the business community of America. Their main attack was aimed at the State Department, demanding that Robeson's passport be returned to him, forthwith. They claimed, in effect, that Robeson was a citizen of the world, therefore, what happened to him was the concern of everyone.

Other groups tried different methods to liberate Robeson from "house arrest" in the United States. Several universities, including Andrews and Edinburgh, offered him the position of Headmaster. The Shakespeare Company, at Stratford-upon-Avon, invited Robeson to come to Stratford for a third production of "Othello." The State Department, caught between a rising tide of criticism from abroad and an uncompromising Robeson at home, remained adamant and turned a deaf ear to the petitions.

Robeson's first invitation to attend the Welsh Miner's Eisteddfod arrived in 1953, just before his Second Peace Arch Park concert. The Welsh invited him to be their honored guest at their 1957 Eisteddfod. Again, the request was denied, but Robeson and his friends had an alternative plan. They arranged a trans-Atlantic telephone hook-up between New York and Porthcawl, Wales and Robeson sang on schedule. The American press, by and large, ignored this event. Just the opposite was true in England and Europe. Thousands listened to the program in Wales. Millions in England and on the continent read about the concert in their newspapers; and the miners recorded. the concert for posterity. The record jacket states:

The purpose of the trans-Atlantic telephone link-up between the 1957 Miner's Eisteddfod at Porthcawl and Paul Robeson in New York was two-fold. It was to bring his voice in song and his speech direct to the music lovers of South Wales and to fortify him with the knowledge that the hand of friendship is extended to him by thousands of Welsh people who are longing to see and hear him in person again. With him in the studio were his wife and son, his son's wife, and their two children.

The historic program opened with words of welcome from William Paynter, a miner's miner. Although at the time of the program he was president of the South Wales Miner's Union, Paynter had started at the bottom. The son of a miner, he got his start in the Rhondda Pits in South Wales. He participated in the hunger strikes in 1931, 32 and 36. In 1937 he joined the International Brigade in Spain and fought for the Loyalists. When he retired in 1968, Paynter was at the head of the National Union of Miners of all of England.

William Paynter (Porthcawl):
Hello, Paul Robeson? This is Will Paynter, President of the South Wales miners speaking. On behalf of the South Wales miners and all the people gathered at this Eisteddfod, I say to you, "greetings of friendship and respect." We're happy that it has been possible for us to arrange for you to speak and sing for us today. We would be far happier if you were here in person.
Our people deplore the continued refusal of your government to return your passport and deny you the right to join us in our festival of song. We shall continue to exert whatever influence we can to overcome this position. We look forward to the day when we shall again shake your hand and may you sing with us in these valleys of musical song. As one of our songs predicts, we dedicate it to you,

We'll keep a welcome in the hillside,
We'll keep a welcome in the vale
This land of ours will still be singing
When you come back to Wales.

Now, Paul, we'd like you to give a message of greeting to the Welsh miners and to the great audience here assembled. After that you'll sing for us. After you have sung, we have here on the platform the Treorchy Male Choir, which is one of the premier male-voice choirs in Wales. They will sing for you one of the beautiful Welsh songs, "Y Delyn Aur." Over to you, Paul.

Paul Robeson (New York):
Thank you so much for your kind words. My warmest greetings to my people of my beloved Wales and a special "hello" to the miners of South Wales. It is a great privilege to be participating in this historic festival. All the best to you as we strive toward a world where all live abundant, peaceful, and dignified lives.

Robeson then sang:

"Didn't My Lord Deliver Daniel?"
"This Little Light of Mine."
Schubert's "Lullaby."
"All Through the Night."
"All Men Are Brothers."

The trans-Atlantic telephone program brought into sharp focus, for millions of Europeans at least, the unjust treatment to which Robeson was being subjected. Relentless pressure from diverse directions continued to mount. Eventually the State Department granted Robeson the right to travel to Canada and Mexico.

In May of 1958, the Welsh miners sponsored another trans-Atlantic concert betwen Robeson in New York and an audience of nearly one thousand in St. Pancras Town Hall, London. Cedric Belfrage of the *Manchester Guardian* filed this report of the event:

> Didn't Jericho's walls tumble when Joshua fit the battle and didn't my Lord deliver Daniel? The assault on the cold-war walls around America took a new turn here on May 26, and many wondered what the defenders would do to meet it. In any case . . . the American Telephone and Telegraph and the General Post Office in London . . . helped Paul Robeson to make the U.S. State Department look silly.
>
> The audience of nearly one thousand . . . were never so conscious of being in the presence of the sublime and the ridiculous at the same time. Here was a great artist, a captive in his own country whose most widely beloved son he is, finding a way through the Wall via trans-Atlantic cable.
>
> Robeson told the audience that when the walls that were holding him crumbles he would come back to "pound on the table with love to sing for you and for you to sing for me." A thunderous applause greeted his words. The Miner's Choir, who had come from Wales to honor Robeson and faced an all-night ride back to make the morning shift, sang the ever-popular "There'll Be a Welcome In The Valleys When You Come Home Again To Wales."
>
> At the end of the program, the audience would not let Robeson go until he sang "Ole Man River." They did not care if the broadcast was costing them six dollars per minute. "We want it; we'll pay for it," they yelled. True to their words, they emptied their pockets of their scant savings to hear Robeson sing the song that was written for him.

At the end of the program, Robeson vowed to keep up the fight until he was dying – "I'll be in Wales, Glasgow, on the waterfront, everywhere, singing."

This program touched off a wave of new protests against the State Department for their "scandalous" treatment of Robeson and others who criticized the government's anti-Communist foreign policy abroad and the racist policies at home. The weight of world criticism became an embarrassment for the U.S. Government, especially in our foreign embassies. Within a few weeks, the Supreme Court ruled (Kent vs Dulles) that the State Department had acted illegally in voiding the passports of dissidents. Robeson, along with many others, regained his passport during the summer of 1958. He left for England almost immediately.

As promised, one of Robeson's first considerations was the autumn Eisteddfod in Wales. He was guest artist, in person, at the October convocation of the event. The program notes recall the historic occasion: "For many years it has been the custom of the singing country of Wales to invite Paul Robeson to be a guest of honor at the National Eisteddfod, their famous musical event. Paul made a beautiful film about the lives and work and music of the Welsh miners, many years ago, called 'Proud Valley'; and they have never forgotten him."

The *Heath Guardian* (Wales, October 10, 1958) speaking of Mr. Robeson at the 11th Miners' Eisteddfod, in Portcawl, Wales stated: "ROBESON BRINGS THE RAFTERS DOWN . . . . When he appeared on the stage, surrounded by the choir of Welsh children . . .

the mighty audience joined the children in singing 'We'll Keep a Welcome in the Valley For Him.'"

A reporter from the South Wales *Evening Post* was there: (10/6/58): "President of the South Wales area, Mr. William Paynter, told the big audience that they were honoring a great man and a great artist. Mr. D. D. Evans, the Area General Secretary, presented Paul Robeson with a miniature miner's lamp. Printed on the base of the lamp is the following inscription – 'Greetings To Paul Robeson From The South Wales Miners, October, 1958.' The singer had a great ovation from the miners and the members of their families." Robeson went on to Glasgow and Stratford to keep over-due appointments with his public, but time was not in his favor. More than a decade of constant oppression and villification had taken a terrible toll on Robeson. His health began to fail. Robeson's friends in South Wales, as elsewhere, maintained their interest in justice for black Americans, even after he retired from the scene. Dia Francis, chief administrative officer of the South Wales Miners' Union wrote in "The Miner," Sept./Oct., 1963, Vol. 11 No. 5):

> WHY THE AMERICAN NEGRO IS ANGRY . . .
>
> Where do the trade unions stand in this struggle (for racial justice)? Not all the unions affiliated to the CIO and the AFL practice racial discrimination, but many craft unions do. There are thirty-two large cities in which unions exclude Negroes. They are known as "lilly-white" unions. Negroes are excluded from skilled jobs in the construction industry, mine, plumbing, metal work and electrical trades. The railway unions (with the exception of the car porters which is almost wholly black), exclude Negroes from better paid jobs.
>
> The American Negroes are not prepared to remain second-class citizens. They have clearly indicated their determination that fundamental changes will go through American thinking and the American way of life.

SCOTLAND

Robeson established strong bonds of friendship with the mine workers in Scotland as he did in Wales but unfortunately, the evidence for this is scant and incomplete. According to Seton (1958), he made his first concert tour to Glasgow and Edinburgh in 1930. Over the next eight years, he made several trips to Scotland. After 1934, most of his time was spent with the working classes.

On August 19, 1939 Robeson and Larry Brown appeared in concert at the City Hall of Glasgow. Before the concert, Robeson stated how happy he was to work for the things he believed in. The concert was very well received.

The Scots did not forget their champion. Ten years later, he returned to England and participated in a protest demonstration against the racist practices of the South African government. A fund drive was set up to assist the hard-pressed, working-class black Africans. Various labor unions contributed a total of $1,500. More than $500 of this amount was contributed by the Scottish unions!

Robeson returned to Scotland in 1960 for their May Day celebration. According to the *Daily Record* (5/6/60) . . . "The magic of Paul Robeson gave Scotland one of its biggest May Day demonstrations for years . . .". At the end of the program, the miners honored Robeson by presenting him with a miniature miner's lamp. Printed on the base was the inscription . . . "From The Scottish Miners to Paul Robeson, 2-5-1960."

ROBESON IN MANCHESTER, ENGLAND

During the 1930s, Robeson visited Manchester, England and carried words of hope to the millworkers of that industrial city. They remembered. A group of workers met in 1956 to plan a tribute to Robeson. Their goal was to focus world attention on his "persecution" by the American government.

Ambitious beyond their means, the group scheduled the tribute for the Free Trade Hall in Manchester on March 11, 1956. Robeson was invited to come to the affair, but he sent a letter of regret that the U.S. State Department refused to grant him a passport. Instead, he recorded songs and a statement that were played at the concert. Local fascists threatened the group and pessimists predicted abysmal failure for the project. The sponsors worked diligently and all 500 seats at the hall were filled. A large portrait of Robeson dominated the stage. When Robeson's taped message was played, the audience fell into a deep silence, trying to catch every word:

> Though I must send you these words from far, I can say that never have I felt closer to you than I do today. The warmth of your friendship reaches out across the barriers which temporarily separate us and rekindles the memories of many happy years that I spent among you. I recall how a Manchester friend explained to me how closely we two were bound by the web of history, and human suffering and aspiration. He told me of the life of bitter hardship and toil which his father and grandfather knew in the mills, and of how the cotton which his forefathers wove linked them with other toilers whose sweat and toil produced that cotton in far away America, the Negro slaves, my own father, my own people.
>
> . . . I, myself, believe, that the pressure of democratic opinion, here and abroad, will compel the State Department to relent in their refusal to permit me to travel to other countries . . . I am eager to be on my way, to be free to sing, to act, to be at your side and at the side of the people everywhere, whose hearts sing peace and freedom, brotherhood and love!

The sound of Robeson's voice, silenced for so many years, aroused the public to action. The sponsoring group unanimously passed a resolution to send the following message to President Eisenhower: "This meeting requests you, Mr. President, in your high and honorable office, to intercede with the department involved to secure for Mr. Paul Robeson a passport so that once more we can hear that great American singer." The *Manchester Guardian* carried portions of Robeson's taped message in its issue of March 12, 1956:

> Here in my home in New York, I recall your own great city as another home to me, a place where I came so often to sing and where I always was inspired by the flourishing cultural life of Manchester the splendid orchestras, the outstanding contribution to classical music and the other arts, the great newspapers and by the richness of the folk culture of Lancashire, which has given to England and the world the artistry of dear Gracie Fields and so many others.

The *Guardian* continued to quote Robeson by reporting that he deeply appreciated the concern that had been expressed for his civil rights by the *Manchester Guardian* and other British newspapers and magazines and by all the many groups who had urged the State Department to grant him a passport.

Most of the other speakers looked upon him as the symbolic victim of American reaction to maintain its hold on the old order. Mr. G. Vaughn Davies, prospective candidate (Liberals) from Withington, saw Robeson's incarceration as a threat of state tyranny. "He is really the symbol," said Mr. Will Griffiths, M.P., "of thousands of unnamed and unknown who are . . . languishing in Spanish gaols, in Kenya, in South Africa and Northern Ireland." And Cedric Belfrage, the former editor of the *National Guardian* said, "Robeson in captivity is fast becoming the symbol of the hypocrisy of the free world."

Under the banner "Let Robeson Sing," the workers' movement spread throughout the British Isles and the world. The ordinary workers sent sixpence and shillings and the Welsh miners donated fifty pounds. "Let Paul Robeson sing" became the demand of people throughout the land, from the shipyards of Scotland to the London docks; from Yorkshire mines to the Welsh valleys.

Later in 1956 a group convened in St. Pancras Town Hall, London to petition for Robeson's freedom. In December, 1956, a conference for the founding of a National Paul Robeson Committee was called in Manchester. In a few months, the movement for Paul Robeson had grown from a mere handful to a million strong. Among the supporters were such well-known personalities as Mr. Aneurin Bevan; the Bishop of Birmingham; the Canon of St. Paul's Cathedral; the Chairman of the Labor Party, Mr. Tom Deiberg; the Composer, Benjamin Britten; the painter, Paul Hogarth; and many others. Artists, scientists, and many members of Parliament joined the working classes in the effort to restore Robeson's right to sing.

At the end of the program, the group showed the film "Proud Valley," depicting Welsh miners struggling for survival, a generation before, with Robeson as the star. The program ended with songs from a choir of Welsh miners who had traveled many miles, voluntarily, to add their voices to the rising wind of protest against the United States government. The miners returned to Wales that same night and arrived home in time to enter the mines on schedule. Other groups of workers followed the lead of the mill people of Manchester. Some organizations used tape recordings and gramophone tape recordings that Robeson had made, to inspire millions of peope.

WITH KRISHNA MENON, JAWAHARAL NEHRU, AND THE INDIA LEAGUE

A parallel study of the lives of Krishna Menon and Robeson reveals some remarkable similarities. It is not surprising that they supported each other's struggles for the freedom of the common man. Krishna Menon's father was a lawyer who resisted British colonial oppression of his fellow Indians. He set a fine example of courage for his son. Robeson's father escaped from the slave system of North Carolina through the Underground Railroad and taught his son the value of freedom at any cost.

Krishna Menon first came to England in 1927 as a delegate to a Boy Scouts' jamboree, expecting to return to India after the convention was over. He remained in England for 28 years before returning to India. The Robesons, Paul and Essie, came to England in 1927 for his appearance in "Showboat." They had not planned to stay in England but the play ran for several months. They took a house in Hempstead Heath and lived in London for the next twelve years. Before his arrival in England, Krishna Menon had fallen under the influence of Annie Besant, a practicing Theosophist. Her support of the cause of Indian freedom endeared her to millions of Indians everywhere. Krishna Menon entered the London School of Economics and became a favored pupil of the Socialist teacher, Harold Laski. He became a member of the Labour Party and cultivated their friendship. Robeson was influenced toward Socialism by William Patterson, Bernard Shaw, George Padmore, Mei Lan-Fang (a Chinese actor) and Harold Laski. Krishna Menon studied law and was admitted to the bar in 1934. He never established a law practice. Robeson took his law degree at Columbia University in 1923. He soon discovered that the practice of law was not to his liking.

Sensitized to the degrading effects of British colonialism before he left India, Menon began his crusade for the freedom of India, including Pakistan, while still a student. His base of operations was the India League, the surviving half of the Commonwealth of India League. Henry Polak, a Theophist solicitor, was the guiding force in the old League before 1928. His moderate position on Indian independence was unacceptable to the impatient Krishna Menon. He split the League and carried with him the more militant members to form the new India League.

Robeson was born in 1898 and Krishna Menon in 1897. They first met around 1935 in the home of Marie Seton, in England. Both men took single-minded, uncompromising positions on the question of freedom for the common men of all races and colors. Each man sought help from the political left and was accused of being Communist. Both men were famous public speakers. Thousands flocked to hear them whenever they appeared in public. Both men incurred the enmity of the American press and suffered from the hostility of the news media.

On the other hand there were significant differences in the men and their experiences. Krishna Menon has been described by his detractors as a cold, irascible brain, incapable of human warmth. Even Robeson's enemies admit that his charisma was legendary. Krishna Menon's close relationship with Nehru drew him into the circle of power after Indian independence. He served his country as Lord High Commissioner to London, Indian Representative to the United Nations, and Minister of Defense. Thus, his ideas helped to shape the policies of the Indian government, especially in the area of foreign affairs. Robeson discovered that neither the Democratic nor the Republican party had any sincere interest in the welfare of black people. Unable to work with either, he helped to form a new political group, the Progressive party in 1948. When the effort failed, he tried to influence America's governmental policies, domestic and foreign, from the outside, sometimes with frightful frontal assaults.

When the two men first met in 1935, Robeson had recently walked out of the opening of his film "Sanders of the River" at the Leicester Theatre, in protest of the way that his role had been distorted. His identity as a freedom fighter was on the rise. Seton (1958) has reported that the two men got together as if they had many things to talk about. She recalled that Robeson became a regular supporter of the India League, financially and otherwise. Krishna Menon reciprocated by supporting West Indian and African groups in London. He spoke at the League of Colored People on several occasions.

Jawaharal Nehru made a fateful visit to the west on the eve of World War II. Krishna Menon met him in Marseilles, and they toured the Loyalist encampments in Barcelona and Madrid. Nehru saw the Spanish Civil War as the "upheaval which would embrace the national and social problems of the world." Everywhere he went he spoke for the Loyalist's cause and against Fascism with the same sincerity that he championed the cause of Indian independence. They returned to London late in June. A welcome meeting was held for Nehru at the India League on Monday, June 27, 1938. Speakers for the occasion were:

Marjorie Corbett Ashby
The Dean of Canterbury
Stafford Cripps, M.P.
H. H. Elvin
R. Palme Dutt
Harold Laski
Paul Robeson
Ellen Wilkinson, M.P.

Upon hearing of Nehru's anti-fascist position, Robeson was pleased to appear on the program. He sang several songs. This was probably Robeson's first meeting with Nehru. The appearance of this list of people at the India League, especially Nehru, caused many Indians to join and support the India League for the first time.

On March 25, 1949, a protest meeting was held at the Friends' House, London, against the racist policies of the South African government. It was organized by the South African Committee of the India League in cooperation with the League of Coloured Peoples, the West African Student's Union, and the East African Student's Union. Krishna Menon sat with the Souh African Indian leader, Dr. Dadoo, and the Rev. Michael Scott. Julius Silverman, M.P., acted as chairman and Paul Robeson led the protest meeting of 3,000 people.

Krishna Menon and Robeson crossed paths again when Krishna Menon was appointed United Nations representative from India in July, 1952. He arrived in New York shortly after the outbreak of the Korean War. His criticism of U. S. intervention in Korea made him suspect by many Americans. Just as Robeson attacked the U. S. Government for its pro-colonial, anti-Communist, racist policies in his public appearances, Krishma Menon did the same as an official delegate to the United Nations. Both were castigated by the American press. Menon was described by some observers as the diplomat without diplomacy. He was rather blunt in his denunciation of racial discrimination. He supported the Council of African Affairs, which Robeson founded. He continued the fight that Nehru started to gain a United Nations seat for Communist China. When Mrs. Vijaya Lakshmi Pandit, Nehru's sister, became President of the United Nations in 1953, she joined Krishma Menon in an unrelenting attack on the West's colonial policies in Africa, especially South Africa (The *New Statesman and Nation,* 11/22/52).

Robeson's passport issue had become an international issue by 1958. Eight years of confinement to this hemisphere had cast Robeson in the role of an unfortunate victim of the punitive State Department. Many world leaders joined in the constant criticism of the U.S. Government for this abridgement of the right to travel. Nehru wrote an open letter to Robeson in 1958, on his sixtieth birthday.

> . . . . This day should be celebrated, not only because Mr. Robeson is one of the greatest artists of our generation, but, also, because he fights and suffers for a cause which should be dear to all of us: for

human dignity. To celebrate his birthday means to honor both a great man and at the same time the cause for which he stands and which he suffers . . . .

Nehru's letter caused an international furor. The American Ambassador went to India's Ministry of External Affairs to register his protest in person. An official of the State Department called the Indian Embassy in Washington to file a formal complaint against this "intervention in a domestic affair." Less than three months later, the State Department announced that it was bowing to the ruling of the Supreme Court and Robeson's passport was returned to him. Soon after regaining his passport, Robeson returned to England. One of his first public appearances was at a concert in St. Paul's Cathedral in support of a Fund for the Defense of South African Political Prisoners.

THE NATIONAL MARITIME UNION

Robeson returned to New York in 1939, ending a twelve-year exile in London. Already his work with the Welsh and Scottish miners, the mill workers in Manchester, the dock workers in London, and the laboring classes in Europe had established his identity as a staunch friend of labor. Soon after his arrival, he lined up with the trade union movement in North America – the United States and Canada and, eventually, Panama and Hawaii. The unions accepted his help with open arms as they struggled for survival in the hostile environment of the late 1930s and early 1940s.

In a personal interview in Honolulu, Eddie Tangen, International Representative of the Longshoremen's and Warehousemen's Union (ILWU) recalled: "I first heard about Paul around 1940 when he was helping the National Maritime Union (NMU)in Houston, New York, and other east coast ports. As you know, whenever Paul came around, a crowd always gathered. Then the unions could tell their side of the story."

Prior to leaving London, Robeson had starred in the play "Stevedore" which brought him into direct contact with laborers in the shipping industry. With this background and the fact that NMU headquarters was in New York, his hometown, it is easy to understand why the NMU was one of the first labor organizations to receive Robeson's support. Moreover, the two men who headed the union were Robeson's friends. Joseph Curran, President, and Robeson grew up in the same New Jersey town. Curran underscored his warm affection for Robeson by naming his son, Joseph Paul, in honor of Robeson. Ferdinand Smith, a black West Indian, was Executive Secretary of the NMU. He and Robeson became fast friends and supported each other in their wide-ranging struggles for the rights of black workers in the NMU and elsewhere.

Robeson was attracted also by the history of the NMU's fight for democracy in the shipping industry. He referred to this when he spoke to the Sixth National Convention of NMU that opened in Cleveland, on July 7, 1941: ". . . I came here today because I feel close to the Maritime Union . . . . I know the whole background of your union, and I would like for you to know that among the colored people of this country, your union stands foremost for giving complete equality and for the advancement of colored people. (Proceedings of NMU Convention, 1941.)

The first trade union among black seamen was the American Seamen Protective Association, formed April 15, 1863 (Wesley, 1967). In 1868 there were an estimated 3500 black seamen living in New York, some of whom carried masters' licences. One, Captain George Brook, sailed from New York to Europe and Africa with an entirely black crew and returned home after a successful voyage (The Negro in the Trade Union, The *Pilot* – 5/30/40).

The working condition in the shipping industry was so poor, before the Civil War, that many black seamen mutinied, losing their lives along with their white fellow-workers (The African Repository, Pub. 1830-60). During the Civil War, the southern ship owners released their white seamen and hired black crews. When the war was over, the blacks were fired and the whites were rehired.

An outstanding example of interracial solidarity among those early seamen was shown in Baltimore during the 1930s. The crew of the Diamond Comet struck the ship, and the owner shanghied a group of unorgainzed black seamen to put her out to sea. The black seamen did not learn of the strike until after they left port. As soon as they reached Philadelphia, the entire crew jumped ship. From Baltimore, black and white seamen marched together to Washington, D.C. in support of the relief system that they had fought for two years earlier. The ships' owners made every effort to divide them along racial lines and play one group against the other. The seamen resisted all such efforts, sleeping in union halls rather than accept segregated flop houses. The Baltimore seamen abolished discrimination against blacks in the distribution of relief. Black seamen enjoyed the same rights as others in Baltimore shipping through the centralized shipping bureau.

This kind of rank and file activity facilitated the formation of the Maritime Union in 1937. The organizers chose Joseph Curran as their first president. Having come up through the ranks, Curran had won the respect and confidence of the seamen. Many years later, he recalled the strike of 1936 that led to the formation of NMU: ". . . Militant blacks, Jews, Puerto Ricans and others stood shoulder to shoulder with the rest of the rank and file to form our union. Goon squads and police clubs left their marks, but they were unable to crush the union." For their own protection, the seamen set forth in their constitution a list of clear objectives. One that interested Robeson, in particular, was: ". . . To unite into one organization, regardless of creed, color, sex, nationality or political affiliation, all workers eligible for membership directly or indirectly engaged in the maritime industry."

Ship owners fought, with every resource at hand, all attempts at unionization. Labor spies, specially trained in fomenting racial and religious strife, were planted in the union. When they were exposed and expelled, Curran warned: "Trade union history has proved that racial, color and religious discrimination have always been an obstacle in the path of unity, dividing workers into smaller groups which are vulnerable to all types of employer attacks."

Robeson was pleased to learn that the NMU's constitution stood up to severest test from many quarters, especially when it became necessary to translate the words of the constitution into deeds:

> Wages of $50.00 per month were paid to riverboat firemen and dock hands in 1842. They remained the same until NMU began negotiating in their behalf.
> In September of 1940, the Captain of the SS President Garfield decided to have a Neptune Party as the ship crossed the equator. All of the members of the crew were invited, except the blacks. When the white unionists refused to attend the party, the Captain offered a compromise. "The black seamen could attend the party if the others would agree not to throw any of the black seamen into the pool! The white seamen refused to accept the compromise and the party was called off" (*Pilot,* 9/22/40).

Robeson was pleased with the position of the NMU with respect to World War II:

> . . . The NMU and Transport Workers Union united in a 40,000 man anti-war demonstration for peace in Madison Square Garden, early in 1940. When their representatives tried to lay a wreath at the Eternal Light, in honor of seamen lost in the war, they were arrested. Those arrested included Ted Louis, R. J. Sullivan, James Edwards, Frank Cupeuro, Merle Chase, Edward Tyler and Harry Wensted (*Pilot,* 4/19/40).

On June 14, 1940, the NMU issued its statement of war policy: "We oppose America's entry into the war. We, as trade union men, believe that to really be able to defend our nation we must defend all the social economic and political rights of our people and fight against all steps to drag our country into war."

Hundreds of seamen, longshoremen, harbor workers, and fishermen left New York for Chicago, in early June of 1941, for the Emergency Peace Mobilization Rally. Robeson was the featured star at the affair. Following Robeson's presentation, a mass meeting was held to mobilize for peace. More than 20,000 delegates attended.

Just two and one-half weeks before the NMU convention, on June 20, 1941, President Curran sent a letter to President Roosevelt protesting the discriminatory hiring practices against black workers that was so rampant throughout the United States. The union threw its full support behind the March on Washington, led by A. Philip Randolph, to force the President to issue an executive order for a fair employment practices act. Robeson referred to the Union's support for the black worker in his speech before the NMU convention on 7/7/41:

. . . I know that we are all one in the things for which we stand. Here at home, of course, for complete rights for labor, for complete equality for the colored people of this country and for a right to a better life for every worker in this land of ours.

. . . This is my first time among you. And whenever your next convention comes – I see by the papers it may be in 1943 – I will be back again.

Mr. Robeson sang the following songs requested by the audience:

"Bill of Rights"	"It Ain't Necessarily So"
"Water Boy"	"Fatherland"
"Joe Hill"	"Spring Song"
"Ole Man River"	"Song to Joe"
"Jim Crow"	"Ballad For Americans"

After Robeson's presentation, President Curran made a suggestion:

. . . I would recommend that we give consideration to extending to Paul Robeson, for the work he has done in all the fields of endeavor, an honorary membership in the National Maritime Union [extended applause].

M/S/C to extend to Paul Robeson honorary membership in the National Maritime Union. The convention, again, rose amid a demonstration of applause, as Paul Robeson left the hall.

(Proceedings of the NMU Convention, July 7, 1941, Cleveland, O.)

Over the next several months, Robeson had many reasons to be proud of his membership in the NMU. On January 2, 1942, the owners of the troopship, Kugsholm (United States Lines), called the NMU hall for 140 seamen to man the liner. Of the 140 sent, 115 were white and the remainder were black. All of the white seamen were accepted; all of the black seamen were rejected. Joseph Curran, President of NMU, acted without hesitation. He sent a telegram to President F. D. Roosevelt protesting the racial discrimination. The following morning, officials of United States Lines telephoned the NMU hall to report that the black seamen were now acceptable. When the ship sailed, all 140 men were aboard.

A few days later, four able-bodied, black seamen were sent by the NMU to help man the Mor Mac Post, a new, government-built cargo ship of the Moore-McCormack Lines. They were told that they were not wanted. The remainder of the crew held a meeting and voted not to sail unless the black seamen were hired. The ship, eventually, sailed with the black seamen aboard.

When asked about his company's racial attitude, Robert C. Lee, Executive Vice-President of Moore-McCormack Lines answered,

Lee: We'll take colored men provided the whites don't object. That's positively the only basis I'd accept .

Rep.: Did the white men object in this case?

Lee: Probably not, they're all commies.

(NMU Bulletin, December 1943)

Early in 1942 six seamen, three white and three black, signed on the SS Selitz, of the Grace Line. The white seamen were hired immediately, but the black seamen were rejected with the explanation that the white crew would not accept them. NMU members polled the crew and the black men were accepted unanimously. The union issued a statement that made its position clear: "They pay their dues and meet all of their obligations to the Union and are entitled to equal shipping rights on a rotary basis."

It was mid-April, 1942 when Ferdinand Smith, Executive Secretary of NMU and Earl B. Dickerson, Chicago Alderman, met with officials of the War Production Board and offered a program to train and hire 50,000 black workers in the war industry. A follow-up meeting was held early in June with Gen. Frank McSherry, labor aide to Donald Nelson, Chief of the War Production Board. Smith made a progress report to A Unity for Victory Rally, at the golden gate ballroom on June 27, 1942. He reported that McSherry gave every indication that their plan was being implemented. Among the speakers at this rally were New York City Councilman Adam Clayton Powell and Joseph Curran.

The NMU was equally vigorous in fighting bias against Jews, Chinese, Filipinos, and other minorities among its membership. The case of Philip Nazareth, a fireman, brought the NMU into conflict with the racist practices of the Gulf Oil Company. The case lasted several days and involved several doctors. Justice triumphed when spurious medical reports from anti-semitic sources were disproved and set aside.

The most celebrated case in which the NMU played a decisive role was the mistreatment of Captain Hugh Mulzac. Hugh Mulzac had twenty-five years of experience at sea on steam and sailing vessels. He had sailed as A.B. Quartermaster, bos'n third mate, second mate, and chief officer, on British and American vessels. A graduate of the U.S. Shipping Board School, he earned his certificate in 1918. He held a diploma in navigation and radio from the International Correspondence and Nautical School and a Certificate from the Sperry Gyro Compass School.

In 1922, Mulzac passed his examination as Master of Ocean-going Steamers, Unlimited, and was, therefore, qualified to command any merchant ship of any tonnage on any ocean.

None of these qualifications was sufficient to overcome Mulzac's major handicap, his blackness. His applications for positions as Master were treated with contempt by all ship owners. So, for twenty years, Mulzac sailed as cook or steward.

The NMU fought this case "with all its strength, from every port in the country, from ships on every sea." Resolutions and telegrams of protest flooded many government offices in Washington.

In cooperation with the Negro Labor Victory Committee, and other interested groups, the NMU helped to organize delegations that went to Washington to argue the Mulzac case, in person.

Victory came on September 23, 1942, when Captain Edward McCauley, of the War Shipping Administration, announced the appointment of Captain Hugh Mulzac to command the new liberty freighter, Booker T. Washington. She was launched by Miss Marian Anderson, noted concert singer.

Thus, through these and other involvements, the NMU earned the distinction of being one of six groups in the country, chosen by a national poll, that had done most for the improvement of race relations in terms of real democracy. The Director of the Schomburg Collection of Negro Literature, in making the results known, cited the NMU: ". . . For supporting Captain Mulzac in his fight for recognition and for its uncompromising stand against racial discrimination in the employment of its members."

President Curran's response was clear and consistent: "One hundred and fifty years ago, the founding fathers of this country wrote, 'All men are created equal.' We believe that is true. And we are prepared to carry out the fight to prove it."

The NMU did not sit on its laurels. After several months of bitter struggle, the Union backed by ships' crews, enacted a non-discriminatory policy in all of its contracts with ship owners. The contract became effective on July 15, 1944. It provided that . . . There shall be no discrimination because of race, creed, color or national origin.

In an editorial entitled, "Negro Record on Merchant Ships," the *New York Herald Tribune* reported:

> On July 15, the NMU placed in operation a contract which prohibits discrimination because of race and color or national origin. This contract, Secretary (Ferdinand) Smith says "has been accepted by 124 ship companies." Here, sure, is a long step taken in a right direction. Neither storms, mines nor torpedoes have shown discrimination. Ships which sail every ocean may fitly be officered and manned by all such free men as have shown themselves able to steer a course, save a life and win a war.

In July 1946, the national CIO formally paid tribute to the NMU's effective fight against race prejudice. At that time CIO president Philip Murray, presented to president Curran the Annual Award of the CIO National Committee to Abolish Discrimination for "outstanding service to the cause of economic and political democracy in the field of relations." Serving notice upon the enemies of Freedom and Justice, a union spokesman replied: "Within our own industry and on every front in our national life where discrimination raises its ugly head, the rank and file will be in there pitching, as always, to uphold the democratic principle which has made this Union strong."

Robeson was cheered and encouraged by the anti-fascist activities of NMU and other unions. His earlier conviction that the future of the black workers was closely tied to the future of labor was confirmed by these activities. His pro-labor involvements became more frequent and more widespread.

On April 8, 1942, Robeson, Joseph Curran, and Pearl Buck addressed a mass meeting in New York City's Manhattan Center, called to "mobilize Negro and colonial people in the fight against Fascism." The meeting was chaired by Channing Tobias and the keynote speaker was Hubert Agar, editor of the *Louisville Courier Journal.* After singing the songs of many lands, Robeson spoke to the audience: "There is a need to clarify some of the confusion that exists today, regarding Negroes and the war. Negroes have every need to be active in a people's war. To fight Fascism is to fight for every right of the Negro people." Three weeks later (May, 1942), Robeson sang and spoke to 51,000 laborers in Yankee Stadium in behalf of a second front to shorten the war. He stressed unity at home, unity at the United Nations, and international trade union unity (*Pilot,* May 7, 1942).

Robeson sang at the close of the sixth annual dance of the NMU in mid-November, 1942 at the Royal Windsor Hall, New York City. One thousand people were present to swell the coffers of the United Servicemen's Clubs and Allied War Relief Organizations. President Curran thanked Robeson for coming, in spite of the fact that he had just finished a concert in another hall that same night. Robeson praised the union for its fight for human freedom and urged the group to call on him at any time.

Over 54,000 people attended a labor victory rally at Yankee Stadium, on May 2, 1943. Robeson as guest artist sang folk songs and the songs of freedom. He urged the group to fight to defeat Fascism at home as well as abroad. He closed his remarks by saying, "We are here because we believe in the dignity of man and the right to freedom of all mankind."

Robeson was a special guest at the Eighth Annual Sessions of the NMU convention that began in the Grand Ballroom of the Manhattan Center on July 8, 1943. President Curran introduced him:

> . . . Paul is an old friend of mine. We both came from the same little town; only he left the little town a few years before I did. We each knew all the people in that little town.
> Paul Robeson speaks for himself. He speaks for the American people. He speaks for all of the people and he sings for all of the people. Paul Robeson is a member of our union. I can safely say that we are extremely proud that he is a member of our union, and we hope that he will always be a member of our union (applause). He will be, we know.
> Brother Robeson is an extremely busy man. He is all over the place . . . . Whenever there is a need or help wanted for fighting for freedom, he is busy helping out. I said once before that Paul Robeson's voice is one of the strongest voices in the world for democracy, today.

Robeson strode to the rostrum and smiled as he waited for silence. He told the group that he had remained in New York, in spite of commitments in Michigan, just to attend their convention. He expressed great pride in his membership in the NMU: "I am proud because we are a union that understands and is striving to understand better, every day, the issues that confront the world. There is no organization that is doing a better share in the whole world struggle. We are on the right side."

Recalling the support the NMU had provided in the struggle of blacks for first-class citizenship, Robeson concluded: "I am proud of the record you hold in America today. In these days when there is some undercurrent of feeling arising in our country, you stand as a bulwark, showing how people can really work together, how thousands and thousands of men can stand side by side, whatever their color, believing deeply in common rights of men." (Proceedings of NMU Convention, July 8, 1943.)

Robeson sang eight songs and departed amid thunderous applause. Two days later, the convention voted to support the Anti-Poll Tax and Anti-Lynch legislation, then before the Congress. The text of the resolution read:

> Therefore Be It Resolved: That this convention wholeheartedly supports the Marcantonio Anti-Poll Tax Bill and the Gavagan Anti-Lynch Bill. That the efforts, funds and energies of our organization be used to carry on an intensive campaign for the passage of these measures as an essential program for winning the war. M/S To Adopt. (Proceedings of NMU Conv., 7/10/43.)

Robeson's next appearance before the NMU convention was during the session of September 22–October 15, 1947 in New York City. Joseph Curran, still president of NMU, again introduced Robeson:

> . . . He has been with us since the beginning, has assisted our organization in its growth, has always been ready to help and has done a great job.
>
> We feel with deep pride that we can say he belongs to our organization; and, no matter how far away he may be, or no matter how busy he has been, when we needed him, he came. He even stopped in the middle of concert tours to speak to our people and to sing for us.
>
> He is a great representative not only of his own people but of all working people the world over. He has sacrificed a great deal for his principles; and he stands head and shoulders out in front in the fight to promote peace, to promote an end to discrimination and, at the same time, to give of his great talents to help advance the progressive causes. So I would like to introduce an old friend of ours, a working man, a great artist and a great man – Paul Robeson. (The delegation rose in a demonstration of cheers and extended applause.)

Robeson started by saying: "Thanks so much, fellows. I needn't say I am proud to be back and say hello to my parent union. I do feel myself a part of the struggle; and, as a union man, I am first a member of the National Maritime Union" (applause). Robeson sang "The Three Mariners," "Waterboy," "Joe Hill," "Lullaby," "Ole Man River," and "The House I Live In." Following the songs, he continued his remarks:

> . . . . That is the reason I have come into the struggle, so that I can go back today to the people, to the Negro people, to the forces of labor. Speak to them not from the Carnegie Hall stage, not in the so-called big places, but in their small meetings, in their

> churches, wherever they may be — and it is with them that I will stand until the final victory (extended applause).
>
> So we are fighting today. You are fighting every day for a decent kind of living, not just for bare security. This is the wealthiest and greatest nation in the world. We have a right to some fair share, so that our children don't have to live in condemned houses and go to condemned schools. Suppose a deep depression were to hit tomorrow, how many workers' homes would be so secure that they wouldn't have to worry? . . . .
>
> I have always been proud to say I have been on the side of those who were in the anti-fascist struggle.
>
> This struggle goes on everywhere where the forces of privilege still rule. You realize what the struggle is in your fight against the Taft-Hartley Law (applause). But beyond that, it goes to the very basis of American democracy, to the very basis of American faith . . . .
>
> And so I stand with you today, and I know somehow you will find a way to fight these forces that are attempting to change our democratic America. I must say to you, whenever I can be of help, call on me, and don't worry about the pressures that come . . . .

President Curran gave the final word as Robeson prepared to depart:

> I am sure that we can assure Brother Robeson that this Union will always remain in the fore-front in the fight against discrimination and the fight for people's rights throughout the world (applause). At this time, I think we ought to have a rising vote of thanks to Paul Robeson for coming to our Convention and speaking to us. (Delegates rise amid extendede applause.)

Before this convention ended, a resolution on minorities was passed which affirmed the Union's commitment to fight discrimination . . . . "in any form against any member or group of members of our organization . . .".

The 1947 NMU convention was the last one to which Robeson was invited. His relationship with the Union, like the good intentions expressed in the Minorities Resolution, was influenced by the realities of the cold war. A destructive power struggle, dormant for many months, became public early in 1948. The liberal faction lost and the victors moved the Union into the position of compliance with President Truman's anti-Communist foreign policy.

Robeson's name came up for discussion on two occasions during the 1949 NMU convention. Michael Quill, President of the Transport Workers' Union, addressed the NMU convention on September 12, 1949 one week after the Peekskill violence. He suggested, during his speech, that the Democratic Party had lost New York state because of the (Henry) Wallace campaign. He expressed the opinion that the Communists were likely to run Wallace or Robeson for the Senate from New York, thereby siphoning off support from his candidate, Gov. Lehman. He made an impassioned plea to the delegates for the candidacy of Lehman. Later in the same convention, Thomas McDonald, NMU delegate, moved that Robeson's name be stricken from the NMU's Honorary Membership list. The motion was sec-

onded by Israel Putman. Chairman Curran intervened: "I don't believe that motion is in order at this time. I can't see any sense in that motion at the present time. I don't see any reason for jumping all over the place and doing things of that type right now." McDonald: "I will withdraw it." Curran: "The motion is withdrawn."

THE INTERNATIONAL LONGSHOREMEN'S AND WAREHOUSEMEN'S UNION

More than 100,000 disgruntled dock workers struck the West Coast ports in 1934, paralyzing the shipping industry for many days. The strikers won, and their working conditions were markedly improved. The success of this effort gave birth to the Longshoremen's and Warehousemen's Union (ILWU). In time it would include sugar and pineapple workers, cannery workers, and fishermen. Among the most steadfast supporters of the dock workers were the members of the Maritime Union. This common struggle forged a bond of friendship and support between the two unions that would last for more than a decade.

The Union's 30th Anniversary, in 1964, was a major event. Congratulations flowed in from such distinguished persons as Oregon's Senator Wayne Morse, California's Gov. Edmund Brown, and Paul Robeson. Robeson's statement was representative of the messages received: "Warmest greetings to the Union and thanks for your magnificent contributions, over the years, in the struggles which have benefitted so many workers, not only my people, but the whole labor movement. It has been a great joy and privilege to have been able to participate from time to time. Warmest congratulations and best wishes for many years of continuing successful struggles and progress" (The *Dispatcher*, 5/1/64).

Robeson did, indeed, "participate from time to time" in ILWU activities. As early as 1942, he appeared on the west coast in support of the trade union movement in general and the advancement of the rights of black workers in particular. Speaking to a press conference in Los Angeles on September 18, 1942, The *Labor Herald* (9/25/42) quoted Robeson: "CIO unions throughout the country are in the forefront of the fight to smash barriers of racial discrimination in hiring . . . . Everywhere I go, I find labor unions, particularly those in the CIO, leading the fight to get my people jobs."

Robeson had just returned from a visit to the Englewood, California plant of North American Aircraft where he sang and spoke to several thousand workers. Encouraged by the presence of several hundred black workers in the audience, he thanked the officials of local 887 UAW-CIO for having invited him to speak and congratulated the plant officials for their use of black workers:

> A victory for Hitler would be the worst thing which could happen to my people. It would mean we would all be consigned to slavery for I don't know how long. Therefore, the salvation of Negro people lies in the overthrow of fascism. . . . We must see that we're not engaged in just a struggle of the colored peoples. Our fight for freedom embraces the common men all over the world – in the Balkans, among the Welsh miners, in the slums of London, all oppressed peoples in all lands. There are those in the south who say that this war is being fought for a new kind of life, but which doesn't include the Negro. But you can't talk about a war for new freedoms which do not include not only my people but the people in India and Africa and everywhere else. It is impossible to say we're fighting for a freedom that excludes the colored people. (*Labor Herald*, 9/25/42).

The Bay Area CIO gave a luncheon in Robeson's honor in San Francisco the following day. He seized the opportunity to challenge the labor leadership: "The unions can make it clear to the Negro that this war is his war because the democracy that he wants is staring him in the face in the unions. I hope your organizational work will extend among my people. It is the one great hope to make them see that America can be theirs, too."

As he had done on many occasions before, Robeson tied the cause of the black man to the cause of labor: ". . . . But the problem of Negro people is generally a problem of working people. Their future lies with labor. They must work side by side with labor."

Robeson's friends on the West Coast told him many stories about the racial policies of ILWU. It was common knowledge that the most profitable ship lines on the West Coast were allocated to white seamen (Alaskan Lines) while the longer, less profitable runs to the Philippines, China, and Japan were given to black seamen. There was a real crisis when the Admiral Lines discontinued some of its ships that had black crews. No one knew what to do with all of those idle black crewmen. Fortunately, there were some white union officials who had the conviction and the courage to meet such crises head-on. One such official was Eddie Tangen, international representative of ILWU. He described a crisis that came his way in 1940:

> I was working at the union office in Seattle when I dispatched a black seaman named Norman Paine to a job on the passenger ship, Alutian. The job was in the pantry and it had never been held by a black man before. Neither the crew nor the company wanted a breakthrough on the color line. The problem was that the pantryman slept in the "glory hole" with the rest of the crew and they didn't want a black down there. This is the big room in the after-end of the ship that sleeps sixty or seventy people.
>
> No one else would apply for the job. Since the ship was sailing that day it gave me the opportunity to declare an emergency and send anyone I wanted to fill the job. Here was a guy who was very active in the union, a college graduate, had a masters degree and a very skilled craftsman for any job on that ship. He was very articulate and the ideal man for the job.
>
> Norman knew that there would be trouble, but neither of us knew

how much. All hell broke loose in about half hour. There were ninety-five men in the stewards department. When they saw Norman, nearly all of them walked off the ship. As fast as I hired on new crewmen some of the old ones would quit. The old crew began to waylay the new crew members and turn them around. We even had to escort the new men on board. In the end, we had to comb the streets of Seattle for men with seamen's papers. Instead of sailing in two hours when Norman dispatched, the ship did not sail for 2½ days. By that time we had dispatched over 300 men.

There was a lot of pressure on Norman, but he stayed on the job. Then, of course, one of the finest things happened that occurs many times. During the voyage the steward department's delegate became ill and was taken off ship in Alaska. The crew held an election, and they chose Norman as their delegate. That was the breakthrough. Within 6 months Negroes were in all jobs they were capable of handling.

Tangen spoke of the risk that white unionists took in supporting the cause of black seamen:

All of us who were involved in building up the union were labelled as reds and especially those of us who were involved in the fight for Negro rights. These charges were made by the steamship companies, labor spies within the unions, the press and even some of the leadership among the middle-class blacks who would agree with what we were doing but thought that we should be criticizing Russia, instead of fighting discrimination at home.

After we had won the fight aboard the ships we had to fight what was happening in the communities. We had a situation in Portland, Oregon, an out-and-out Jim Crow town until after the war. I could come into that town on a trip with a Negro; he couldn't eat anywhere in the Pacific Railway station. He couldn't go into any bars up to 1948 and 49.

Now this was a town in our union area. The people over there went along with it for a long, long time. Finally, we mustered enough forces, along with others, to break down the Jim Crow in Portland. What we accomplished, at first, only benefited the Negroes who were in the union. The others were subjected to the same old injustices. So we participated with many other groups such as the National Negro Labor Council and the National Negro Congress. At one time, way back, we even tried to work with the Urban League. By getting into the communities, being involved and using some of the mechanics of our union, we were able to get some things accomplished.

Tangen described Robeson's influence on their union activity:

I think that some of our successes were due to Paul's clear thinking on this thing. You see, we were sort of content in many ways with the gradual reform. We were supposed to be way out in front. We were what people called rebels.

Paul had this great quality. He didn't try to tell us how to run our unions. He would just discuss matters with us. That came out in a meeting we had in San Francisco, where he pointed out that the fight for Negro rights was a special problem and needed special solutions.

This was a breakthrough. We had been involved in this thing for a long time, but we had never looked at it that way. We had just taken the position that all men are created equal. That ought to do the trick. And as we began to see what he meant, our programs were stepped up considerably.

Another thing that Paul, very forcibly, brought to our attention was that this whole fight had to be led by Negroes, now, not after the friendly white society molds the whole ball of wax and says ok, now, you can take your rightful place. He took this position; and, certainly, it turned out to be right. Whites could be allies; they could assist wherever they could.

I recall one time I told Paul "Say, look! I understand the problem. I've lived with it for a long time! Why can't I lead?" He answered, "You're not black, that's why."

It was a little difficult for me to accept this at first; but I had to agree with it. So we changed some of the things that we were doing. This was the motivating force for me to step aside so that Joe Johnson could become the secretary-treasurer of the union. He appeared before our people on many, many occasions. When we had something special and he couldn't come, he would make a tape or sing to us by long-distance telephone. Part of what he did for us as seamen and black workers resulted in some of the injustices being put on him. This was about the time that that horrible campaign against him really began.

Much of the credit for the liberal position of the ILWU must go to Harry Bridges, the durable, controversial leader of the union. Among labor leaders, he is considered by some to be one of the best the country has produced. Tangen gave his assessment:

Harry has been one of the builders of the democratic unions on the waterfront of the west coast. He became the president of the ILWU when it was founded on the mainland and became involved in the organizing campaigns that took place in Hawaii.

I am sure historians will compare people who have been labor leaders, in this century, who have accomplished and done something to change the way that particular part of the world reacts. If Harry's name isn't at the top of the list it will be among the first. He went through more than Paul Robeson went through. There were three long, long attempts to deport him, all of which failed. There were arrests, and villifications, right and left. Things are better now. From the very first, the ILWU was integrated under Harry Bridges.

On November 12, 1943, President Harry Bridges conferred honorary, lifetime membership in the ILWU upon Rockwell Kent and Paul Robeson. The event was reported in The *Dispatcher* on November 19, 1943:

President Harry Bridges (of ILWU) bestowed honorary, life-time membership on the world famous singer (Paul Robeson) and the well-known American artist (Rockwell Kent) at a luncheon in their honor at the Hotel Roosevelt, while 50 leaders in the fields of labor and the arts rose to their feet to pay tribute to the men who were being honored and to the organization which had singled them out in recognition of the good anti-Fascist fight which these two great Americans have fought in every way.

For hundreds of years colleges and universities have conferred degrees on leaders in all walks of life except labor. Today, the ILWU, a great, militant trade union, showed that, in labor's eyes, those who fight for the common man are also deserving of respect and esteem. No college ceremony was ever more dignified and impressive than this one. The caps and gowns that are traditional in college functions were not missed here. The warmth and spirit of the honored guests, their heart-felt love for the people, were all that was needed to give the ceremony a tone of simple dignity. Quietly, and with honest pride, Harry Bridges explained that honorary membership in the ILWU was not conferred indiscriminately. It was a token of the respect and admiration of the whole membership. "To be awarded honorary membership in the IWU," said Bridges, "one must receive the unanimous vote of the delegates to the convention. Paul Robeson and Rockwell Kent, leaders for many years in the fight against Fascism, received that vote. They are the only living honorary members of the ILWU. Their membership entitles them to the full support of our union. And although our union is small, our members make up in activity what the organization lacks in size."

Robeson responded:

I want to tell you how proud I am to become a member of the ILWU and a brother of Rockwell Kent. I have labored, and I come from laboring people. I have hooked many a load, taken many a tray . . . . I know what poverty is.
I am already an honorary member of another great labor organization, the National Maritime Union. Now, I am happy to join the Longshoremen and Warehousemen who have done so many things. When I walk along the Front in San Francisco, I will be proud that I can put out my hand and say "Hello, brother."
I know what Harry Bridges has done, and I know what the fight for Harry Bridges means. We must not lose that fight. This is our great responsibility.

(These were the first Life Memberships bestowed by the ILWU. Three have been awarded since that time: to Attorney Vincent Hallinan, Dr. Linus Pauling, and the Rev. Dr. Martin Luther King.)

The touring company of "Othello" played in San Francisco in 1945 at the same time as the Sixth Biennial Convention of the ILWU, March 29–April 2, 1945. Robeson was invited to speak to the delegates. Despite his responsibilities as an actor, he readily accepted. After Harry Bridges' introduction, his "fellow members" greeted him with a standing ovation. This time, Robeson brought a political message:

Thanks, Harry! Thanks, fellows!
I came along, today just to say "Hello" as a member coming to the Convention. There is no need to tell you how proud I am, especially here in San Francisco, to be able to walk around and know that I am a member of a Union that has done the job and is doing the job that you are. . . . I have been excited the last couple of days at the prospect of the Charter Agreement that is coming between business and labor, certainly with the full cooperation of the government.
That should make us pretty proud, I think, because it is a well known fact that the charter signifies a great advance in the whole functioning of a labor-management relations, and the high standard it has achieved certainly points to a future of a very different kind in this America of ours.
Most of the stimulus here has been the insistence on the part of your Union and your executives, especially Harry, to unify and really build a decent life for the working people and all the people of our country.
So, I have felt very, very, proud these last couple of days, seeing that all America must now realize that this is the future pattern that we must follow if we are going to work out these problems.
I want to say again that it is quite obvious that this policy must be carried through and carried through fast. I know that you

will take the initiative in providing for this period of change and readjustment and that you will bear in mind the necessity again of never forgetting and never relaxing in this feeling which we have here, in actual fact, this necessity of complete unity of all groups in our country.

What at one time was a germ here has grown to be a national policy; so, maybe within our Union here, we can solve the problems that will make it perfectly clear to colored workers, white workers, Latin American workers, Chinese workers and all that we can really work in complete harmony, everywhere, as we do in our Union, itself.

Maybe we can have a little faith that way down through the whole union rank and file, if it is necessary, we can make some kind of sacrifice, just as in the old days we had to do when it was tough going and we had to get out and fight in a different way for our rights. We can tie this bond of fellowship that will carry us through this long range thinking to a real America with a job for every American.

There is just that tough part in between, and I think this Union might be able to solve it when it seems as though business might not solve it, and government might be a little slow on the up-take. Maybe you can work it out; because, certainly, the record is a mighty fine one up to this point.

I am sorry I cannot come into a lot of the sessions and get down to bed rock and sort of see how it works. One of these times I will. I have a pretty tough job over here with "Othello."

Robeson sang a group of songs and left the convention with everyone standing and cheering. (Proceedings. ILWU Conv., San Francisco, 3/29–4/2/45.)

Robeson continued to support the ILWU whenever the opportunity arose. During the west coast longshoremen's strike of 1946, he aided the strikers with a concert that included the universal favorite "Joe Hill." Also, in 1946 ILWU officials asked Robeson to make a concert tour of the Hawaiian Islands, described in greater detail on p. 49. It was crucial time for the union's efforts to organize the pineapple and sugar cane workers. The fifteen-concert tour was a great success and the proceeds were given to charitable causes.

Robeson addressed the Longshore and Shipclerk's caucus on August 21, 1948, in San Francisco, California (The *Dispatcher*, 9/3/48):

The struggle never seems to stop. It gets sharper and sharper. I pick up the papers today and find that we and our Union have a real job to do. I have watched your struggle, watched the consistent stand you have taken, and I know that you are going to continue to do that.

Taft-Hartley means death to the trade union movement. The two parties have been playing around; and, at every moment, we see that Truman steps in, and uses every provision he can to do his part of the job. You have a real problem. I understand. It means that you are going to tell them, as you have told them before, that you want no part whatsoever of this kind of legislation, which not only would break the back of the labor movement but would set back the whole struggle of American people for generations. And I understand that you are going to tell them that you want no part of voting on what the employers have offered to you, that you will set the terms yourselves. That I am very proud to see. In travelling about the country it is quite clear that the struggle for economic rights, the struggle for higher wages, the struggle for bread, the struggle for housing, has become a part of a wider political struggle. They have moved men in to high places in government; and, today, the enemies of labor control the working apparatus of the state. They have to be removed. There has to be a basic change. I feel that this can only be done by seeing that we put into power those who represent a political party which has the deep interests of the people at heart. I am sure you understand that this cannot be separated, that we must understand, politically, that Truman is in office through one party, the Republicans are in through one party and are responsible for Taft-Hartley, and that somewhere you have to see another group in there that fights for the rights of the American people.

. . . I am proud of the leadership that you have given to the whole labor movement. I want to thank your courageous leader, Harry Bridges, for his consistent stand.

The final word is that as a member of the ILWU, we have a tremendous responsibility. I cannot tell you how the Labor movement throughout the country looks to you as an example. And so there is added responsibility for you to carry on the fight in the next few days, in the next few weeks, in the next few months. What you do here in this Union can very well determine the future of the whole labor movement in these United States. It can mean victory for the American people in these times. And I, as one who comes from an oppressed people, one who has identified himself with the whole progressive struggle, know that you will carry on.

Robeson's support of labor aroused the ire of the giants of the business world. His friendship with the Russians created enemies within the government and veterans' organizations. The hostiltiy of these groups reached a peak at Peekskill, New York in late August and early September, 1949. Trade unionists gave Robeson immediate and sustained protection and support. The *Dispatcher* issued the following editorial on September 16, 1949:

Two attacks upon peaceable assemblies have been made at Peekskill, New York. In the first instance veterans' organizations announced that they would parade in protest against a concert by Paul Robeson. Apparently the veterans had been incited by false newspaper reports and editorials regarding statements which Paul Robeson has made. In the first attack the veterans and hoodlums stoned, kicked and beat Negroes, even including aged women.

In the second instance, after Paul Robeson had announced that he would not be intimidated nor would the people who backed him be intimidated, certain dirty elements operating under the name of "veterans" organized another attack and Governor Dewey of New York supposedly ordered the State Troopers to keep order. From many eye witness accounts we know now that at the second concert State police actually led the attack. We know that they guided the automobiles of concert-goers into blind alleys where they knew hoodlums were waiting for them. We know the State Troopers then broke windshields with their billies and gave tickets to drivers with broken windshields. Even the photographs taken by the apologetic venal press show State Troopers grinning broadly as skulls are cracked by misguided fascist youth.

* * * *

Does all this have anything to do with us as a uinon? We believe it does. It started this way in Germany, and what happened in Germany is certainly well known to all of the members of our union, many of whom lost their sons or brothers in the fight to put it down.

. . . . Dewey well knows that his own State Troopers did most of the skull cracking in the second Peekskill incident. He well knows also that he himself incited it by his very announcement that he would assign policemen, in which he indicated that in his opinion Robeson had no right to sing at a concert – presumably because Robeson is not of exactly the same political persuasions as Mr. Dewey. The injuries inflicted at Peekskill are injuries to all of us. If this sort of thing can be allowed in New York it can be allowed elsewhere. It can mean that all liberty is at an end, as, indeed, it once came to an end in Germany.

The ILWU's support for Robeson was reciprocated in November of 1952, when the delegates at the convention of the National Negro Labor Council accused the federal government of a frame-up in the charges against ILWU leaders Harry Bridges, J. L. Robertson, and Harry Schmidt. Each delegate was given a pamphlet entitled, "American Minorities and the Case of Harry Bridges."

The ILWU, through The *Dispatcher*, kept up an unrelenting fight against the State Department in behalf of Robeson's right to travel abroad. Regular coverage was given also to Robeson's appearances before the House Committee on Un-American Activities. They called attention to the similarities of treatment of "two of the greatest freedom fighters of our time," Harry Bridges and Paul Robeson. The editorial staff of The *Dispatcher* rejoiced when the Supreme Court handed down its decision, Dulles vs. Kent, and ordered the State Department in 1958 to validate the passports of their two lifetime members, Rockwell Kent and Paul Robeson.

ROBESON IN HAWAII

A well-worn expression in the Hawaiian Islands is "The American missionaries came here to do good and did well." The names of such men as Dole and Judd support the truth of this statement. American missionaries first came to the Hawaiian Islands in 1820. Among the first wave was the Reverend Daniel Dole, preacher and educator. His ecclesiastical impact on the Islands was small compared to the political impact of Sanford B. Dole, of the second generation, toward the end of the century.

Sanford B. Dole was well known as a Justice of the Supreme Court of Hawaii. Less well known was his membership in the Annexation Club, a secret society of haoles (transplanted white Americans) formed in 1892. This group worked actively, but clandestinely, to annex the Hawaiian Islands to the United States, ". . . the only hope for a stable government in Hawaii." Members of the Club gained key positions in the government and bided their time. It was not long coming. Taking advantage of a political upheaval the next year, members of the Annexation Club overthrew Queen Lilikalani and took over the government on January 17, 1893. The coup was bloodless. A provisional government was formed with Justice Sanford B. Dole at the head. President Dole quickly set into motion the Club's pre-arranged plans. A hand-picked delegation was sent to Washington to formalize annexation. Unforeseen problems arose to thwart their scheme.

The *New York Times* took a strong position against annexation and stirred up public opposition to it. Princes Kiakalani, the deposed Queen's niece, rushed to Washington while the Annexation Committee pressed its case before the Federal Government. She told reporters:

> If American people are the noble-minded people I have learned to regard them as, they will not be a party to the outrage by which I have lost my birthright. Seventy years ago, Christian America sent over Christian men and women to give religion and civilization to Hawaii. Today . . . sons of those men are at your capital asking you to undo their father's work. Who sent them? Who gave them the authority to break the constitution they swore they would uphold? (Webb, p. 137).

With an ear toward the *Times* and an eye on the beautiful princess,

President Grover Cleveland withdrew the Annexation Bill from the Senate and ordered an investigation. The findings caused him to oppose annexation. There followed a brief, futile effort to restore the monarchy in the Hawaiian Islands. The members of the provisional government were to prove more durable than the British, who occupied Honolulu for five months in 1843, and the French who occupied Honolulu for ten days in 1849 (Webb, p. 59).

When it became apparent that the chances for annexation under President Cleveland were scant, the provisional government was converted into a constitutional government, patterned after that of the United States. In 1894, the Republic of Hawaii was formed with Sanford B. Dole as President. Political fences were mended before the next presidential election. Annexationists teamed up with the increasingly powerful imperialists on the mainland to support the candidacy of William McKinley for the presidency. After his election, the sovereignty of the Republic of Hawaii was transferred to the United States over all objections. The signing of the treaty gave official sanction to a major theft that does approximate, if not exceed, the heist of Panama. In 1898, Hawaii took her place as a satellite in the uncertain American orbit. That same year, Paul Robeson took his first steps into a future of even greater uncertainty as an American citizen.

The major domestic problem that faced the new government was the shortage of laborers. Climate and geography meet in happy harmony in Hawaii to provide optimum conditions for the growth of pineapples and sugar cane. The passage of the Wilson Act in 1894 and the opening of the Panama Canal a bit later boosted Hawaii's sugar industry to new heights of productivity and profitability.

As early as 1864, Hawaii had labor problems. The plantation owners' dissatisfaction with Chinese coolies, their principal source of labor, led to the establishment of the Planter's Society to help solve the labor problems of the area. Robert C. Wyllie helped to form the organization. His ownership of the large Princenill Plantation, in Kauai, made him more than an interested bystander.

The government set up the Bureau of Immigration to oversee the importation of foreign workers and to promote and encourage the introduction of free immigration from abroad. Laborers worked under contracts authorized by the "Acts for the Government of Masters and Servants," which was passed in 1850. Under this law, a laborer who did not satisfy the letter of the law could be arrested, brought before a judge, and imprisoned until he consented to abide by the law. Widespread employer abuse of the law aroused public resentment: and the rules were softened two years later.

Recruiters went out to China, Japan, the Philippines, and the South Sea Islands to hire laborers for the plantations. Working conditions were extremely poor; strikes and protests were common. Plantation owners, mostly Americans and Europeans, dealt with labor unrest by keeping the various racial groups separated, and one group was used against the other to discourage protests and to break strikes (Kuykendall, pp. 280-281). The following case demonstrates the difficulties of unionization:

> In May of 1909, about 7,000 Japanese workers left their jobs on Oahu plantations and stayed out until the strike was broken, three months later. The strikers demanded to be paid the same wages as Caucasian workers doing the same jobs. Other nationals were hired, at premium wages, to break the strike. As soon as the Japanese gave in, the strike-breakers were fired and the Japanese were rehired, at lower wages (Kuykendal, p. 281).

Prior to World War II, the Congress of Industrial Organizations (CIO) tried to organize the plantation workers but failed. They were defeated by the well organized employers who maintained strict control of their employees.

The Japanese attack on Pearl Harbor on December 7, 1941 resulted in rigid regimentation of the common laborer. A military government took over after the attack and issued General Order No. 38 on December 20, 1941. This directive froze wages as of December 7, forced all workers who had left their jobs since that date to return to their former employers, and demanded that employees must report to the jobs to which they were ordered by the military government of the U.S. Three months later, the workers' rights were further proscribed by General Order No. 91 which in effect bound the employee to the employer until the latter released him. The worker had no right of appeal; and if he was released with "prejudice," for any cause, the doors to defense jobs were barred to him.

Men who failed to report for work as ordered, or who were absent without leave, were subject to a $200 fine or two months in jail, or both. Under threat of arrest by military police, a delinquent worker was ordered to appear before a labor control board within 48 hours. On January 1, 1942, an agreement between the Army and the plantation owners permitted the United States' Engineers to requisition labor and equipment from the plantations, without question. Although seething with the resentment of the helpless, the workers gave priority to the war effort. Eventually, their anger exploded against these repressive measures. Strikes were illegal, but charges of illegal servitude, government slavery, and militarism filled the air. The common laborers outgrew the paternalism of the pre-war working arrangements. Many felt that the "Big Five" (American Factor, Ltd.; C. Brewer & Co., Ltd.; Alexander & Baldwin; Castle & Cook, Ltd.; and Theo H. Daniels & Co., Ltd.) had abused their rights during the war. The workers demanded a measure of self determination in order to avoid a repetition of the pernicious war-time practices.

Working conditions on the plantations were ripe for the arrival of organizers of the International Longshoremen's and Warehousemen's Union (ILWU) at the end of the military domination. They profited from the pre-war failure of the CIO. Their coffers were amply full, and they were led by that resourceful, durable, and controversial freedom-fighter, Harry Bridges. Among Bridges' aides was Eddie Tangen, International Representative of ILWU.

In a 1946 pamphlet entitled, "Raising Cane," the ILWU recalled the violence of their earlier organizing drives in the territory of Hawaii:

> After the successful organizing drive of 1934, the waterfront workers moved inland to organize their brothers on the plantations. Their efforts were halted by Pearl Harbor when Martial law and Military Government were used by the "Big Five" in an industry-busting campaign.
> Plantation owners took advantage of the Japanese ancestry of many of the workers to intimidate, manhandle and jail "on suspicion" those sympathetic to the union. In 1942, the average wage of plantation workers was $928.00 per year.
> With relaxation of military controls, the union movement spread like fire. Because the Wagner Act did not cover agriculture workers, the ILWU, on the Territory, organized their own political action committee and elected a new legislature which passed a Little Wagner Act to cover agriculture workers. In one year, 20,000 plantation workers, mill and farm hands were organized in Territorial ILWU.

Early in 1948, officers of Territorial ILWU invited Robeson to tour the Hawaiian Islands under their sponsorship. Already an honorary member of their union, Robeson had supported the longshoremen for many years on the West Coast. Robeson agreed to make the tour in March. Although the tour lasted less than two weeks, Robeson's group visited three islands and made twenty-seven public appearances. Why was Robeson asked to come to Hawaii at that particular time? Perhaps a study of the labor conditions at that time may yield some answers.

A long and costly sugar-workers' strike ended in victory for the workers on November 19, 1946. The "Big Five," controlling over 90% of the sugar production of the islands, were surprised and challenged by the strength of the ILWU. Plans were laid for a counter offensive against the Union. Jack Hall, Regional Director of ILWU for Hawaii, was asked to resign his commission with the police department. He resigned after the sugar strike, accusing the governor, Ingram Stainback, of using his Territorial appointments to build his political machine. In December of 1946, 137 sugar workers were arrested and faced criminal charges for their role in the victorious sugar strike the previous month. One-hundred-one ILWU members were charged with serious felonies that carried penalties of up to twenty years. Seventy-nine were charged under Riot and Assembly statutes that were passed in 1869, and no prior convictions had come before the Supreme Court.

Jack Mior, Manager of Pioneer Sugar Mill, decided that he would "pick and choose" those who would return to work after the sugar strike ended. One thousand sixty-five workers remained out until until January 2, 1947 (*Dispatcher*, 1/10/47).

On 1/9/47, ILWU representatives charged that the "Big Five" brought an ex-Hearst newspaper man, Lee Ettleson, to devise secret schemes for destroying the Union. After learning of his plan, the union issued a directive for counteracting the proposed attack. A month later, as a result of increased "red-baiting" in the newspapers, ILWU issued a pamphlet entitled, "The Big Lie," designed to "counteract the efforts of Governor Stainback, the Elks Clubs, the American Legion, and the Chamber of Commerce, to smear the Union as Communist." Union officials recalled that the "Big Five" first made the charge after the successful sugar strike the year before.

Two events, elsewhere, had a demoralizing effect on plantation workers in Hawaii. Jesus Mendenez, leader of the 350,000-strong Cuban Sugar Workers' Union, was murdered on January 22, 1948 by Capt. Joaquin C. Casillas. Mendenez was on an organizing tour of the sugar plantations in preparation for the fight for the 1948 wage scale. The soldier emptied his gun into the back of the union official, as he emerged from a train. Labor officials blamed the "reign of terror" conducted by the government of Grau San Martin and the Latin-American policies of the United States' State Department.

The National Secretary of Philippines Congress of Labor, Manuel Joven, was kidnapped and murdered on February 24, 1948, as a "beginning assault on organized labor by imperialist-inspired local reactionaries." It was recalled that a Philippine National peasant leader, Juan Felei, was murdered in 1946 and no arrests were made. News of these murders spread through the Hawaiian Islands with great rapidity. Many of the workers on the plantations were from the Philippine Islands and all of the workers felt a common bond with their fellow workers in Cuba.

ILWU officials hoped to counteract the disruptive influence of these murders and other anti-union activities by sending Robeson on an extended tour of several islands early in 1948. He was accompanied by Lawrence Brown and Earl Robinson. Seton (1958, p. 182) recorded the comment of Brown and Robinson relative to this tour and both agreed that Robeson was very well received throughout the islands. The trio drew huge crowds wherever they went. Their programs stressed folk songs of many countries. Robeson sang songs in Chinese, Filipino, Japanese, and Hawaiian. Thus, Robeson opened up lines of communication among the various ethnic groups of laborers.

The industrial bosses recognized that Robeson was a threat to their domination of the work force. Through the news media, they attacked him and tried to drive a wedge between him and the plantation workers. Robeson fought back in a press conference: "I will fight for anybody, anywhere, who is oppressed . . . . For myself, I ask no quarter . . . . I am anti-fascist. I hate Fascism and all it stands for."

Threats against Robeson's life were common, but they never stopped his crusade. Eddie Tangen, ILWU official, accompanied Robeson on some of the more dangerous occasions: "We tried to tell him how dangerous it was to go to all of those places he went to. But there was no way to stop him, except physically. Nobody wanted to try that. So, we all just tagged along, expecting the worse."

As a result of Robeson's concert tours of the islands, the widows of Jesus Mendenez and Manuel Joven each were presented with checks for $1,250.00 by the territorial ILWU from proceeds of the tour. Approximately $500 was given to the Honolulu branch of the Salvation Army (The *Dispatcher*, 7/9/48).

Aside from the formal concerts that charged admission, Robeson made appearances in the sugar cane and pineapple plantation fields to sing and talk to the workers. After sundown, he visited their cabins. Most of his time was spent among the Filipino workers, learning of their glorious fight for freedom against oppressors from Spain, Japan, and the United States. From them, also, he was introduced to the works of the Filipino freedom-fighter, Luis Taruc.

Robeson assisted the ILWU in becoming a permanent fixture in the life of the Hawaiian Islands. To this day, the sugar cane and pineapple workers are members of the Longshoremen's and Warehousemen's Union.

Nearly thirty years later, the name of Robeson brought bright smiles to the faces of middle-aged Hawaiians. The driver of the tourist bus fills the hours of the long drives with Negro Spirituals that were introduced to the Island by Paul Robeson, when he came to fight by their side in their quest for freedom. His expanding interest in Polynesia eventually took him to Australia where he stood up for the Aborigines against Australian oppression.

Robeson's close contact with Filipino workers in Hawaii had a profound and lasting effect on his future. After his conversations with them, he began an in-depth study of the Philippine Islands and Southeast Asia. He uncovered a sorry set of events that prepared the stage for the rape of much of Southeast Asia and the death of millions of working-class people. He learned that it was Justice William Howard Taft, first American Governor of the Philippines, who entered into a secret agreement with Katsura, representing the Imperial government of Japan. Taft assured Katsura that the U.S. would recognize Japanese hegemony over Korea if the Japanese would not interfere with the United States' colonization plans in the Philippines. Thus, greed and racism shacked up in unholy matrimony, producing a brood of malformed bastards that are still around to haunt us all.

Robeson referred to these matters in his Foreword to Taruc's book,

Born of the People, which he wrote during the height of the Korean war:

> What part does this great land of ours play in those world changes? We see the results of their deadly work in Korea. We hear talk of "no imperialist ambitions," but we see the close ties with the agents of Japanese and German Fascism. We watch with dread the policies of Gen. McArthur and (Secretary of State) John Foster Dulles coming into ascendency. We know that we must widen and deepen the struggle for peace, that we must fight for these United States to help civilization forward, not to attempt to check its march or even threaten to destroy it.

After his Hawaiian trip, Robeson became even more severe in his criticism of a United States' foreign policy that he felt sure would lead his country into war in Southeast Asia. The State Department tried to mute Robeson's criticism by voiding his passport in 1950, but failed. The United States continued its course toward a military misadventure in Southeast Asia and Robeson reviled the government whenever and wherever he could, usually before those few union locals that would still allow him to address them.

THE TOBACCO WORKERS OF NORTH CAROLINA

Active agitation for better working conditions began to alarm the tobacco growers in the early 1930s. Independent at first, groups of workers started unifying to force the reluctant rulers of the tobacco industry to invest more of their profits in the well-being of their employees. A measure of the success of such efforts was an agreement between Liggett and Meyers Tobacco Company and the Tobacco Workers' Industrial Union (TWIU), an affiliate of the American Federation of Labor (AFL). The new wage and hour agreement announced on March 21, 1937 in Richmond, Virginia, represented a major advance for the trade union movement and yielded significant and immediate benefit for the workers. Unfortunately for the black workers, TWIU adopted the racist practices of the AFL and followed the pattern of the tobacco industry by segregating black workers into impotent, isolated locals. It was clear to the black tobacco workers that their relief had to come from elsewhere.

Since colonial days, blacks have been employed in the tobacco industry. They made up the bulk of the work force until the industry became mechanized. Jewish immigrants, too, were among the early workers in the industry; but the dirty work and low pay caused them to seek employment elsewhere. Their departure left a vacuum that was filled with unskilled black workers. So long as management could keep its employees on skimpy wages and avoid the expenditures of improving their working conditions, there was little incentive for mechanization. Union pressure for higher wages and better working conditions plus the proliferation of cigarette smokers forced the tobacco industry to introduce machines in the late 1930s and early 1940s.

Prior to mechanization, almost all cigarettes were rolled by hand – by black hands. With the introduction of machine rollers, white women were hired to operate them. Thus began an industry-wide reduction in the relative and absolute numbers of black workers in the tobacco plants. The report of the U.S. Bureau of Census reflected this trend:

Employees	1910	1920	1930	1940	1950	1960	1970
Total	29,028	50,453	37,866	42,460	40,463	48,910	69,941
Black	18,910	33,839	25,725	19,438	15,119	13,130	13,233
Percent Black	64.5	67.3	67.9	45.8	37.2	26.8	19

The largest decline of black workers occurred between 1930-40, when machines replaced them. Locked into unskilled locals because of race, the machines made the black workers expendable. This trend has continued, in spite of a steady increase in the total number of workers in the industry, especially during the past two decades.

Black workers welcomed the Food, Tobacco and Agricultural Workers' Union as an alternative to TWIU. They threw their weight behind FTA, supporting it in many ways. The Southern Negro Youth Congress, later listed by the U.S. Attorney General as subversive, provided funds and leadership during the organizational period. Eventually, FTA became affiliated with the Congress of Industrial Organizations (CIO), bringing to the tobacco industry the titanic struggle being waged between the venerable AFL and the young and brash CIO for control of the labor market.

The unions flexed their muscles at Liggett and Meyers, American, and some other tobacco companies with favorable results. R. J. Reynolds Tobacco Company, Winston-Salem's giant of the industry, was unimpressed by such calisthenics and became the Flanders Field of the unions' organizing efforts.

TWIU did organize RJR during World War I, but Company resourcefulness prevented the union from gaining a strong foothold in the plant. Since TWIU made very little effort to represent black workers, the company was given a decided advantage in playing one group against the other.

In the early 1940s, a group of black women, disgusted with their dirty, poor-paying jobs, tried to organize workers within the RJR plant in Winston-Salem. They called their group Local 22. Fear and intimidation made the work of these courageous women extremely difficult. It was only after a worker fell dead on assembly 65 that Local 22 sprang to life. They gained in strength and numbers; and around 1944, FTA made them an affiliate. An election soon followed at RJR and FTA defeated TWIU and won the right to represent the tobacco workers. FTA listened to the grievances of the workers and tried to negotiate with management for relief. The Company, "resilient and paternalistic," appeared to listen but refused to grant any meaningful concessions. After weeks of fruitless discussions, Local 22 called a strike in 1947.

RJR countered the strike move by laying off hundreds of workers, chiefly black workers, especially those who had organized Local 22 years before. The strike was long and costly. A settlement was announced on June 8, 1947 but it failed to materialize. The agreement soon fell apart, and some labor leaders accused RJR officials of bad faith. The besieged FTA picked up editorial support from the West Coast:

REYNOLDS COMPANY VOIDS F.T.A. STRIKE PEACE

> Close to 500 camel cigarette workers were locked out of the Winston-Salem (N.C.) plant by R. J. Reynolds Tobacco Co., in violation of the ten-day strike settlement.
> The contract violation was reported by Local 22, of Food, Tobacco, Agriculture and Allied Workers (CIO) in an appeal for continued strike aid from unions.
> R. J. Reynolds filed mass separation notices to 408 Negro workers and 73 white workers, with the statement that "others were hired on their jobs during the strike."
> A union spokesman said, "Reynolds hopes to destroy our strike victory and permanently break the union by continuing their attacks at a time when our funds have been exhausted and news of the strike settlement has spread to our friends and supporters. The contract we won with national support will mean nothing unless we get funds to defeat this union-busting drive (The *Dispatcher*, June 27, 1947).

Their funds and morale exhausted, representatives of Local 22 sent a desperate appeal for Robeson to come to their rescue. Their call reached him about mid June of 1947.

On the one hand, the appeal arrived at a very bad time for Robeson. A rising tide of resentment against his plea for a peaceful co-existence with world communism had forced cancellations of concerts in Peoria (Ill.) in April, and in Albany (N.Y.) in May. A chain-reaction had set in; and by the time the tobacco workers' plea arrived, his eighty-concert tour was in shambles. Moreover, Robeson had just returned from a tour of the Panama Canal Zone at the request of the United Public Workers' Union and he was busily berating the federal government for its malignant neglect of its non-white employees in the Canal Zone. These and other political and economic pressures provided ample, legitimate reasons to decline the invitation. On the other hand, Robeson's interest in North Carolina and the tobacco industry was both profound and personal. His paternal roots sprang from the soil of North Carolina and his relatives "toiled in tobacco and indigo" for many years.

Unlike some members of the current crop of black leaders, financial considerations did not enter into Robeson's decision to answer a call. He arrived in Winston-Salem on June 29, 1947 and appeared in an open-air concert in the Woodland Avenue school playground. In spite of a "boiling sun," thousands came to hear Robeson sing. Loudspeakers carried his voice well beyond the schoolgrounds.

The concert opened with one of the all-time favorites, "Water

Boy," followed by work songs and Negro spirituals. In spite of the oppressive heat and the high humidity, the crowd responded to the songs with amens, clapping hands, and stomping feet. For a brief moment, they forgot the menace of R. J. Reynolds. At the end, Robeson gave a dramatic interpretation of the song that was written for him, "Ole Man River," and became as one with his beleagured brothers and sisters. The crowd erupted with shouts of approval and understanding that ventilated months of repressed frustrations.

The singing over, Robeson spoke to the people. He told them that he was glad to be singing to a North Carolina audience because his father had lived near Rocky Mount. He reminded them that the achievements of one member of his race counted for nothing when he looked at the way other Negroes were treated. He continued:

> If anyone wants a reason for my singing here, there's the reason. I'll never forget my father . . . . If it can happen to boys in Greenville [S.C.], it can happen to me anywhere in this country . . . . I am devoting two years, more if necessary, to fighting for my race. I have come back to my people, and I am fighting not as an artist, but as one of you . . . . If fighting for the Negro people and their trade union brothers, if that makes me the subversive that they're talking about in Congress, if that makes me a Red, then So Be It! (The crowd roared approval).
> Our national leaders are wasting their time trying to break down independent nations in Europe . . . . There's nothing going to happen to Tito, nothing going to happen in the Balkans or in China or in the Soviet Union. Those people have the land in their hands, and they're not going to take it away from them. We're going to build a world of equal men . . . living in a true American democracy (Winston-Salem *Journal Sentinel,* June 30, 1947).

A collection was taken at the end of the concert, with the proceeds going to those workers not rehired after the strike or locked out after the settlement. Mrs. Velma Hopkins, in charge of arrangements, made it possible for Robeson to meet with groups of workers after the concert. He listened to their grievances against the tobacco company and gave advice and encouragement.

Robeson was invited back to Winston-Salem in April, 1950. The occasion was the funeral of Mrs. Morando S. Smith, one of the principal organizers of Local 22. The nation in general and the trade union movement in particular had undergone major changes since Robeson's visit to Winston-Salem, three years before. The Truman Doctrine, The Marshall Plan, and the enforcement of the Taft-Hartley Law of 1947 had made the life of the radical trade unionist difficult, if not impossible. Officials of FTA had incurred the displeasure of the CIO by refusing to sign non-communist affidavits as was required by Taft-Hartley. On February 15, 1950 just two months before Robeson's return, the CIO expelled the FTA from membership in the Congress under a charge of being "Communist dominated." The CIO confiscated FTA's jurisdiction and divided it among three conformist affiliates.

By the time of the above events, Robeson was well on his way to the title of "public enemy No. 1." His challenges to President Truman on lynching and poll-tax legislation, his appearances before the House Un-American Activities Committee, and the more recent violence at Peekskill made Robeson one of the most controversial figures of the period. His appearance as a speaker at the funeral was not universally approved:

> . . . . My visit here is very symbolic to me. I'm coming to a State where my people were born and reared – where my father was a slave – where my cousins are tobacco workers in the eastern part of the state.
> It is hard to believe that this person [Mrs. Morando Smith] who has given so much to the Negro workers is gone. Yet there are thousands of us to carry on her labor. Her name will remain deep in the hearts, not [only] of Negro people, but all people.
> She is a symbol of the best in the land. Winston-Salem will give her the greatest victory. Her name will remain a part of the city. She is a symbol of the dignity of full expression as human beings. We must dedicate ourselves to the struggle as she did – to see that this will be a bounteous, peaceful world in which all people can walk in full human dignity . . . (*Journal Sentinel,* April 17, 1950).

Robeson's charge to the funeral audience foundered on the events of the period. The black tobacco workers found the world less than bounteous. Their numbers in the tobacco industry had been reduced to 15,119 in 1950 from a high of 33,839 in 1920. Just a few weeks later, the Cold War burst into flame in Korea and the prospects for peace disappeared. Robeson's own chance to walk in "full human dignity" was dealt a severe blow on August 3, 1950. Accusing him of meddling in the foreign affairs of the U.S. Government, the State Department cancelled his passport.

Another event occurred a few weeks after the funeral that was to have a decisive effect on the future of tobacco workers in Winston-Salem. On June 27, 1950, an enterprising black reporter of a local paper wrote an account of a Robeson interview by a Russian reporter of the *Pravda News Agency.* Robeson, identified as a member of the Permanent Committee of World Peace Congress, spoke of his recent trip to Winston-Salem. Robeson was quoted as saying:

> Last week I visited the southeastern part of the United States – the city of Winston-Salem in the state of North Carolina. In this town, which is one of the centers of the tobacco industry, a large number of people gathered at the meeting, both white people and Negroes, workers and members of the intelligentsia. They warmly welcomed the proposal for peace and friendship with the Soviet Union.
> . . . . Great responsibility rests on all who are fighting for peace and for democracy, and on the partisans of peace in the United States. Should the instigators of war in the United States succeed in unleashing a new and bloody slaughter, it would inflict incalculable horrors and suffering on millions of Americans (*Journal Sentinel,* 6/27/50).

The red scare, emanating from Washington, had all but paralyzed our national government. Senator Joseph R. McCarthy (D-Wis.) was a regular visitor in the living rooms of the nation. Anyone who made statements favorable to Russia or China attracted unfavorable attention and came under the surveillance of sundry loyalty groups. The resourceful, anti-union forces in Winston-Salem saw this news report as a golden opportunity to discredit union activity at RJR and strengthen their hand. They recalled that the original support for FTA had come from the Southern Negro Youth Congress, now suspect. In spite of their painful house-cleaning, the CIO was accused of harboring revolutionaries. Forced to defend their positions on all fronts, CIO officials had little time for mundane matters of union business.

In the absence of radical-liberal union activity in the tobacco industry, blacks have continued to be shortchanged in the marketplace of workers' rights. After World War II RJR placed a few blacks on machines to make cigarettes. Six percent of machine operators were black in 1951. Pressure from the Committee on Government Contracts, in the middle 1950s and the civil rights movement later on forced Liggett and Meyers and American Tobacco companies to open up a few jobs that had been all-white. Both companies were reported to have entered into "gentlemen's" agreements with white locals to permit token upgradings of blacks in order to relieve the pressure on them.

Acting alone at first and in concert with the AFL after the merger, CIO officials attacked the RJR citadel on many occasions with disastrous results. An Associated Press dispatch of June 14, 1974 reflects the unions persistence, if not their prosperity: "The R. J. Reynolds Tobacco Company reported today that its workers voted 2:1 against the AFL-CIO's Tobacco Workers' International Union. Of 8,400 eligible production and clerical workers, 7,930 or 94% cast ballots. The vote was 65.5% against unionization and 34.3% in favor. This was the latest of many atempts of the union to organize R. J. Reynolds."

R. J. Reynolds Tobacco Company today remains unorganized, unconquered and, apparently, unconquerable.

THE UNITED PUBLIC WORKERS' UNION

Public workers — employees of federal, state, county and municipal governments — have fared badly in the market place of organized labor. They have been forced to wage constant battles for marginal gains in their working conditions. Robeson aligned himself with the United Public Workers of America (UPWA), soon after he returned to America in 1939. He addressed their founding convention in 1939 and over the next twelve years attended many of their national and local meetings throughout the country. Abram Flaxer, former President of UPW, in a private communication recalled Robeson's involvement with his union at all levels: "As he travelled about the U.S., he never failed to address our local union meetings, state council meetings and our picket lines, when the need arose."

UPW members responded to Robeson in many ways. On May 8, 1944, the State County and Municipal Workers of New York established the Paul Robeson Scholarship Fund at New York University to train black students in business management. Robeson attended the New York State meeting of UPW's biennial convention at New York's Astor Place on June 23, 1946. The 300 delegates, representing 28,000 state and city employees, adopted a resolution calling for the defeat of Governor Thomas E. Dewey in the Fall election. The Governor was charged with systematically opposing the rights of governmental employees. His elimination of $120,000,000 in state income taxes was labelled a "soak-the-poor" taxation program. During the convention, Robeson pledged his continued support to the union's efforts to improve their working conditions. A group of UPW officials, led by Ewart Guinier, International Secretary-Treasurer, put Robeson's pledge to an immediate test. They asked for his help on behalf of the non-white (silver-roll) public workers in the Panama Canal Zone, the victims of harsh segregation and discrimination at the hands of the federal government. Robeson listened attentively and promised to help. As usual, Robeson did his home work. He studied the history of the area, while formulating a plan of action. When the French effort to build a canal across the isthmus of Panama bogged down, United States' officials decided to take over the project. A working treaty was prepared, with Secretary of State John Hay representing the U.S. and Dr. Tomas Herran, Charge d'Affairs, representing Colombia, whose territory included Panama.

The treaty authorized President Theodore Roosevelt to acquire rights and property of the French company for not more than $40,000,000 and to acquire from the Colombian government a strip of land six miles wide along the route of the Canal. The U.S. would have administrative control over the Canal for 100 years, if needed. The U.S. would pay Colombia $20,000,000 in gold plus $250,000 annually, beginning nine years after the treaty. Colombia would retain her sovereignty over the land. Both men signed the treaty and took it to their respective governments for ratification. The U.S. Senate ratified the pact without delay; but the Colombian government discussed, dissected, and delayed action on the treaty for months.

Meanwhile, seeds of revolution, already dormant in the territory of Panama, began to germinate, thanks to self-seeking Americans and a wily, daring Frenchman, Phillipe Bunau-Varilla. He had been the fourth chief engineer for the French effort to build a canal. Not only did Bunau-Varilla know the terrain and the people, he had a personal, financial interest in securing a favorable treaty. His contacts and his cunning enabled him to play a leading role in the take-over of the Panamanian isthmus by local insurgents. As had been true in Cuba and the Philippines earlier, the U.S. Navy was the balance of power in our territorial expansion in Panama. In this instance it was the Cruiser *Nashville* that steamed into the Port of Colon in time to neutralize the Colombian soldiers dispatched from the mainland to prevent the coup. Other pro-revolutionary Americans sent the only available train across to the other side of Panama, effectively imobilizing the Colombian troops. Thus, Dr. Manuel Amador, physician and leader of the revolutionary forces, had a free hand in taking over the government. Within a few hours, he was able to announce the independence of Panama. The U.S. government recognized the new government of Panama two days later.

Bunau-Varilla's price for engineering this bloodless heist was his appointment as Envoy Extraordinary and Minister Plenipotentiary of Panama. His credentials were readily accepted in Washington despite serious questions of their legitimacy. One of Bunau-Varilla's first "official" acts was to rewrite the Hays-Herran treaty, making the U.S. an offer "it could not afford to refuse": "The Republic of Panama grants to the United States all rights, power and authority within the Canal Zone which the U.S. would possess if it were the sovereign of the territory . . . to the exclusion of the exercise by the Republic of Panama of any such sovereign rights, power and authority." The new treaty became known as the Hays-Bunau treaty and was rushed to signature while Panama's legitimate delegation was detained in New York.

Thus began decades of ill will, bitterness, and bloodshed. The new canal builders came into the territory and brought the technical skills for building the canal; they also brought the unhappy trappings of racism. When transplanted into this virgin soil, the seeds of racism produced, in some instances, a more vicious hybrid than the original root back home. Victims of this unfortunate development were black Americans, West Indians, and native Panamanians who flocked into the Canal Zone seeking employment. The UPW dispatched organizers into the area to do battle with federal employers on behalf of the government workers. It was an uphill fight, but UPW gave a good account of itself until it was destroyed in 1951.

Early in 1947, Robeson and the union agreed that he would make a tour of the Canal Zone to observe the working conditions, first-hand. It was certain that his presence there would strengthen the UPW's Panamanian affiliate, local 713 (CIO). Moreover, the UPW had introduced legislation in the Congress for the relief of canal workers. Robeson's report of his trip to the Canal Zone could be expected to arouse public support for the legislation, HR 227. Robeson's visit was scheduled to follow a good-will tour of the Canal Zone by Thomas Richardson, International Vice-President of UPW-CIO and head of the union's anti-discrimination division. The fact that both Richardson and Robeson were black enhanced the union's position among the workers that they were trying to organize.

The May 3, 1947 issue of *Star and Herald*, Panama City, Panama announced:

> Thomas Richardson, Negro trade unionist, who is now an International Vice President of the UPWA-CIO, is scheduled to arrive in the Canal Zone Terminal for a stay on the Isthmus. The CIO official, according to an announcement by J. L. Strobel, Local 713, is coming to the Isthmus to visit UPWA locals, on a good will tour and to assist in organization works and the Union's programs for better working conditions for silver-roll (non-white) workers. He will address a number of CIO meeting during his stay.
> Richardson had been active in the trade union movement and the CIO in the USA for many years and had a wide experience as a labor leader and organizer.
> This is the fourth high official of the UPWA to visit the Canal Zone to perform works in connection with Local 713. The other visitors were Len Goldsmith, Director of Education, Robert Weinstein, International Director of Organization and Vice-President J. L. Strobel.

Richardson appeared in Cristobal on May 7, 1947 to build up support for the union's bills then pending before Congress on behalf of the silver-roll workers of Panama. The union's six-point program for the Canal Zone was designed to:

1. Support the doctrine of equal pay for equal work.
2. Insure equality of opportunity for all, regardless of race or national origin.
3. Establish 25¢/hour as the minimum wage.

4. Place HR 227 on the congressional calendar.
5. Construct decent housing for non-white employees.
6. Institute a decent retirement plan for silver-roll workers.

Robeson was presented in concert by UPW-CIO local 713 at the olympic stadium on 5/27/47, and at the Colon arena on 5/29 and 5/30/47. One aspect of these appearances by Robeson has been described by Seton (1958, p. 181):

> Robeson left for Panama late in May to give four concerts under the auspices of the United Public Workers of America CIO, which was seeking to unionize the workers of Panama. As soon as he arrived, on May 25, the anti-union forces began to attack him, saying that he had not come as an artist. Tickets for the Robeson concert were selling for $1.00 each. It was said that as such a low price, Robeson must have been paid by someone else. However, these people did not realize that 10,000 would turn out to hear Robeson sing. One of his concerts was held in Panama's open-air stadium which Don Enriquez Jiminez, the President of Panama, attended. The concerts were a great event: for not only did he sing, but he gave excerpts from "Othello" which the people wildly applauded.

These appearances were mass meetings where Robeson sang and spoke to the workers, assuring them of the continued interest and support of the parent union as well as his own. Aside from the three large meetings, Robeson spent much time with smaller groups, learning of their plight and offering encouragement.

When Robeson returned to the USA, he went about describing the vicious practices of discrimination and segregation against non-white employees, Panamanian as well as migrant workers, that was worse than that in Alabama and Mississippi. In the Canal Zone, segregation was complete, as reflected in substandard housing, poor schools, and unequal pay for non-white federal employees. "Even the post-office had separate windows for buying postage stamps."

Panama's Local 713 ran into financial difficulties during the latter part of 1947 and the organizing drive slowed down. They sought financial help from the national office in New York. Again, Robeson assisted with a benefit concert in January of 1948, and the proceeds went to the Panama local.

The federal government took strong exception to UPW's activities on behalf of its mistreated members. Political pressure against the union began to mount during the latter part of the 1940s. The Union fought back, often with Robeson at their side. The *Dispatcher* (2/20/48) recorded one such event on the West Coast: "Paul Robeson is scheduled to appear at the Scottish Rites Auditorium, under the auspices of the United Public Workers (CIO), on February 21, 1948, to help in the fight of government workers against loyalty purges and terrorization by the government and its un-American Committee."

The UPW officials did not give in to the governmental intimidation. The UPW newspaper, the *Public Record,* reported in its issue in October, 1948 and March, 1949 efforts taken to end segregation and discrimination in the Canal Zone. These included the formation of a committee to end silver-roll jim crow in the Canal Zone with Robeson, W. E. B. DuBois, Ewart Guinier, and Abram Flaxer as members. A national legislative assembly to end segregation was formed in Washington, D.C. on 2/11/49 with Judge Hobson Reynolds as head of the nineteen-member committee. Upon their visit to the Canal Zone, they were told by Governor Francis X. Newcomer that there was no discrimination in the Canal Zone. The discussions ended with the delegation denouncing the Governor and pledging to campaign within their own organizations for public support to change the government's policies in Panama.

The UPW became directly involved with the Federal Government on the Washington front when the Bureau of Engraving and Printing, division of the Treasury Department announced on June 1, 1948 that it was firing 1300 employees within a year. The apprentice program for printers would be scrapped, and printers would be recruited from private sources. The Bureau estimated that these economy measures made possible by modernization programs would save the government $5,000,000 per year. The Bureau's discriminatory practices against black workers had already come under attack from UPW. The Union reported that none of the 500 printers employed in the Bureau were black. Moreover, there had never been a black printer in the department nor in the apprentice program. Since most of the black workers were frozen in the unskilled categories, they would be affected most by the cutback. For several months, representatives of UPW tried to discuss this matter with Treasury officials, with little success. Eventually, they were able to mobilize widespread support, and picketing of the Treasury building began in June of 1949.

The pickets were organized and led by Teresa L. Robinson, Grand Directress of civil liberties of the Elks Lodge. The picket line attracted widespread support. A photograph of the event showed Mrs. Robinson with Charles B. Howard (Des Moines publisher) and Robeson carrying protest signs in the picket line. The *Public Record* in August, 1949 reported the picketing and the denouncement of the denial of civil rights in government by Rep. Vito Marcantonio. Among the pickets were many Negro veterans of World War II. Picketing continued through the fall of 1949 and early into 1950. In February, 1950, CIO officials became embarrassed by the UPW's actions against the federal government and urged Richardson to drop the militant fight. Alan Hayward, CIO Director, told Richardson that the union was violating civil service regulations. Richardson refused to give in. The UPW's fight to end discrimination in the Bureau of Engraving was crowned with success on February 24, 1950 when the Fair Employment Practices Board upheld the union's complaint and ordered the Treasury Department to cease biased personnel practices.

As a result of the above ruling, more than thirty qualified Negro veterans were hired as apprentice printers for the first time in history. No blacks had ever been employed anywhere in the nation as apprentice journeymen plate printers. According to the *Public Record* of February, 1950, the FEP Board reported that the victory created an electric atmosphere in the printing plant that was comparable to the issuance of the Emancipation Proclamation. For the first time, black employees with 30 to 40 years of service had the chance to win ratings providing $24.00/day salary.

The union's jubilation was premature. The House Un-American Activities Committee stepped up its already active interest in the UPW. The Committee had already sent subpoenas to Abram Flaxer and Ewart Guinier, officers of UPW, and to Robeson. The latter first appeared before the Tenny Joint Legislative Committee on un-American activities in Los Angeles on 10/6/46 on a charge of affiliating with Communist-front organizations. The UPW was listed as one such organization. According to the *New York Times* of 10/7/46, Robeson replied: "I am not a member of the Communist party; but as a Negro, I am inevitably attracted to anti-Fascist movements."

CIO officials were displeased with the militant position that the UPW had against the Federal Government in support of its black members. The Union ignored the CIO's order to abandon its fight for racial justice. Union officials refused to become intimidated by the high-pressure from the Federal Government. Unexpectedly, UPW got pressure from another source.

In the February, 1951 *March of Labor*, Ewart Guinier wrote: "In January, 1950, on the initiative of the NAACP, over 5,000 delegates assembled in Washington for what was undoubtedly the most representative and largest lobby in the history of American politics. But Mr. [Roy] Wilkins, at the instigation of the CIO, went in for a wholesale purge." Tom Coleman, head of a Detroit affiliate of UPW, reported that the NAACP refused to seat delegates to the NAACP convention from his union, despite the fact that some of the delegates had been members of the NAACP since chapters were founded in their areas.

The Washington *Afro-American*, in a front-page editorial, on January 21; 1950, stated: "Having allowed themselves to become drunk with power and charged with super-patriotism, they (NAACP officials) turned like head-hunters upon their own membership and chopped them to pieces, while the real enemy looked on with unsuppressed glee."

Guinier pointed out that the NAACP leadership completely ignored a UPW-sponsored resolution introduced the year before that the NAACP would "recruit national groups and citizens from every walk of life to the end that both the President and the Congress shall feel the wrath and demand of the people for the speedy enactment of a comprehensive civil rights program." The Washington Edition of the *Afro-American* continued: ". . . The purge succeeded in demobilizing the NAACP, weakened its leftist support and removed its position as the only powerful spokesman of colored people."

The repercussions from the NAACP action were felt throughout the country. In Detroit, Thomas Coleman, a purged delegate from a UPW local in the Motor City, protested his outrage in an open letter to NAACP officials in New York. A year later this letter was a part of the evidence used by the Detroit Loyalty Commission to "prove" that Tom Coleman "follows the Communist line."

Meanwhile, the CIO continued to charge the UPW with being Communist and by a 34 to 2 vote of its Executive Board on 2/15/50 expelled the UPW on charge of Communism (the *New York Times*, 2/16/50). Earlier, the CIO had expelled the United Electrical, Radio and Machine Workers; the United Farm Workers; and the United Office and Professional Workers' unions. On 2/21/50, the State Department and the Veterans Administration announced that they would no longer recognize the UPW as bargaining agent for their employees. The end of the UPW as a labor union was in sight.

The first meeting of the UPW as an independent union occurred in Chicago on 5/27/50 under the leadership of Abram Flaxer with some 300 delegates in attendance representing 60,000 members in 27 states. Thomas Richardson accused both the AFL and CIO of direct attacks upon the UPW. The union became so demoralized from pressures from both internal and external sources that it ceased to exist in 1951.

In closing this chapter on the UPW, a synopsis of the trials and tribulations of Abram Flaxer will disclose the fate of many non-conformist American labor leaders on the national scene in the 1950s.

7/9/52 – Flaxer indicted in Federal Court for failing to produce his organization's membership list. The specific charge is contempt-of-Congress.

11/18/52 – Contempt-of-Congress charges quashed against Flaxer.

11/21/52 – Grand Jury, again, indicts Flaxer.

3/25/53 – Flaxer acquitted of two of three original counts of failure to give Sen. Arthur Watkins (R-Utah) list of union's members on 10/5/51.

10/16/53 – Flaxer fined $1,000 and sentenced to two months in jail for contempt-of-Congress. Appeal was filed and bond set at $1,000.

6/22/56 – Appeals Court upholds contempt-of-Congress conviction of Flaxer.

6/25/57 – Supreme Court sets aside the contempt-of-Congress conviction of Flaxer and orders case returned to trial court.

4/4/58 – Appeals Court, by a 4 to 3 majority, upheld the contempt-of-Congress conviction of Flaxer for second time.

6/10/58 – Supreme Court agrees to review case against Flaxer.

11/19/58 – Supreme Court unanimously reversed the Appeals Court ruling.

The Thomas Coleman affair typified the fate of many local nonconformist labor leaders during the same period in our nation's history.

THE THOMAS J. COLEMAN AFFAIR

The first in a series of traumatic events that completely changed the life of Thomas J. Coleman, destroyed the Detroit affiliate of the United Public Workers (UPW), and eventually cost the Detroit taxpayers over $400,000 was announced by the *Detroit News* on 9/19/50:

> **GARBAGE UNION BOSS FIRST CITED IN RED HUNT**
>
> The President of a garbage worker's union today became the first City employee cited to appear before the City Loyalty Commission, which is charged with weeding out subversives in the municipal service.
>
> He is Thomas J. Coleman, Negro, who lives at 35854 Vinewood Ave., Romulus Township. The seven-member Loyalty Investigating Committee charged Coleman with a series of affiliations with Communists and activities on their behalf.

The Tom Coleman story is presented in some detail as a prototype of the fate of many working-class people throughout the United States who were identified with Robeson. Three events occurred in 1949 which were to play significant roles in the life of Tom Coleman.

1. Tom Coleman had attended a peace convention in Chicago where Paul Robeson spoke, picketed a downtown hotel after Robeson was refused accommodations, and was seen near the scene of a Robeson concert the year before.
2. An amendment to the Detroit City Charter was adopted in November, 1949, establishing a City Loyalty Commission consisting of the Mayor, City Clerk, City Treasurer, Chief of Police, and the President of the City Council. It also provided for the establishment of a Loyalty Committee, appointed by the Mayor with a budget to hire an executive secretary and other help, as needed, to investigate the loyalty of city employees.

   Under the provisions of the Amendment, the Loyalty Committee could file charges against any city employee with the Loyalty Commission, charging the employees with disloyalty. When such charges were filed, and only then, would the charges become public. The Loyalty Commission was then required to proceed to a public hearing to determine the validity of the charge.

   The Loyalty Amendment provided that the accused have the right of counsel and the right to examine witnesses, except for "security reasons." It also provided that the accused shall be entitled to a fair trial and shall be presumed innocent until proved guilty.

   Disloyalty to the government was defined under the amendment as membership in or active association with any organization

owing its alliance to a foreign power, any organization on the Attorney General's list or the F.B.I. list. The amendment in its final form was drafted by George Edwards, then President of the City Council and candidate for Mayor.
The City Fathers and the press were proud that Detroit was the first city to follow the federal example of the Senate Sub-Committee on Internal Security and the House Committee on Un-American Activities. They were seeking the right case to try out the new Commission.

3. On February 15, 1950, the Executive Committee of the CIO cancelled its affiliation with the UPW charging "Communism." While federal investigative bodies brought heavy pressure on the national office of UPW, local loyalty agencies and rival unions made life difficult for the local affiliates of UPW.

Tom Coleman, President of Local 285, UPW, was in a bitter struggle with the City government for better working conditions for his garbage workers at the time that he was accused of subversion. Fifty-years-old at the time he was married and the father of four children, one of whom was fighting in Korea. Two were in college. He came to Detroit from Memphis, Tennessee in 1919 and started to work for the Sanitation Department in 1925 ("the only department of the City government where a black man could get regular employment"). Coleman had been very active in organizing city employees during the 1930s. Fellow garbagemen chose him as their president even before their local was affiliated with the AFL – a brief, unsatisfactory, and demeaning relationship ("A black man couldn't even buy a drink at the AFL bar"). For the several years prior to the charge of subversion, Coleman had served as International Representative of the UPW-CIO on a full-time basis.

Almost from the start, Coleman had been a "thorn in the side" of several city administrations as he tried to change the city's policy of no seniority, sick leave, paid vacations, holidays, or retirement for garbage workers. Relations between the City and garbage workers reached a new low on April 5, 1950 when the City Council cancelled a tentative appropriation of $100,000 earmarked for adjustment of the wages of sanitation workers. All efforts to restore the appropriation failed. This and other unmet grievances resulted in a wage demonstration at City Hall before work time on the morning of August 31, 1950. The garbagemen marched around City Hall and returned to their trucks in ample time to start the day's work on schedule.

Mayor Albert Cobo and Detroit Public Works (DPW) Commissioner Carl Varner reacted swiftly. They invoked the Hutchinson Act (a state law that prohibits work stoppage by government employees), declared the demonstrations strikes and empowered foremen to order the garbagemen off their jobs. Tom Coleman and his staff moved with equal dispatch. They convened a meeting of the local and voted to strike, accusing the mayor of a lockout. By nightfall, pickets were stationed at all DPW yards and many city offices.

In an effort to avoid direct bargaining with Tom Coleman, Mayor

Cobo talked to top city officials and members of the AFL Sanitation Drivers and Helpers. His policy was one of "carrying the issue to the men involved rather than to their unreliable leadership." When the Drivers and Helpers refused to cross the garbagemen's picket lines, the mayor had to seek another remedy.

All three daily newspapers supported the mayor and commended him for his swift, decisive action in invoking the Hutchinson Act. Louis Segadeli, President of the Joint Board of UPW, and Tom Coleman bore the brunt of editorial criticism for the garbage tie-up. Irate housewives and mountains of uncollected garbage soon forced the mayor to agree to meet with UPW officials. Although the mayor made his arrangements through Segadeli, Segadeli did not show up for the meeting. On one side of the table were Mayor Cobo, Frank Szymanski (Corporation Counsel), and departmental superintendents of public works, all white. On the other side of the table sat Coleman, Guy Chapman, A. J. Cooper, a man called Manning, Arthur Poplar, and Wiley Thompson, all black.

The bargaining session began early on Wednesday, 9/6/50. Progress was slow and difficult. At one point, an exasperated Manning stood up and shouted, "Man, we're wasting our time. These guys don't understand no talk. Let's hit the bricks again." The marathon meeting lasted until Thursday morning before agreement was reached on everything except the union's request for a 20¢ wage increase. Tom Coleman called a ratification meeting later that morning at the Tabernacle Baptist Church, Beechwood at Milford. The rank-and-file members voted to accept the agreement, with the provision that the wage matter would be settled as soon as possible. This issue was still being debated, twelve days later, when newsmen met a surprised Tom Coleman at his office and showed him the bold headline in the afternoon paper: **"GARBAGE BOSS FIRED IN RED HUNT."** They asked for his reaction to this charge of subversion. Coleman refused an official comment, choosing to study the charge and seek legal advice. A day or so later, Coleman received an order to appear before the Loyalty Investigating Committee. He refused to obey the order on the grounds that he had been tried in public already . . . "so why go behind closed doors so they can cut my throat." He appealed to the Loyalty Investigating Commission for a public hearing.

The legal firm that offered a sympathetic ear to Coleman was the Goodman, Crockett, Eden, and Robb organization, with Ernest Goodman handling the case. One of Mr. Goodman's first acts, as Tom Coleman's legal representative, was to request a bill of particulars from the Loyalty Commission. He was told that the particulars were confidential. Finally, the Commission sent the charges back to the Committee for further investigation.

A few days after the charges were publicized, J. R. Jackson, former co-worker, spoke up in Coleman's favor: "I have been personally associated with Tom Coleman for the past twenty-four years, and his activities have been those of a man sincerely and courageously interested in the advancement, politically and economically, of his race" (*Pittsburgh Courier,* September 30, 1950).

On October 2, 1950, the Thomas Coleman Defense Committee was formed with the Rev. Charles A. Hill, pastor of Hartford Avenue Church, and State Senator Patrick Walsh, as co-chairmen. The Committee prepared a fact-sheet on Coleman to show his involvement with the fight for freedom –

figure in establishing the chapter
chigan. He led the fight against
cipation in the founding and con-
enter in Romulus Township.
endent organization of garbage
rking conditions in 1926.
to get the C. F. Smith stores to
in jail as a result in 1932.
ery and potatoes from a friend's
needy families in the Eastern

drive at the Ford Motor Co.
Wagner Act, he spent his lunch
n plant organizing the workers

workers for the UAW strikers
rs strike of 1946.
Progressive Association, he col-
ontgomery Bus Boycott.

mass meeting at the Calvary
au on October 15 to protest the
rges of subversion against Tom
ame to his defense with weekly
hey made some psychological
doesn't raise our pay checks,
n 'Red' doesn't lower the rent,
ders 'Red' won't stop us from
r. Cobo. It didn't when Kim
on't work, Mr. Cobo. Nothing
" (Issued by Local 238, United

The Americans for Democratic Action scored Atty. G. W. Schudlich, head of the Loyalty Investigating Committee, for violating the spirit and letter of the charter amendment by prematurely and irresponsibly releasing to the press certain ". . . evidence which we understand should have been reserved for inclusion in the charge to the Loyalty Commission proper. Our concern . . . is to protect the basic rights and reputation of all innocent employees . . . . We must not protect ourselves into a police state. Mr. Schudlich's arbitrary disregard for the procedure stipulated in the Acts he operates under is a long step in that dangerous direction" (*Pittsburgh Courier*, October 6, 1950).

Attorney Goodman echoed the findings of the ADA, in pointing out some of the interesting coincidences of the Tom Coleman case: "It was while the negotiations were going on with the city for higher wages that the charges were filed against Tom Coleman. Despite the fact the Charter Amendment provided that no publicity be given to such charges until after they were received by the Loyalty Commission, charges were in the headlines before either the Commission or Tom Coleman had received them."

Goodman labelled the case against Coleman an "Alice-in-Wonderland procedure of first making charges and then looking for evidence to support them."

The Loyalty Commission hearings on the charges of subversion against Coleman began on 10/18/50. After a two-day parade of witnesses against him, he took the stand in his own behalf: "If you think that it will be of service to God and country to find me guilty, find me guilty! But if you think that when I leave this room I'm going to change one bit, you're wrong. I don't believe that I've suffered before as I have suffered during the last three months. But if that suffering can make you five men (Cobo, Boos, Leadbetter, Williams, and Miriani) understand how I feel, I will have accomplished something; because I will have made you understand how the average Negro feels. I am representative of the average Negro."

Coleman went on to challenge the Commissioners to make democracy a reality by hiring more Negroes on the police force and in the fire department. Testifying just before noon, Coleman invited the Commissioners to lunch with him at a near-by restaurant. "They will not only refuse to serve me, they won't serve you either if you come in with me." The Commissioners declined both offers.

One of the witnesses for Coleman during the early hearings was Justice of the Peace Hazel Harrison, from Romulus (the only black female Justice in the state at that time). She was horrified to see . . . "well-heeled agents of the prosecution, just outside the hearing room, trying to bribe people to go in and testify against Tom." It took only a few days for the prosecution to recognize the flaws in its case. In order to gain time, the Commission adjourned the loyalty hearings without date. The City's attack on Coleman opened up on a new front.

On 10/24/50, the *Detroit Times* reported that the Civil Service Commission of Detroit produced voter registration documents from Romulus Township purporting to show that Coleman did not reside within the city's limits. On 11/1/50, the *Times* reported that the Civil Service Commission had fired Coleman in a unanimous decision. The Civil Service Director, Donald Sublette, admitted that the Commission took "extraordinary" action in firing Coleman since he was not given an opportunity to move into the city as was usually the case. Sublette admitted that the Commission knew of 132 other city employees who lived outside the city limits.

The Rev. Charles A. Hill and State Senator Patrick Walsh issued a protest statement on the Coleman firing on 11/2/50. Five days later, Coleman was restored to his job as a city garbageman. His first assignment was in a residential area at $1.56/hour. He recalled his first days to this writer:

> I wasn't a young man anymore. After three years in the office my muscles were pretty soft. They assigned me to the toughest district in the city. I had to go to places like Palmer Woods where they don't have any alleys. We call this "carry-out" districts. You have to go to the rear of the deep lots and carry the heavy tubs on your shoulder to the truck into the front. I tell you it was rough. The boys helped me out all they could. I remember, especially drivers Arthur Poplar and Cecil Johnson helping me out. I guess it took me about a week to get back into the groove again.

The hearings against Coleman were re-scheduled for December 12, 1950 but did not get underway until December 20. The original list of charges had undergone a three-month revision and expansion. Before submitting the bill of particulars, all members of the Loyalty Investigating Committee signed it execpt the Rev. Malcolm Dade, the only black member of the first Committee. Tom Coleman and Atty. Goodman answered each of the Commission's charges as presented:

Charge: Coleman belonged to the UPW, an organization that had been kicked out of the CIO because of its "Communistic practices."

Response: "When my union got fed up with the anti-Negro practices of the AFL, we asked the CIO to grant us affiliation with their organization. The CIO advised us to join the UPW. Although they have kicked us out of the CIO, we're still happy to be in the UPW," said Coleman.

Charge: Coleman attend a Communist meeting in the office of Atty. Lebron Simmons in a downtown office building.

Response: The "key" witness to this charge was a Thomas Jackson. During his testimony, Atty. Simmons came into the hearing room. The witness was asked to identify anyone in the room who was at the meeting in question. He failed to do so despite help from his brother who was a city policeman.

Charge: Coleman was one of the leaders who protested the shooting of Leon Mosely.

Response: "Leon Mosely was shot in the back by a Detroit policeman before they knew that he had done anything wrong. When the citizenry fails to protest cold-blooded murder, the city is in serious trouble. Sure, I went to city hall to swear out a warrant for the arrest of the officer. In this state it is easier for a man to go to jail for shooting a pheasant out of season than for killing a Negro," responded Coleman.

Charge: Coleman attended a Civil Rights Congress picnic. The name of the park and date of the picnic were given.

Response: Attorney Goodman was able to prove that the picnic that Tom Coleman attended occurred in another park with a difference of three months in dates.

Charge: Glenn M. Irving, who admitted that he was an FBI agent and a former member of the Communist Party, testified that he had attended a Communist party meeting in Detroit, some time before, where he was introduced to Tom Coleman by the state youth organizer of the Communist Party.

Response: On cross-examination, he got mixed up and testified that he had not know Tom Coleman until he saw his picture in the newspaper in connection with the Commission's charges. When asked how his two statements could be reconciled, he answered that he was not introduced to Tom Coleman personally, but in a general way. (Later it was disclosed that Irving had been arrested eight times since 1940, and placed on five-years probation for prowling near home. In 1951, he was sentenced for soliciting funds for an anti-Communist "crusade" without a license.)

Charge: A member of the police Red Squad testified that he saw Tom Coleman at a Civil Rights Congress meeting, along with 800 other persons. On the basis of this testimony he presented hundreds of pages of documents and testimony of various congressional and state investigations, from as far away as California relating not to Tom Coleman but to the Civil Rights Congress; to officers of the Civil Rights Congress; and to organizations to which such officers claimed to be affiliated. The testimony of this witness needed no response.

Charge: Tom Coleman supported the candidacy of the Rev. Charles A. Hill for City Council.

Response: "True. I wanted a black man in the City Council. Rev. Hill was a good man; so I campaigned for him and voted for him," said Coleman.

Charge: Coleman wrote a letter of protest to Roy Wilkins of the NAACP in which he criticized Governor Dewey.

Response: "After the Boston meeting of the NAACP, my local got a letter from Roy Wilkins that our delegates would not be accepted at the next convention of the NAACP because of the charges made by the CIO. I did write to Roy Wilkins, telling him that the NAACP was penalizing members who had been supporting the organization since it began.

"I told him that the NAACP should spend more time protecting its members from unfair practices, rather than following the CIO. They could have started by asking Gov. (Thomas) Dewey, who at the time was visiting Owosso, Michigan, his birthplace, to lend his efforts to make it possible for a Negro to stay overnight in Owosso.

"Mr. Wilkins was asked to contact Gov. Dewey while he was still in Owosso to see if he could open up that jim crow town."

Charge: Coleman attended a Chicago Peace Conference at which Paul Robeson sang and spoke. (Note – House Report 378 of the 82nd Congress lists Thomas Coleman as a member of Michigan's Communist "Peace" offensive. Seventeen other members of Michigan included Rev. Charles Hill and William Hood. Tom Coleman and delegates from many other cities met in the Ashland Auditorium in Chicago on 10/1/49, on the eve of the Korean War.)

Response: Paul Robeson had taken a strong position for peace. The labor unions supported his position. This so-called Communist Peace Offensive was in reality, a national labor conference for peace. Many unions from all over the country were represented.

"I saw nothing wrong with being for peace. My son was fighting in Korea at the time of the hearings. If the peace efforts had succeeded, he would not have had to go to Korea.

"I told the Loyalty Commission that even if my son should get killed in Korea, the unborn child that his wife is carrying will never be able to enjoy first-class citizenship in this country. Those things he would die to preserve will be denied to his child," said Coleman.

Charge: Detroit Police detective Warner Taylor reported that Tom Coleman attended a concert featuring Paul Robeson at the Forest Club on 10/9/49.

Response: "No, I didn't go to that concert, but I tried. I rode the bus from downtown that night. There were so many people in the street that the bus had to be detoured over to Woodward at Canfield. Now this is five blocks from where Robeson was appearing. All crosstown and north – south traffic had to be rerouted. There were hundreds of people filling the streets all around the Forest Club. Policemen were everywhere.

"No matter how I tried, I couldn't get into the club. I learned that Robeson was coming down to the Shiloh Baptist Church later and I went down there to wait for him. So I did see him at the church, but not at the Forest Club."

The hearings originally scheduled for 12/12/50 were re-scheduled for 12/20 and got under way with John Dunn as Corporation Counsel presenting the city's case against Coleman. The chief witness for the city was the admitted part-time FBI worker and ex-Communist – Glenn M. Irving. Following this witness, the hearings were postponed to 1/3/51. The *Detroit Times* of 1/4/51 reported that detective Sgt. John Palek placed Coleman at a Civil Rights Congress and Progressive party picket line on 10/13/48. Under cross-examination, Atty. Goodman drew from Palek the admission that there was no evidence that Coleman belonged to any organization other than the UPW. The *Times* reported on 1/5/51 that Jefferson Jackson, an admitted ex-Communist, testified that Coleman had attended a Communist party meeting in 1946. On this date of the hearing, three prominent black citizens took the stand in Coleman's defense (Collins George, editor of the Detroit edition of the *Pittsburgh Courier;* the Rev. William Hilliard, pastor of the St. Paul A.M.E. Zion Church; and the Rev. Jessie J. McNeil, pastor of the Tabernacle Baptist Church).

Meanwhile, Coleman sought support from other organizations and individuals. Edward Turner, president of the Detroit NAACP, pointed out that his organization was under heavy pressure and could not take any chances. Coleman tried to enlist the aid of the teachers' local in his fight against the Hutchinson Act. He was told that he had the wrong lawyer. Coleman then issued a position paper in his own defense:

> I have only one comment on this hectic business of the last two months and that is that I shall continue to fight for full and equal citizenship for my people. Some may call this treason but I think it is a contribution to true Americanism which I can make to my country.
>
> As a city employee and citizen of Detroit, I had hoped to live long enough to see this city begin to eliminate racial discrimination in city jobs such as the fire department and to see our Negro citizens integrated into all branches of city employment, including the Civil Service Commission itself.
>
> When my son, Tommy, and many other boys of his race come home from Korea, I'd like to know that they have all the chances afforded every American. To this end I shall devote much of the remainder of my life, as I have in the past twenty-five years. This is and shall be my contribution to my country.

The trial hearings ended on 1/19/51 but a decision was not to come for some two months later. During his summation, the Corporation Counsel for the city did not argue that Coleman was a member of the Communist Party, but that his activities and associations were such as to make him disloyal to the United States Government, as defined in the city amendment. Attorney Goodman's summary pointed out that the "trial" could hardly be considered a fair one since one of the "judges" was the police commissioner who employed one of the principal witnesses used against Coleman, while the mayor was Coleman's protagonist in a labor dispute. He also pointed out that a witness had testified that he had been offered a bribe to appear against Coleman and that the other evidence made it appear that the case agaisnt Coleman was a persecution from beginning to end.

In a later summary of the case submitted to the *National Guardian*, Goodman said:

> While the press was hostile to Tom Coleman up to the first day of the testimony, even the press could not conceal the perjury of the witnesses against Tom Coleman. At each session, additional evidence of perjury was so dramatically presented that the reporters present at the hearing were forced to play up this part of the case; and the newspapers, in their published reports, were somewhat objective and in some instances actually favorable to Tom Coleman. The Negro press played the case up, and there was no question that their feeling was that Coleman was an object of persecution because of his race and because of his fight over the years for equality.

Two days before a verdict was reached, the *Pittsburgh Courier* summarized the hearing for its readers. Several city officials were quoted as saying that the case had taken up more time than they thought it deserved. The five-man Committee spent more than five days hearing testimony that produced a 400-page transcript.

Finally, six months after the charges were levelled against Coleman, a verdict came; Coleman was cleared of subversion charges. The *Detroit Free Press* of 3/22/51 reported that Mayor Cobo announced that the charges had not been substantiated by the evidence presented at the public hearings. The unanimous verdict came after some six hours of secret deliberations by the Commission. On 3/22/51, the *Free Press* carried the following editorial:

> In these times of hysteria, when the pursuit of justice might easily become a witch hunt, the city's Loyalty Commission has done something salutory in clearing Thomas Coleman of subversive charges.
>
> Coleman is the president of Local 285, United Public Workers, representing a large group of employees of the Detroit Department of Public Works. The United Public Workers is a left-wing organization which was kicked out of the CIO because of its reddish tinge. The fact that Coleman was a high officer in this union, coupled with the fact that Coleman appeared at open meetings of leftist organizations made him suspect.
>
> It is because of his affiliations that he was cited by the Loyalty Investigating Committee, a screening group to the LoyaltyCommission. Had he been found guilty by the latter, the penalty would have been dismissal from his job.
>
> The Loyalty Commission, composed of five top officials, none of

whom has the slightest leftist learnings or sympathies, might have been looked upon as a biased tribunal, from Coleman's point of view. In fact, left-wing groups opposed the establishment of the Commission on the grounds that it would be used unfairly against accused persons.

> The Commission held long, tedious hearings in the Coleman case, the first to be brought before it. The obvious fairness of its verdict should allay fears that it is a witch-hunting body and should build confidence in it.

As a matter of "principle," Tom Coleman resigned from the Sanitation Department immediately after his exoneration. He had worked for the city twenty-five years, but pension was denied on the grounds that the first four years were part-time. His memory of the event is still fresh:

> With two kids in college, I really needed the job, but there are some things a man just can't do. Furthermore, the ctiy had done its dirty work. By the time they got through with me, the UPW was completely demoralized. We had a strong union and could have handled the red baiting and union raids from the CIO and the AFL. But when the government came in on their side that was too much for us.
>
> You already know what happened to Abram Flaxer and Ewart Guinier at the national level of UPW. Well, we had the same thing happen to us here on the local level. It wasn't too long before the two unions were fighting each other for the scraps of what had been our union.

Coleman not only left city government, he did not seek employment in the city. He took his manual lawnmower and went to Ann Arbor . . . "where nobody would recognize me," and spent all day trying to get employment as a gardener. Nobody would hire him. Toward sunset, he offered to trim a lady's lawn without charge, if it did not please her husband when he came home. She agreed. "When I finished, there wasn't a single blade of grass out of place in that whole yard," he said. When Coleman returned the following week, not only did the lady hire him for her regular gardener, but she lined up many of her neighbors for him. In a short time, he was earning as much as he had made on the garbage truck. Impressed with Tom Coleman's industry, the husband of his first employer offered him a job in his tire company. Coleman went to school to learn the skill of vulcanizing. He became a much-valued employee and remained with the company for many years.

The members of the Loyalty Investigating Committee blamed their failure to convict Coleman on their lack of subpoena power. They requested that this additional power be given in the interest of public safety and national security. The matter was placed before the Detroit voters in the April election of 1951. It passed on April 2, and was enacted on April 12.

Spirited objections to this extension of the power to the Loyalty bodies came from the UPW, the ADA, and many private individuals.

Both the Loyalty Investigating Committee and the Commission

continued to function until September of 1962, but in secret. In May, 1962, a Charter amendment was presented to the Common Council by the Corporation Counsel. The proposed amendment concerned abolition of the Loyalty Commission and Investigating Committee and included submission of that question to a vote of the people at the primary election to be held in the City of Detroit on August 7, 1962. The proposal was approved by the voters.

The Loyalty Committee began operations September 12, 1950. Total expenditures were:

	Totally Actually Spent
Sept. 12, 1950–June 30, 1951	$ 24,781.54
July 1, 1951–June 30, 1952	50,835.52
July 1, 1952–June 30, 1953	47,844.25
July 1, 1953–June 30, 1954	50,961.66
July 1, 1954–June 30, 1955	48,383.05
July 1, 1955–June 30, 1956	42,685.15
July 1, 1956–June 30, 1957	38,533.30
July 1, 1957–June 30, 1958	33,395.00
July 1, 1958–June 30, 1959	21,773.00
July 1, 1959–June 30, 1960	22,885.00
July 1, 1960–June 30, 1961	23,132.00
July 1, 1961–June 30, 1962	22,641.00
July 1, 1962–Sept. 10, 1962	4,405.00
Total	$432,255.47

In carrying out the terms of the 1962 Charter Amendment city officials have made it difficult to determine what the Detroit taxpayers got for this expenditure of $432,255.47.

Occasionally, the City Council demanded progress reports from the Loyalty Investigating Committee. One such report was given by Alfred A. May, Chairman of the Committee, on October 31, 1955. A summary of this report provides some ideas as to how the Committee served the Detroit community during the 11 years of its post-Coleman existence. Since 1950, 26 persons resigned city positions after being requested to appear at a closed hearing of the Committee. Some 3,198 names were searched through the indices of the Committee. Of the names searched 161 were given preliminary investigations. Only two of the 161 cases were given full investigation.

Coleman felt that his identification with and support of Robeson added to his woes in the late 1940s and early 1950s. Still in the forward trenches of the fight for freedom in spite of his 75 years, Coleman summarized for this writer his position in 1974:

> I consider it an honor to be identified with Paul Robeson. If I had to do it all over again, I would do the same thing.
> The whole federal government was after Robeson. Congressional investigating committees, The Federal Bureau of Investigation, the

Immigration Service, and the Treasury Department were out to destroy him, not to mention the local groups in the cities that he visited. Yet, he stood up to them all.

You see, Robeson was the bird in the pivot of the formation. They had to try to shoot him down to try to demoralize the flock. This system will try to do that to any black man who shows signs of true leadership. They have bought off or shot down many black men, but Robeson was too tough for them. What a Man!

THE UNITED AUTOMOBILE WORKERS

Of all the appearances Robeson made in support of the labor movement, none was more dramatic or decisive than his presence at the United Automobile Workers' (UAW) organzing drive rally in downtown Detroit on May 19, 1941. Only two days remained before the final showdown between the UAW and Henry Ford for control of the world's largest industrial unit, the mighty Rouge plant in Dearborn, Michigan. Already, the UAW had won bargaining rights from such industrial giants as Briggs, Hudson, Chrysler, and General Motors. The experiences gained from these preliminary skirmishes would be put to good use in the main battle ahead. The UAW's founding fathers fought hard to establish their union during the great depresison of the 1930s. From its beginning, their major goal was to bring Henry Ford to heel and "organize the Rouge."

In the early days, industrial bosses took a dim view of labor unions. Recruitment was clandestine – man to man. Small groups met from time to time in secret to discuss their many problems and seek solutions. Recruitment was even more difficult among the foreign-born workers who spoke little or no English and lived, for the most part, in enclaves of their own people. Grateful to be employed in a strange land, they were not inclined knowlingly to arouse the wrath of their employers.

Workers who did join the union did so at considerable hazard to themselves. If their union affiliation became known, or strongly suspected, they were likely to be fired, beaten or both by company agents. Thus, fragmentation and fear were two formidable weapons in the arsenal of the anti-union forces. The industrial unions had an additional, internal problem that demanded resolution if they were to reach full flower. Prior to 1936, most labor unions operated under the umbrella of the American Federation of Labor (AFL). Geared to the needs of the smaller but more powerful craft unions, the AFL tried to discourage the expansion of the larger but less powerful industrial unions.

John L. Lewis, head of the Miners' Union and leader of the industrial faction within the AFL, was the only non-craft union member of the AFL Council. Even after he forced the Council to increase its membership to 17, the craft union majority regularly overruled every effort Lewis made on behalf of industrial unions. This unhappy and uneasy situation caused angry rumblings within the AFL for many months. The inevitable, volcanic eruption occurred on November 19, 1935.

The Rubber Workers had petitioned the AFL for an industrial charter at an earlier convention in August. Instead, they were offered an unacceptable modification of the craft union charter. When the convention resumed its deliberations in October, the Rubber Workers reopened the debate for an industrial charter. The convention chairman tried to cut off discussion, but Lewis ignored the chairman and kept the issue on the floor. William S. Hutcheson, President of the Carpenters and Joiners, a strong craft union, confronted Lewis and tried to shout him down. The bushy-browed leader of the United Mine Workers suddenly lost his temper and Hutcheson suddenly lost his upright position. When the smoke cleared, Hutcheson, a bit the worse off, was bleeding briskly from a laceration of the face; and he sustained a contusion of the lip.

When order was restored on the convention floor, the Council voted to suspend Lewis. He was charged with engaging in dual unionism and fomenting insurrection within the labor movement. Other industrial union leaders threw their support behind Lewis. These included the 200,000-member International Ladies Garment Workers' Union, the 150,000-member Amalgamated Clothing Workers of America, and six other industrial unions within the AFL. They, too, were supended.

On November 23, 1935, Lewis sent the following telegram to William Green, President of the AFL: "Dear Sir and Brother:

Effective this date, I resign as Vice-President of AFL.

Yours truly, John L. Lewis."

Lewis said that his group was determined upon "as bitter a fight as necessary to win practical recognition for industrial unions." Eventually, he stormed out of the AFL, and most of the industrial unions followed in his wake to form a new labor organization more suited to their needs. They first called themselves the Committee of Industrial Organization but later changed it to the Congress of Industrial Organization (CIO).

The fissure that Lewis caused in the central body of the AFL by his disruptive departure spread down to the locals with great rapidity. The Lewis fissure reached the UAW on August 3, 1936 when the general Executive Board of UAW voted, unanimously, to sever their connection with the AFL and join the CIO. The Board sent William Green the following telegram: "The UAW are loyal to the AFL but realize that the automobile industry can be organized, successfully, only along industrial lines." The UAW's parting shot was a reminder to the AFL Council that it had acted illegally in suspending Lewis and the other union leaders. "Only the National Convention can order such suspensions."

This was the beginning of nearly two decades of AFL vs CIO warfare. Their conflicts would be sharpened, during this period, by the militant, pro-labor position of the CIO, on the one hand, as opposed to the more conservative, pro-industry position of the AFL on the other. Toward the end of the period, however, the CIO's latter-day-saints were destined to exorcise the militant demons and, prodigal-like, return to the fold.

Many UAW locals, meanwhile, were the scenes of abrasive AFL/CIO confrontations. Percy Llewellyn, formerly President of Ford Local 600, UAW-CIO, recalled the comedy of errors when the split came to Dearborn:

> Homer Martin was the leader of the AFL wing of our local, and he had control of the membership files and the union charter. We had to get the lists. For all we knew, they might turn up in the hands of Harry (Bennett) and Henry (Ford).
>
> A group was sent to scout the building, where the files were kept, and plan for forcible entry. The building was located on Michigan Avenue in Dearborn. They reached a decision and sent for a local locksmith to help with the safe.
>
> Our group got in, all right; but Martin's people arrived before the job was finished. Fortunately, our people had locked themselves in. Unable to gain entry, the other crowd called the Dearborn police and reported a breaking-and-entering. Each group produced proof of membership in the union and disputed the others' right to the premises.
>
> The confused policemen threw up their hands and suggested the advice of a nearby magistrate. While the AFL group went to summon the magistrate, the CIO group completed their heist and fled.
>
> They brought us into court. All of a sudden, something hit me. I had our lawyer subpoena the lease of the building. It showed that I had signed the original lease for the building when we first rented it. The case was thrown out. We kept the membership lists and the charter and got down to some serious organizing in the CIO.

Not the least of the problems facing these early organizers was the creator of the Rouge, Henry Ford, and the men who surrounded him, Harry Bennett, Don Marshall, and I. A. Capizzi, just to name three. Harry Bennett, Director of Personnel, exercised nearly absolute power within the Ford organization. He could make or break men and is reported to have done both with impunity. Don Marshall, a black chip off the white block, was Bennett's assistant in charge of black personnel. Together they ran a tight ship, as many Ford workers of the period can attest. Capizzi an attorney, provided the legal breastworks against all kinds of assaults on the citadel of the Rouge and other Ford holdings.

Other deterrents to unionization at the Rouge were conditions inside the plant. Ed Lock, one of the first Ford organizers, described these conditions before the organizing drive began to succeed:

> Terror prevailed inside the plant. You couldn't talk to a fellow-worker. Ford's service men (security force) followed you everywhere you went, even into the toilet. If you didn't produce enough evidence to justify the trip, you could get fired on the spot. A worker could be fired for almost anything. Take the case of John Gallo; he was fired for smiling. (*Ford Facts,* March 5, 1941 reported that John Gallo was fired by the general foreman, Harry May, for smiling while screwing nuts in steering gear. May admitted to referee Charles Rubinoff that Gallo's production did not suffer because of the smile. Rubinoff did allow that any worker who could find anything to smile about in the Rouge should be regarded with suspicion. But when all the evidence was in, Rubinoff had to rule that Gallo had not committed a crime. Not only did Gallo get his job back, but the UAW forced the rehiring of 40 other men who had been fired for similar reasons.)
>
> The whole idea was the speed-up. You could be fired for almost anything. It was so bad that the employment office kept a steady stream of new men coming in one gate while the men who just got fired went out another gate.

William "Bill" Mackie was one of the first and most effective champions of the workers in the automotive industry. The men loved and trusted Bill. His technique was to recruit members individually and in small groups for their early organization. He carried the membership lists in his pockets and guarded them with his life. As new and more daring men joined the union, they moved toward open, mass recruitment of members. Men like Lock and Llewellyn knew that strength in numbers would be required to conquer the Rouge. Despite the danger and difficulties, they decided to come out in the open. Llewellyn recalled their first effort to hold a public meeting:

> A decision was made to come out in the open for union activity and defy the fear mongers in the plant. A mass meeting was called for Dearborn's Fordson High School. Our application for a permit to use the school's auditorium passed the Board by only one vote. There was quite a fight.
>
> The United Allied Veterans of the City of Dearborn objected to the Board's decision on the grounds that the meeting would be a "Communist meeting." The Board withdrew its approval and offered to reconsider if we would bring in a petition signed by property owners in Dearborn.
>
> This created a problem for us. We couldn't ask Ford employees to sign up for fear of reprisals. Also, many workers did not own property. Fortunately, there were enough workers in other plants, willing to sign, to get us the names we needed.
>
> The petitions were submitted to the Board, and an even bigger fight followed. But, we won again by one vote. The call for the meeting went out and thousands came. The front rows of the auditorium were filled with members of the Knights of Dearborn, led by Sam Taylor. I think they had planned to disrupt the meeting; but when they saw the size of the crowd, they changed their minds. We had to open up two more halls, to accommodate the crowd; and our speakers went from room to room. After that we were on our way.

There were many such victories, many at the rank and file level, that gave strength and stability to the youthful UAW. In due course, the matter of bargaining rights, in the other major automotive industries, had been settled in the Union's favor. The last of these was the General Motors confrontation, where the UAW-CIO won out over the AFL on April 17, 1940 by a 3:1 majority.

Now, the moment of truth was at hand. For the Union it was an all-out, all or-nothing-at-all effort in which nothing, men nor money, could be spared. For if they failed to take the Rouge, the cradle of mass production, their claim to power in the field of labor would have a hollow ring. R. J. Thomas was re-elected President of UAW-CIO on August 5, 1940. Six weeks later, the Union appropriated $100,000 to help finance the Ford organizing drive. An organizing team was recruited from their most experienced personnel. Phillip Murray, President of CIO, sent a sizeable purse to aid the drive and dispatched one of his best men, Michael Widman Jr., to direct the entire operation.

One of the Union's first moves was to challenge the City of Dearborn's administration which was, understandably, sympathetic to its most illustrious benefactor. Three UAW officials defied the city's ordinance against distributing hand bills by passing out leaflets near the Rouge plant supporting unionization. They were promptly arrested and charged with violation of the City Charter. The case went to trial and the Municipal Court ruled that the City Ordinance was illegal. Charges against the UAW officials were dropped. The Dearborn city police ignored the Court's ruling and arrested 25 additional workers for passing out leaflets. In December, 1940 the Federal Court ruled that the Dearborn ban against the distribution of leaflets was unconstitutional. This was the beginning of a carefully-planned, multi-pronged attack on the Ford dynasty that would last for five months before a final decision.

At the same time and on another front, the UAW and Ford were grappling in the Federal arena over an issue with national ramifications. The UAW had convinced the officials of the National Labor Relations Board (the investigative arm of the Wagner Act) that the relationhip between the Ford Motor Company (hereafter called the Company) and its employees left much to be desired. Over the objections of the Company, the NLRB scheduled hearings; and they were underway while the organizing drive gained momentum.

Testimony of Ford workers from diverse sections of the country supported the Union's charges that the Company engaged in anti-union activities that were in violation of the provisions of the Wagner Act. Especially revealing were the stories from witnesses of espionage, tarring and feathering, arrests and beatings of unionists by Company agents in Dallas, Kansas City, and elsewhere. Union officials reported that Bennett and Homer Martin were fostering the AFL as the Company Union, another violation of the Wagner Act. The

NLRB issued a cease and desist order to the Company. On February 19, 1941, Company representatives posted a notice that it would no longer discourage union organizers. Union observers could detect no change in the Company's behavior. After five days, they complained to NLRB again. Earlier testimony had convinced the NLRB that the Company was unfair to organized labor. The case went to the Circuit Court which ruled in favor of the Union. The Company appealed the ruling to the Supreme Court. In February, 1941, the Supreme Court confirmed the lower court's decision.

Reeling from this unaccustomed defeat, the Company temporarily relaxed its rigid discipline in the plants. The workers, equally dazed with victory and unsure of the limits of this new-found freedom, overstepped the limits that the Company allowed. In short order, the old order (no smoking, sudden and unexplained changes in jobs and shifts, precipitate firings, etc.) was restored. The rank and file, having had a sweet but brief encounter with freedom, could not wait much longer for the slow, uncertain results of the negotiating teams. On February 26, 1941, two days after they had complained to NRLB that the Company was ignoring the cease and desist order, the Union filed a strike notice with the State Mediation Board. They would need all of the thirty-day waiting period to arrange the thousands of details of a walk-out.

In a desperate, last-minute effort to demonstrate to the Union that the Company would bargain in good faith and that a strike may not be necessary, NLRB officials sent a subpoena to Henry Ford and Harry Bennett to appear before them on March 25, 1941. Neither man appeared. Instead, the Legal Department of the Company issued a statement to the effect that the Union and Communists were in a conspiracy to take over the Company. Only three days of the thirty-day waiting period were left.

The time was not opportune for a strike. German Panzer divisions had just conquered Crete with terrible British losses. Dive bombers and unmanned missles were making shambles of the British countryside. Ford Motor Company was working on approximately $150,000,000 worth of defense contracts; a strike could cripple the war effort. Then, too, there was the unknown factor of the black employees at the Rouge plant, estimated at about 14,000. Many of them felt an almost slavelike loyalty for Mr. Ford. Would they answer a strike call from a Union that they neither knew nor trusted?

R. J. Thomas, UAW President, had already issued an official union challenge that made retreat or restraint impossible: "People say that UAW-CIO has taken on an almost impossible job in trying to bring Ford workers the benefits of unionism. They say Ford is unscrupulous, that he will stop at nothing to keep his employees from joining the union. They say that Ford does not care about the law or the government, that his army of thugs and stool pigeons will work overtime to terrorize the workers out of their legal rights. The UAW-CIO will do the job" (*Ford Facts,* 1/26/41).

Many people recalled Henry Ford's appraisal of his operation in 1937: "We have never had any strikes in any of our plants; because our conditions do not create them." The evidence that he may have changed his mind was less than overwhelming.

Early on the morning of April 1, 1941, Norman W. Smith went to Gate 4 of the Rouge plant and shouted an order that many people thought would never be given, "Evacuate the plant!"

First-hand testimony from people who were there suggests that the UAW brass were just about as surprised by the strike call as the Company. Apparently, the final decision was made at the plant level, without "official" sanction or knowledge. Several hours of high-level quandry elapsed before UAW officials announced what was already an established fact: the Rouge was struck! Thousands of workers dropped their tools and walked out of the plant. Kitchens, set up in nearby buildings, and first-aid stations, placed at strategic points, were ready for battle action.

Fighting soon broke out between the strikers and several thousand workers who elected to remain in the plant and "hold for Mister Ford." Some of the Ford loyalists, predominately black, climbed to the roof of the plant and fired a hail of nuts, bolts, and other metal missles down on the strikers. Other loyalists armed themselves with steel bars and knives and attacked the line of strikers in two waves. More than a score of strikers required treatment at the "field hospitals" (*New York Times,* 4/2/41).

Attorney Capizzi charged the Union with illegal seizure of the plant that would cripple the war effort. Widman answered with the following telegram to the Defense Department: "The striking Ford workers are anxious not to permit the illegal anti-labor policies of the Ford Motor Company to impede our National Defense Program. If you can obtain the Company's cooperation, we are ready to assume the work necessary for National Defense."

Harry Bennett countered with a condemnation of the strike: "For several months this Communist-controlled Union has been clamoring for an election at Rouge. This strike, on the very eve of a decision by the National Labor Relations Board on the Union's petition, is very significant. It is clear that the Union's main objective is not an election but is, rather, to tie up another large American industry and cripple the National Defense Program."

This was a masterful piece of strategy on the part of the Company. It was true that the highest priority item of the Union management was an NLRB-sponsored election at the Rouge. A strike was not an essential part of their strategy. As a matter of fact, the strike could prove to be an embarrassment to the developers of the organizing drive as well as an impediment to its progress.

Realizing that Bennett's statement, if allowed to stand, could drive a wedge between the rank and file unionists and their officers, Thomas and Widman issued a quick, joint reply: "Mr. Bennett has allowed himself to be goaded into releasing the kind of red herring that the Ford attorney, Mr. Capizzi tried, unsuccessfully, to use in recent election hearings before the NLRB."

Failing to stop the strike at the local level, Bennett made a bid for an executive order in a telegram to President F. D. Roosevelt that said, among other things: ". . . Communist leaders are actually directing this lawlessness." The President assured Bennett that he was aware of the situation at the Ford plant, but he did not consider the matter crucial in so far as the war effort was concerned. He stated that his attention was absorbed by the more critical strike at the Allis-Chalmers plant. (Michigan Democrats were pleased with the President's response. Some of them recalled Governor Alf Landon's presidential campaign-tour through Michigan in 1936. Speaking before 10,000 people at Navin Field, he praised the leaders of the automobile industry for resisting the compulsory terms of the National Recovery Act. Special commendation was reserved for Henry Ford whom he praised for never signing the "Code of the Blue Eagle." Landon predicted that Roosevelt and his New Deal would destroy the nation. Ford invited Landon to lunch.)

The Ford strike forced the black community to make a difficult choice between Ford and the Union. Horace White, Pastor of the Plymouth Congregational Church, recalled the events of the strike in an article in the *Michigan Chronicle* on September 4, 1954:

> Many Negroes refused to come out on strike for recognition of the Union by the Company. They were holding for Mr. Ford. Those Negroes felt that if the Union failed, the Company would feel a kind of loyalty which would work to their advantage.
> Let it be noted that all Negro Workers did not remain in the plant and draw premium pay to hold the lines against the Union. Many of them sided with their fellows on the worth of the Union. Also let it be said, to the eternal credit of the majority of the workers in the plant, that when the Negro workers did relinquish the right to hold for Mr. Ford, they were received into the ranks of the organized workers without recrimination.

A more detailed study of the explosive situation inside the plant and in the Detroit area at large was provided by the Hardin Report. Walter Hardin, one of the unsung heroes of the strike and the organizing drive, was International Representative and Director of Negro Activities, UAW-CIO. His report is in the Appendix section on pp. 154-155.

On the third day of the strike, the Company carried its case into the black community. Homer Martin and Don Marshall spoke to 3,000 Ford workers, mostly black, at the Forest Club – Hastings at Forest. The listeners were advised to "assert your rights as American citizens and go back to work as members of the AFL." At the time of the Forest Club meeting, the delegates of an AFL convention at the labor temple were passing a resolution to ask the National Council to force Homer Martin to cease representing himself as the authorized agent of the AFL.

Some Union officials expressed the opinion that the press gave unequal coverage to the Company's side of the struggle, especially the charges that the Union was unpatriotic and dominated by Communists. Ernest Goodman, attorney for the Union, issued the following brief in favor of his client:

> Ford attempted to sabotage the National Defense Program by its Nazi connections and foreign investments. The strike was provoked by the Company that does not come into court with clean hands. It has violated State and Federal laws. Ford's espionage system breeds discontent and fear among the workers.
> The Company has refused to mediate the labor disputes, as required under the Norris-LaGuardia Act. The Ford Motor Company encouraged violence, during the strike, even to the point of putting race against race and bringing gangs of Negroes in as strike breakers.

Bennett accused the strikers of violence against those workers who had remained loyal to the Company, and he charged the strikers with $100,000 worth of damage to the plant and its equipment. Union officials accused Bennett of outflanking their picket lines by bringing in supplies and strikebreakers via the Rouge river. In specific response to the charge of Union atrocities, R. J. Thomas said: "The pure invention of a mind that has never been noted for a high regard for the truth. As you know, the Ford Motor Company has been found guilty in eight cases by the National Labor Relations Board. Three cases have revealed violence and terrorism as a regular feature of Ford's labor policy. Ford, today, is still in violation of the Wagner Act."

Despite the charges and counter-charges, some positive things were happening in the strike, itself. Michigan Governor Murray Van Wagoner quickly put aside the mundane matters of state. He came to Detroit and teamed up with James Dewey, NLRB arbitrator, and spared no time or effort in trying to bring the opposing factions together. State Senator Charles Diggs pledged his full support to the strikers. Rev. Charles Hill, highly respected by the black workers, had been able to encourage hundreds of foundry workers to leave the plant and join the strikers on April 4, 1941. Phillip Murray arrived in Detroit on April 5 to aid in the Ford negotiations. It was not long after the arrival of Murray that the NLRB ordered an election to be held at the Ford Motor Company within 45 days. Bennett was enraged. He accused the NLRB officials of favoritism toward the Union and expressed doubt that the Company would get a fair ballot.

Dewey held a press conference on April 7. He felt confident that the strike would be settled soon. He pointed out that this was the first time that Ford officials had faced Union officials across the bargaining table. "Yet, we had two conferences today," he said. The next day, the CIO accepted a three-point peace plan:

1. All employees shall be returned to their jobs without discrimination, at once.
2. Grievance proceedings established before the strike shall be resumed.
3. Both parties, likewise, agree to do all that is in their power to expedite the holding of Labor Board Elections.

Company officials refused to sign the peace plan. One more condition had to be met. If the Union would agree to stop those embarrassing NLRB hearings, the Company would sign the agreement. Union representatives, recalling the many prior postponements and the Company's lack of cooperation in the past, objected. The strike settlement hung in the balance for several hours. Van Wagoner's diplomacy was put to the supreme test. Finally, he was able to convince Union officials that postponement of the hearings would not extend beyond the date of the NLRB elections. Dewey concurred and promised that under no circumstances would the Company be granted another postponement.

The Ford strike was settled on April 10, 1941. Orders went out to the workers and production was resumed on April 13. Everyone was happy, especially the Henry Fords (who celebrated their 53rd anniversary and Mrs. Ford's birthday).

As the Ford workers struggled back to work, strategists for both the AFL and CIO girded for their decisive battle. Whoever won the battle of the Rouge would, eventually, control the automotive industry (*Ford Facts*, 4/15/41). Dewey's announcement made it official: NLRB election at the Rouge and Highland Park plants would be on May 21, 1941.

UAW officials had to guard against complacency and undue optimism because of the strike settlement. The fight was far from over. They had to win the coming election so convincingly that the AFL would leave the arena. The 3:1 margin of victory at General Motors was a minimum goal. A higher ratio would establish their control more firmly.

A key issue for both union and contenders was the ethnic vote. The CIO imported outstanding Polish labor leaders to assist in recruiting support from the 20,000 Polish workers at the Rouge. One such leader was Leo Krzycki, Vice-President of the Amalgamated Clothing Workers of America – CIO, who spoke to a Polish gathering at Polski Hall, Warren at Chene, on January 26, 1941.

The most important unknown in this power struggle for both Unions and the Company was the black vote. Certainly, the events in the recent strike indicated that no group could take it for granted. Without that vote, the UAW's decisive victory was in jeapordy, if not impossible.

For many of Ford's black employees, their jobs had produced home, car and economic stability. His Ford badge was a status symbol which he displayed proudly. Many blacks were recruited from the plantations of the south where paternalism was a way of life. Ford's brand of paternalism was an improvement for them. Was it reasonable to expect such workers to forsake Ford and cast their lot with a Union that was either unknown or suspect? Ford's influence in the black community was a source of much concern for the UAW strategists. Two of Detroit's most powerful black ministers, the Rev. Robert Bradby of the Second Baptist Church, and Father Everad Daniels of St. Matthews Episcopal Church, enjoyed special employment privileges at the Ford Motor Company.

The Second Baptist Church during the 1930s was the largest and one of the most influential black churches in Detroit. With the power of securing jobs, by letter and telephone, Rev. Bradby created a reservoir of good will for Ford, both in the church and the community at large. The relatively small size of St. Matthews Church belied its influence in the community and at Ford Motor Company. Counted among her worshipers were many long-time residents of Detroit who were leaders in the city. Their priest, Father Daniels, had a close relationship with a fellow-Virgin Islander, Charles Sorensen, a high Ford official. Ford, also an Episcopalian, occasionally visited St. Matthews. Rumor had it that he made large financial contributions to the church, but Father F. Ricksford Meyers, Daniel's successor, had serious doubts about such contributions: "It would have been out of character for Mr. Ford to give away substantial sums of money that way." True or not, the rumor enhanced the image of Ford in the black community. Donald Marshall, Assistant Personnel Director at Ford, was vestryman and lay reader at St. Matthews.

Bradby and Daniels used their strong connections with the Company to enhance the Ford legend among blacks. Fact and fiction were imperceptably fused. Yet, they created power and influence that were some of the hard facts of life with which the UAW had to grapple.

The UAW's answer to Bradby and Daniels was Rev. Charles A. Hill, pastor of the Hartford Avenue Baptist Church. A long-time friend of Robeson's, Hill was a fearless liberal who supported labor from the pulpit as well as in the parish. During the strike, for example, Hill stood outside the Rouge plant, megaphone in hand, and convinced thousands of Ford loyalists to come out and join the UAW. The doors of Hartford Avenue Baptist Church were ever open to union groups and other unpopular assemblies who were unwelcome elsewhere.

Another west-side cleric who came to the aid of the Union was Father Malcolm Dade, rector of St. Cyprian Episcopal Church. It was

Dade who raised the question of the future of black workers within the UAW. He was assured that black workers would have the same opportunities as any other members of the Union. Satisfied with their promises, Dade opened his church to the UAW when they needed it most.

Even before the date of the NLRB Elections was announced, the Union began to make strong overtures to the black workers. Copies of Christopher Alston's booklet, "Henry Ford and the Negro," were distributed throughout the black community. The UAW found comfort in the Foreword written by John P. Davis, National Secretary of the National Labor Council:

> In the interest of truth – the decision which Negro Ford workers will make will do much to shape the course of history for Negro workers all over America. In the interest of all Negroes who work in Fords, we take our stand.
> The Ford Motor Company, through its Personnel Manager, Donald Marshall, has openly called upon Negro workers to resist, with their bodies, the onward march of over 80,000 workers in the Ford Motor Co. Seizing upon the actions of the Ford Motor Company, the daily press has played up the activity of a small group in such a manner as to try to create bad racial feelings among the citizens of Detroit and vicinity. We denounce strike-breaking in whatever form it is disguised.

Alston, in the main text, stated that his purpose was to give the lie to one of the greatest propaganda machines ever invented by man:

> We contend, and can prove, that the Ford Motor Company pursues a conscious policy of relegating the Negro to the hardest jobs in the factory, that Ford hires Negroes on a "jim crow" basis and he (the Negro) maintains the status regardless of how many men are employed in his factory.
> In 1937, the Ford Motor Company employed 9,825 Negroes. Of them, 6,457 worked in the worst and hardest jobs in the Company, namely – foundry, rolling mill, and open hearth. The remaining 3,368 Negroes were found in the motor building, the foundry machine shop, the "B" building, the spring and upset building, the pressed steel building, in tool rooms, construction departments as sweepers and on miscellaneous jobs.
> The price that the mass of Negroes working in the foundry have to pay in order for a few of their brothers to work at skilled jobs is too great for a race whose contributions to American life has always been that of labor without honor.

Another strong supporter of the Ford Organizing Drive was the Rev. John Miles, Chairman, Negro Division Ford Organizing Committee. Leading up to the date of the elections, his report was made available to all black workers (see Appendix, pp. 155-157).

Leading up to the NLRB election set for May 21, 1941, the union devoted several issues of its newsheet, *Ford Facts,* to items of special interest to the black community. The issue of April 2, 1941 reported a meeting of black leaders, called by Louis Martin, Editor of the *Michigan Chronicle.* After meeting, the group released the following public statement:

1. We are unalterably opposed to Negro workers being used as

strikebreakers in the present controversy between the UAW and Ford Motor Company.

2. We further denounce the back-to-work movement inspired by the so-called AFL union manager, Homer Martin, which may lead to violence and racial friction.
3. We endorse the position of President R. J. Thomas and other CIO officials who publicly maintain that the Negro worker in the Ford Plant will not lose any of his privileges because of his union membership and stands to gain additional privileges in the way of better jobs through the Union promotion policy based on seniority, regardless of race, color, creed or political beliefs.

Among the signatories were Rev. Charles Hill, Bulah Whitby, Louis Martin, Dr. J. J. McClendon, Attorney LeBron Simmons, Rev. John Miles, Snow F. Grigsby, Attorney Judson Powell, Mrs. Geraldine Bledsoe, Emmett S. Cunningham, Rev. John Crawford, Mr. and Mrs. James McCall, James E. Williams, Carlton W. Gaines, Miss Nellie Watts, William Sherrill, John Buchanan, A. L. Law, Birnie M. Smith, Jr., Peter G. Daniels, Eugene Hall, F. B. Mays, John R. Williams, Lloyd Loomis, and Rev. J. H. Bruce.

Organizations supporting the statement were – First Congressional District Civic Clubs, Michigan Chapter of the AKA sorority, NAACP, Urban League Youth Council, Michigan Federated Democratic Clubs, National Youth Congress, Greater Detroit Youth Assembly, and the Hartford Avenue Baptist Church.

Ford Facts of April 5, 1941 offered the black community a front page photo of black Union organizers at the UAW Headquarters. Another picture showed Sheldon Tappes, then chief union steward in the foundry, leading a biracial committee before management to gain benefits for foundry workers. The editorial in this issue was an all-out effort to win the black worker to the side of labor. A telegram from State Senator Charles C. Diggs was published in its entirety in the same issue (see Appendix, pp. 157-158 for editorial and telegram).

In appreciation for their pro-labor activities, Rev. Charles Hill and Father Malcolm Dade were made honorary members of the UAW-CIO. This event was reported and shown in the April 23 issue of *Ford Facts*.

Dr. J. J. McClendon urged the national office of the NAACP to take a firm stand in favor of the Union. *Ford Facts* published the NAACP statement on April 23, 1941:

> Labor Unions are a necessary and valuable method by which a worker of any race or color can protect themselves from exploitation by the owners of industry and can gain a higher standard of living and greater leisure in keeping with increased output made possible by modern machines and productivity.
> We condemn the efforts of reactionary members of Congress and other public and private agencies to utilize the present world

and national situation to emasculate the Wages and Hours Act, the National Labor Relations Act and other acts of Congress designed to protect industrial workers in their rights to bargain collectively and to secure and maintain decent hours and working conditions. We applaud the slow but steady growth of consciousness of American workers to the realization that white labor still refer to go free until all labor is free.

We deplore the continued short-sightedness, however, of certain labor unions, such as the Railroad Brotherhoods and other Unions which by constitutional provisions ritualistically practice, or by other means, bar workers because of race, creed and color.

We call upon the Congress to enact amendments to the NLRB Act which would prohibit any Union which habitually discriminates in this fashion after January 1, from being designated as the sole bargaining agent of workers in any given industry.

Labor Unions which ask that they not be discriminated against must come into court with clean hands.

Dr. J. J. McClendon was President of the local chapter of the NAACP at this time. He was not only instrumental in bringing Walter White, Executive Director of the NAACP, to Detroit on behalf of the Union, but through the local chapter, sent sound trucks into the black communities to encourage Union membership. Such activities cost McClendon the good-will of Ford officials, and his letters of recommendation for unemployed workers were no longer recognized.

Ford officials were not idle. Loyalty pledges were circulated in the black community which said, "We the colored employees pledge our loyalty and appreciation to the Ford Motor Company."

Other pro-Ford leaflets were circulated in the areas where black workers lived. Here is one example:

ATTENTION! ATTENTION!

ALL LAW ABIDING

AMERICAN CITIZENS

While we are sacrificing every effort and perhaps blood, to aid England, in their fight to crush Hitler. Let's not stand by and let one of our own American born citizens who is trying all he can to aid in this fight, be persecuted in America. Is there time now to fight feuds of years gone by?

Henry Ford is the next man to Abe Lincoln in helping the Colored Race.

Why should we persecute a man when he is a true friend of yours.

STOP! STOP!

And think before you act. Henry Ford has done more for our Race than the Union. What has the Union done for Our Race besides making promises.

We the Colored Race need help and Henry Ford is that man that gives us that help when he hires our men as skilled and unskilled laborers.

Here is what the Union did for the Bricklayers and Cement Finishers. There are twenty-five other men to one Colored, working on a job. Now is that fair to our race? No.

Have you stopped to think who is the Real Head of the Union? And does that race care anything about you? No.

The company and the AFL closed ranks to present a united front against the UAW-CIO. A few days before the elections, Harry Bennett announced that many of the improvements that had been won for the workers had been the result of the AFL bargaining with the Company. The picture became more clouded when the Ford Brotherhood of America petitioned the NLRB for recognition in the coming elections. William Green, President of the AFL, estimated that the majority of workers in the Rouge and Highland Park plants were members of his Union and that they would win the election by a 2:1 majority.

State Representative Colin L. Smith of Big Rapids called for drastic legislation to halt strikes in defense industries. A federal bill to prevent defense strikes and prohibit close union shops for the duration of the war was approved unanimously by the House Naval Committee and sent to the floor. Benson Ford was classified 1-A. Phillip Murray requested that the draft board give Walter Reuther a 2-A deferment for reasons of essential occupation.

These and other threats to victory spurred the UAW-CIO to an all-out effort as May 21 approached. Membership campaigns were held nightly in churches, schools, and homes. Union headquarters became bee-hives of activity that involved both officials and rank and file unionists. Women auxiliaries of the various locals gave financial and material support to the campaign.

The UAW officials felt a desperate need for added assurance that they could count on the black vote. What national leader commanded the admiration and respect of the black masses and, at the same time, was a friend of labor? There was one answer to that question — Paul Robeson.

During the two years since ending his London exile, Robeson spent much of his time concertising throughout the country. Wherever he went, he identified with the black citizens of the town and took an interest in their problems. His outspoken criticism of both federal and local governments for their mistreatment of black Americans had already caused some black leaders to shy away, while the black masses were drawn toward him. A few Detroiters had learned of his pro-labor activities abroad and on the east coast.

As luck would have it, Robeson's concert tour brought him to Detroit just after the Ford strike. A representative of the UAW-CIO approached him, with some misgivings, to get his ideas concerning their struggle against the Ford Motor Company. Most of the stars he knew would be reluctant to speak out against an establishment that helps provide their livelihood. Robeson surprised his hotel visitors. He not only spoke freely but for the record:

> I know about the situation at Ford's and I'll be glad to tell you what I think about it. Most Negroes think of me as a football player and song star. They do not know that before I could get through college, I worked as a bricklayer, on an ice wagon and as a waiter in a restaurant.
>
> My first contact with the labor movement came while I was living in England, because of the problems affecting Negroes. The British Labour Party was intensely interested in problems affecting the Negro workers.
>
> I gained the favor of the labor movement and decided I must do something about the problem of the Negro, their special problem and those that face all workers, white and colored. I came to certain conclusions while watching the movement there.
>
> I am against separate unions for Negro workers. All should belong to the same organization. I am glad that is the policy that has been accepted by the CIO.
>
> Coming back to this country, it seemed to me that the simple right to organize into a Union was a common fact and should be accepted. I was amazed that such a right should be questioned here in the U. S. It is astounding that a man like Ford and a large industry like Ford Motor Company have been able to operate in a democracy and not have to deal with the movement . . . .
>
> The Negro problem cannot be solved by a few of us getting to be doctors and lawyers. The best way my race can win justice is by sticking together in progressive labor unions. It would be unpardonable for Negro workers to fail to join the CIO. I don't see how that can be argued. Insofar as the AFL is concerned, A. Phillip Randolph, President of the Brotherhood of Sleeping Car Porters, a Negro, had difficulty getting the floor at the AFL convention just to present the demands of Negro workers for full rights.
>
> There is no reason in the world why Negroes should not join the CIO. If they fail to do so, they classify themselves as scab labor Negroes and cannot be a part of the American Democracy except through labor unions. A democracy cannot exist without labor unions.

The UAW printed this interview in *Ford Facts* on April 23, 1941, and distributed thousands of copies in the black neighborhoods of Detroit and environments.

Robeson agreed to return to Detroit for the UAW Rally on May 19, 1941. *Ford Facts* carried a full-page notice of the event, just before the mass meeting. Large photographs of Robeson and Murray nearly filled the page. Needless to say, that issue of the news sheet blanketed the black neighborhoods.

May 19 dawned clear, but there was a questionable prediction of rain. It would take more than a downpour to wash away the enthusiasm and optimism of the crowd that was preparing to converge on Detroit's Cadillac Square. By early afternoon, tiny rivulets of people began to coalesce, clogging the main streets leading into downtown Detroit. For some it was a festive occasion. They greeted old friends, made new ones, or shared a few jokes about "Henry and Harry." Others bought the daily papers and took on the gloom of the news. London had just sustained the heaviest bombing of the war, and only one dive bomber was shot down. The unfriendly French threatened to fight if the U. S. attempted to occupy Martinique or Dakar.

The main body of UAW officials and many rank and file unionists gathered at Roosevelt Park, near the Michigan Central station. The crowd was swollen by the women from many locals' auxiliaries. Marching bands and singing groups, gaily festooned, added color and sound to the occasion. At 4:30, the parade left the park and marched down Michigan Avenue to join the crowd already in Cadillac Square. Traffic was paralyzed in the central city while a group of citizens tried to size control of their destiny.

Richard T. Leonard, Westside Regional Director, was in charge of the Rally. He strode to the portable rostrum, begged for silence, and introduced the speakers. Murray delivered the principal address. He predicted that the Ford Motor Company had come to a crossing of the ways and faced the inevitable organization of its workers into the UAW-CIO. He described the coming elections as the best opportunity ever presented to the people of Detroit. In paying tribute to his chief adversary, he said: "There was once a bull who thought that he was the mightiest thing in the world. He tried to ram a railroad locomotive. As the engineer passed over the bull's remains, he said, 'Bull, I admire your courage but you certainly exercised poor judgment.' I think it is safe to say that old Henry is just trying to make a bull of himself."

During Murray's speech, an airplane flew overhead trailing a sign which read, "Vote AFL." The crowd treated the plane with up-raised fists and booed it away. Murray observed that the AFL was always up in the air, so they were running true to form. He suggested that they should parachute down and join the UAW-CIO.

Robeson was loudly cheered as he appeared on the stage. He sang "Joe Hill," "Jim Crow," and a portion of "Ballad for Americans." He repeated many of the statements previously reported and exhorted the workers to reject paternalism and stand up and be counted as men by voting for UAW-CIO on Wednesday, two days hence. R. J. Thompson asked the workers to give the Union a 90% majority in the Wednesday elections. Several other speakers followed with variations on the same theme. Eventually, everything was said and the crowd began to drift away. Officials as well as rank and file had done what they could. Now the decision was in the hands of the gods. Robeson went even further. He visited the Rouge and Lincoln plants and shook hands at shop gates, providing an irresistible personal dimension to his campaign. Unionists placed a tight security guard around Robeson, lest he fell victim to the violence that some of them had known. He had turned a deaf ear to their advice not to go to Dearborn.

For the next seventy-two hours the Rouge and Lincoln plant elections stole the Detroit headlines from the wholesale destruction of people and places in England and Europe. Russell Miller, NLRB elections expert, announced that the Rouge election would be the largest single-plant election in the history of labor. The largest, previous one-plant election had occurred at a Jones and Laughlin steel plant in Aliquippa, Pennsylvania involving 27,000 workers. The Rouge election would be nearly three times that size. He noted that the General Motors election, the year before, involved 125,000 workers, but they were spread out in fifty plants.

Still seething from Bennett's charge that the elections would be rigged against the Company, Frank Bowen announced that the election would be fair to all participants. He went out of his way to keep the public informed of the details of the election procedure.

One hundred special tellers were sworn in at the National Bank building. An additional thirty-five experienced tellers were recruited from other NLRB offices from as far east as New York City, and as far west as Milwaukee. This staff was hired for three days at $8.05 per day. The total cost of the elections, salaries, printing, etc., was estimated at $17,000.

Governor Van Wagoner dispatched 120 State troopers to the Rouge and Lincoln plants, under the supervision of Capt. Donald S. Leonard. Fifty-nine voting booths were set up in the Rouge plant and three were sufficient for the Lincoln plant. One State trooper and representatives from UAW, AFL, NLRB, and the Company were assigned to each voting booth. Bowen announced the ground rules of the election: "Under the terms of the Wagner Labor Act the Union receiving a majority of votes cast becomes the exclusive bargaining agent for that election unit, plant wide or craft wide. If there is not a clear majority, a run-off election will be held."

The pre-election issue of *Ford Facts* published a front-page photograph of Paul Robeson congratulating Earl Leath, the newly elected steward of Local 806, United Electrical, Radio and Machine Workers of America-CIO, Dayton, Ohio.

Plant elections began at 4 a. m. on May 21, 1941 and ended at 11:30 p. m. the same day, enabling all shifts to vote. The UAW's demand that approximately 1,200 former Ford employees, victims of the Company's anti-labor discrimination, be allowed to vote was granted. An additional 800 votes came from Ford employees in the military. A flurry of excitement developed during the voting when the UAW representatives charged that 6,000 foremen and service men, their ineligible arch-enemies, were seen at the voting places. Bowen was able to quell the uprising.

When the last vote was cast, the ballot boxes were sealed under the close security of all observers. The boxes were then stored overnight in a cell-block in the federal building. The single door to the cell-block was guarded by representatives of the Unions, Company, and a U.S. Marshall. A similar escort carried the ballot boxes to the counting rooms, the following morning, where the seals were verified.

The tally began early on the morning of May 22, with challengers from both Unions and Company certifying each ballot. The stakes were too high to rush. An impatient world would have to wait.

At this time, Ford officials made another bid to have the NLRB hearings into UAW-CIO charges of anti-labor brutality postponed again. The Company had made such a delay a condition of their acceptance of the strike settlement the month before. The Union fought such a delay, and the strike settlement hung in the balance for several hours. Finally, the NLRB chief ruled that the hearings would begin on May 22, the day after the elections.

This new pressure for further delay irritated Harold A. Cranefield, NLRB attorney. He recalled that the hearings were originally scheduled for April 14, but had been rescheduled, at the Company's insistance, until after the election. He promised to resist any further delay. The Agenda for the hearings included Union charges that:

1. The Ford Motor Company dismissed 265 employees between 1937 and 1940 at the Rouge, Lincoln, and Highland Park plants in its efforts to destroy the Union.
2. The Company planted high-salaried spies inside the Union, tapped the telephones of Union officials, and used forms of surveillance to subvert the Union and demoralize the workers.
3. The Company recruited groups of strong-armed, muscle-men and persons with notorious proclivities to violent habits to intimidate and assault Union members.

The Union membership was cheered by the government's firm position. They were even happier with the results of the NLRB election returns. The Rouge results showed that the UAW won over the AFL by a margin of 70% to 27.45%; at the Lincoln plant, the margin was 73% to 21.4%. The non-vote figures were 2.55% and 5.3%, respectively, the lowest in NLRB history. Russell Miller stated that virtually every eligible voter cast a ballot.

Robeson was inseparably identified with the laborers and the labor movement in Detroit for the next six years. He met them where they worshipped, and where they lived. Sheldon Tappes related a personal experience to this writer:

> My mother wanted to invite Robeson to her house so she could invite some friends in to meet him. After one of his concerts, she asked Robeson if there was anything she could do for him. Without a moment's hesitation, he answered, "You can prepare breakfast for me.
>
> My mother cooked smothered chicken, rice and gravy, corn on the cob, and biscuits. The neighbors came and were awed by Robeson's size, his charm, and his appetite.

Judge George Crockett, a personal friend of long standing, relates:

> UAW-CIO Local 600 had invited Robeson to come to Detroit for some function. An honor guard went to the airport to meet him and bring him to my house. In the middle forties there had been so many threats against him that a guard went with him at all times. The idea was that the group would eat at my house. By the time that everyone arrived we had twice as many people as were originally expected. So my wife had to prepare more food. While the food was being cooked, I opened up the bar in my basement, and everybody went down there to get ready for the food, everybody but Robeson. When I finally found him he was sitting out on the porch, not a guard in sight, but surrounded by the children of the neighborhood. They demanded, and got, an impromptu concert on the spot.

Ford Local 600 UAW-CIO sponsored a Robeson concert in March, 1942. The Ford Workers' chorus was scheduled to appear with him. Russell Gore, music writer for the *Detroit News*, wrote the following in the March 6 edition: "What has been called the finest musical instrument wrought by nature in our time, will be heard at Olympia on Saturday evening. It is the voice of Negro baritone, Paul Robeson." It was the day after this concert that Robeson got involved in the Sojourner Truth fight, described in a later chapter.

Ford Facts on June 15, 1943 announced that Robeson would be the guest of Local 600 at a giant membership meeting at the Olympia Stadium, called to celebrate the second anniversary of the signing of the Ford contract. Among the speakers at that meeting were R. J. Thomas, R. T. Frankensteen, and Sheldon Tappes, recording secretary. Robeson probably did not make that meeting. His name was not listed among the participants in the news reports of the meeting. It was at this time that Margaret Webster had reached an agreement with Robeson, Uta Hagen, and Hosea Ferrer, for the production of "Othello." Rehearsals could have been underway at this time.

On July 17, 1946, Robeson appeared in Windsor, Ontario and marched in support of a Dodge workers' strike. Before leaving the picket line, he shook hands with every picket.

The automobile workers gave a testimonial dinner for Robeson in January, 1947. Percy Llewellyn, Regional UAW-CIO Director, spoke for the top officers of the International Union:

> I bring you the greetings of several hundred thousand automobile workers and their leadership, who are unable to be present themselves because they have been summoned to Milwaukee tonight to a counsel of war.
>
> As most of you know, there is a battle being waged there at West Allis to win for plain people a real stake in their world.
>
> The first time I ever laid eyes on Paul Robeson was at a meeting in celebration of a victory of another such battle several years ago. A good many of you, I am sure, were at that meeting in the Olympia auditorium. The great hall was packed to the rafters with shouting workers and their wives. It was a crowd made up of the kinds of people Mr. Robeson sings about in "Ballad for Americans," the line that he is a Scotsman, English, Jew, Italian, Negro etc., winding up check and double check American.

> It was the kind of audience drawn together because they had just won a battle by standing shoulder to shoulder. The battle was the drive to organize Ford. And when it was over and the victory was nailed down and the contract was ratified, there was a great service of thanksgiving where Paul Robeson raised his rich voice to the hymn of victory.
>
> It was an impressive moment. Here were the workers in the thousands native and foreign-born, white and black, catholic, protestant, and Jews, and some whose religion was simple faith in the working class. They all sat there quietly as this great American artist raised his voice to sing to them the songs of freedom for all men everywhere. I had never laid claim to knowing about art. There is little enough of beauty in what is called culture in the bitter conflict between those who work and those who clip coupons. On that occasion I knew I was in the presence of art that was great indeed.
>
> It seems to me that the most important part of Paul Robeson's fruit for life is the bringing of art to the services of the common man. While art belongs, first of all, to the plain people, it has been captured by the people who live in big houses on the hilltop. But it always comes back where it belongs, by the people and by the people's sons, the Paul Robesons of every age.
>
> Who has heard Mr. Robeson's voice pouring out the words of "Cheli," of the Chinese guerilla fighter, or the song of the Spanish citizens' army, the Red army, or the quiet, whispering melodies of defiant freedom, without knowing inside that Paul Robeson has brought home music to the people?
>
> A man might sing freedom songs and let it go at that. He could become rich with the good things of this world and to go to bed each night knowing that he had helped make life easier for those who listened. Paul Robeson has done that and much more. He had wedded his golden voice to the politics of struggle. He makes every concert appearance a political foray. He makes a little talk when he is done singing and in these talks he sounds the toscin, sends out a ringing call to arms, which commands respectful attention because his audiences know that Paul Robeson speaks as he sings, the truth.
>
> In a recent Detroit concert, he said there is still a lot of fighting against Fascism to be done at home, right here in Michigan; the fight for jobs without discrimination; the fight for wages high enough so that a man can feed his kids; a school where everybody's kids have a square deal.
>
> This is the Robeson that we honor here tonight, a veteran fighter, not for his own people only but for all of us in every land. A great American by any standard besides whom a Bilbo or Rankin seem mean and contemptible. Here is a giant among us bringing his great strength, his towering prestige, his massive understanding of our world to the service of man.
>
> Mr. Robeson, in behalf of my Union brothers of every race, I thank you for the work you have done in the past, and I bring you the wish that you will carry on for many years, winning more and more recruits for the cause in which all of us have enlisted for the duration.

Robeson rose to thunderous applause. He paid the workers a compliment:

> I have always put my faith and confidence in the working people in all countries and of all colors. I truly believe that they constitute the greatest force in the world for the advancement of all people.
>
> In every people's movement against oppression, the workers have been the backbone of the movement. The situation is no different in the Negro peoples' fight for freedom.

THE NATIONAL NEGRO LABOR COUNCIL

Robeson's all-out support of World War II surprised many of his followers. Some of them accused him of becoming pro-establishment, not realizing that he was continuing his war against Fascism that was begun in the middle 1930s in Spain. Earlier in the war, Robeson gave his position in the expression: "If Negroes are to help to write the peace, they must help to win the war." He had high hopes that black participation in the war effort would guarantee them more freedom after the war was over. Approximately 400 black artists, representing nearly every entertainment specialty, travelled more than 5,000,000 miles and staged 10,000 shows to boost the morale of military personnel, accelerate war production, and raise funds for the war effort.

The 1947 edition of The *Negro Yearbook* (page 436) provides a microcosm of Robeson's participation as an artist: "Paul Robeson sang at the Great Lakes Naval Training Station to 2,000 naval officers and enlisted personnel. He also made a surprise appearance at the Apex Smelting Company, Chicago, Illinois; and he sang for the Biddle Club on Boston Common to a packed house of soldiers, sailors marines and wacs. He sang at a port of embarcation to mothers and wives of boys who were sailing over seas."

Randolph S. Wright, World War II veteran from Detroit, informed me that Robeson's support of the war effort was not limited to the United States:

> Any reference to that great personality, Paul Robeson, immediately brings to my mind a fact which I have never heard mentioned nor publicised and which, therefore, I feel is unfortunately little known. By the same token, I never miss an opportunity to recite this little-known fact, because I have always resented what I feel has been a deliberate mis-representation of this man, his philosophy and ideals, his accomplishments and deeds.
>
> During the Second World War occupation of Germany by allied forces, I chanced to be stationed in the vicinity of Munich, Germany. One beautiful Sunday afternoon, I believe it was during the spring season of 1946, I attended an entertainment provided through the American Army Special Services Branch and commonly known among service personnel as a USO show.
>
> To my amazement and delight, this show was headed by Paul Robeson and comprised, in addition, a black male pianist-accom-

> panist, a white sergeant who sang and a white violinist, a serviceman whose rank I cannot recall. This show or concert, as I prefer to call it, was superbly rendered as all the participants were, like Robeson, artists.
> The concert was held in a beautiful public park near the center of the city and was attended in large numbers by American servicemen and some German civilians. Their appreciation was expressed by long, standing applause.
> It seems to me that Paul Robeson is entitled to acknowledgment, recognition, and appreciation by his countrymen for his contributions to the morale of our American servicemen during this historic involvement and nationally known Americans have been lauded for similar services.

Robeson joined with other artists to stage giant "war-bond rallies" that raised millions of dollars for the prosecution of the war. Frances Smith was just ten-years-old when Robeson led a long list of celebrated artists into Detroit's Olympia Stadium for a war-bond rally. A portable stage was set up in the center of the arena. The place was packed, so Frances was forced to sit at the base of the stage. She recalled the events as if they happened yesterday: "I heard this big voice and looked straight up into Paul Robeson's eyes. He looked like he was fifteen feet tall. He was singing 'Ole Man River' and pulling chains across the stage. Everyone was so quiet. As soon as he finished singing, everybody jumped up and started shouting. I'll never forget that as long as I live."

Despite their heroic support of the war effort on and off the field, it soon became apparent to black Americans that the promise of the peace was not to be fulfilled. In many areas of the country, especially the south, the black veteran found the door to opportunity as tightly closed as before the war. The Veteran's Administration regularly nullified the black veterans' endeavors to secure employment or unemployment compensation. Discriminatory practices by lending organizations virtually eliminated many black citizens, veterans and others, from the housing market. Many vocational schools offered black veterans only a narrow range of courses in fields that were already overcrowded.

Before the war was over, some black leaders began to explore new solutions to the problems of the black worker. To this end a meeting was convened in Chicago on June 25 and 26, 1944. A group of black Americans, along with sympathetic white trade unionists, met to form a Citizens Political Action Committee, an affilliate of the CIO. Among the leaders present were Mary McCleod Bethune, Robert C. Weaver, William H. Hastie, Canada Lee, and Paul Robeson.

On June 17, 1946, some of the same leaders and representatives of 25 national organizations, with memberships totalling 6,500,000, met in New York City to issue a declaration of Negro voters. This declaration cited six issues as being uppermost in the minds of Negro voters at that time:

1. The wholehearted prosecution of the war to total victory.

2. The elimination of the poll-tax by Congress.
3. The integration of Negroes into the armed forces.
4. The passage of anti-lynch legislation.
5. The establishment of a permanent FEPC.
6. A foreign policy of international co-operation that promotes economic and political security for all people.

Unfortunately for black people in general and black trade unionists in particular, a major shift of national priorities occurred in 1947 that was detrimental to their welfare. Many labor unions, seeking conformity with the Truman anti-Communist foreign policy, sacrificed their liberal-radical elements, many of whom were black. By 1949, Ferdinand Smith, formerly Executive Secretary of the National Maritime Union, had lost his position in the Union and was being pursued as a subversive by various loyalty groups. Another high official in the Union hierarchy, Ewart Guinier, a black Panamanian, had fallen from power. His power base, the UPW Union incurred the wrath of the CIO and was slated for expulsion.

The list of other black union officials and supporters who became expendable by the cold war included Revels Cayton, William Chester, Thomas Coleman, George Crockett, Ernest DeMaio, W. E. D. DuBois, Octavia Hawkins, Charles Hill, Carleton Goodlet, William Hood, Joe Johnson, Sam Parks, Hobson Reynolds, Thomas Richardson, Teresa L. Robinson, and Coleman Young, to name a few. Most of these rebels attracted the attention of either the Senate Sub-Committee on subversive activities or the House Un-American Activities Committee. The common denominator and chief rebel of the entire group was Robeson.

The prospects for the black worker seemed very bleak to these leaders when a group of them met in Harlem in 1949 to organize a fight for a larger share of the economic resources of the United States. In a move to establish a national organization, a call was sent out to other cities for representation; and a meeting was scheduled for June 10, 1950 in Chicago. Robeson, one of the organizers, gave a benefit concert in New York to help finance the Chicago meeting. The purpose of the Chicago meeting was to launch a more militant attack on job discrimination than had been undertaken by other existing organizations. The 900 delegates, black and white, were told that they had a common fight against a common enemy, in Robeson's keynote address entitled "Forge Negro Labor Unity For Peace and Jobs":

> Here we are gathered together the basic forces, the Negro sons and daughters of labor and their white brothers and sisters, whose increasingly active attention to national and world affairs is an essential requirement if we are to have peaceful and democratic solutions to the burning issues of our times.
>
> . . . Who built this land? Who have been the guarantors of our historic democratic tradition of freedom and equality? Whose labor have produced the great cities, the industrial machines, the basic

culture and creature comforts of which our voice of America spokesmen talk so proudly about? It is well to remember that the America we know has arisen out of the toil of many millions who have come here seeking freedom, from all parts of the world.

The Irish and Scotch identured servants, who cleared the forests and built the colonial homesteads, were a part of the productive backbone of our early days. The millions of German immigrants, of the mid-nineteenth century, the millions more from eastern Europe, whose blood and sacrifices, in the steel mills, the coal mines and factories made possible the industrial revolution of the 1880s and 1890s.

. . . The workers from Mexico and the east, Japan and the Philippines, helped to make the west and the southwest a fruitful land. And through it all, from the earliest days, before Columbus, the Negro people, upon whose unpaid toil, as slaves, created the basic wealth of which this nation was built. These are the forces that have made America great and preserved our democratic heritage.

Ewart Guinier, formerly Vice-President of The National Negro Labor Council (NNLC), recalled some other aspects of Robeson's speech:

He reminded us that the non-white peoples are more than half of the world's population and that these people, until our foreign policy is changed, typified by the role of the United States in the Panama Canal Zone, the role of the United States government in supporting the imperialists in Africa, the role of the U.S. government in trying to prop up dictatorial regimes in Asia, the struggles of these people for freedom will be more difficult. He said that we, who got strength from the struggles of colonial peoples for their liberties, have a responsibility, as U.S. ciitzens, to try and help change the foreign policy of our government.

Later in 1950, the U. S. State Department cancelled Robeson's passport. One of the principal charges was that Robeson meddled in the foreign affairs of the U. S. government. Robeson retorted, "That's just too bad, because I'm gonna keep on meddlin.' "

The delegates established continuation committees to organize local councils throughout the United States before the next annual meeting. They chose "National Negro Labor Council" (NNLC) as the name of their organization and elected William Hood, Detroit trade unionist, as their provisional president. Preliminary plans were made for an organizational meeting during 1951, at a time and place to be determined. In due course, Cincinnati, Ohio was chosen as the site of the first meeting of NNLC for its historical significance as "the place where Negroes and whites met in the Underground Railroad to help the flight from slavery to freedom." Several weeks before the convention, William Hood issued a National call for the meeting:

Already the determination of the Negro people to fight back against acts of intimidation, terror and mob violence, in legal and illegal form, which has increased with preparation for all-out war, has been demonstrated in many ways. Peekskill, U.S.A. is our answer to those who attempt to cow us. Though Willie McGhee and the Martinsville seven died, the victims of jim crow rule, the hypocrisy of white America, a claim of freedom and justice

for all stands exposed to all the world. Freedom for whom? Freedom to do what?
Negro Labor Councils are needed to forge unity of Negro and white in the struggle against the mounting mob violence that victimizes innocent Negro men and women and in the struggle to achieve equality as we believe America achieves it.

The convention call unleased a niagara of protests from all parts of the country, especially Cincinnati. The *Cincinnati Enquirer* of October 5, 1951 quoted Luke Craig, an official of Cincinnati's AFL building laborers union, as saying that his organization wanted no part of the convention. The *Enquirer* of 10/7/51 reported that Al Whitehouse, an official of District 25 of the United Steel Workers – CIO, sent letters to 300 officers of steel workers in Cincinnati labeling the NNLC as Communist-supported.

The NNLC convention was scheduled for 10/27 and 28, 1951. On 10/17/51, the Cincinnati City Council took a unanimous stand against the convention on the belief that it was part of the Communist party's program to enroll Negroes. The City Council resolution was made by Jesse D. Locker and supported by Theodore Berry, the only two Negroes on the Council. Berry was later to become mayor of Cincinnati. Both the AFL and CIO attacked the NNLC from afar and requested their members to shun the meeting. In spite of these impediments, the convention did convene on 10/27/51 with some 1,098 delegates in attendance to formalize the structure of the NNLC. A liberal sprinkling of uniformed plainclothes policemen as well as FBI observers mingled with the delegates to hear President Hood's opening address which he titled, "For These Things We Fight" (see Appendix, p. 159 for text).

The convention's first day ended with an evening of songs and encouraging commentary by Paul Robeson. In its account of the first-day sessions, the *Cincinnati Enquirer* reported that the Council's purpose was to gain industrial and social equality for Negroes and for all other races. President Hood's address was said to have brought cheers from the delegates, one-third of whom were white. Under the chairmanship of Ernest Thompson, the Resolutions Committee worked far into the night to prepare for the next day's deliberations. The four resolutions that were drawn up are reproduced in the Appendix, p. 159.

On the second day of the convention, Hood continued to respond to some of the criticisms that had been leveled at the new organization:

> To trade union leaders who have condemned the Council as "dual unionism," my answer is that Negroes are still barred from many unions in this country, denied apprenticeship training, upgrading and refused jobs in many, many places . . . .
> We are not represented in the policy-making bodies of most international unions . . . . The day has ended when white trade union leaders in any organization may presume to tell Negroes on what basis they shall come together to fight for their rights.

> Three-hundred years of that have been enough. We ask for your co-operation – but we do not ask for your permission.

The afternoon of the second day was given to a full-length discussion of Paul Robeson's passport issue. The U. S. State Department came under heavy criticism for having cancelled Robeson's passport, and various methods of bringing pressure on the government were discussed. President Hood issued the final statement on the matter: "We shall use all the power of this convention to see that Paul Robeson will have the right to move about like all other citizens."

One of the last items on the conference calendar was the election of permanent officers for the coming year. The officers elected along with the NNLC constitution are on Appendix, pp. 160-161.

The majority of the delegates left the convention full of enthusiasm and drive for the job ahead. The delegates were charged with two major responsibilities: (1) To establish local Councils in those areas of the U. S. where none exists, and (2) to start and extend militant actions on behalf of Negro workers on every front. The group pledged to meet again the following year.

After the convention ended, the *Cincinnati Enquirer* of 10/29/51 reported that the labor issue had been secondary to the racial issue during the convention; that the theme of the entire convention had been the abolishment of jim crow practices and gaining social and economic equality for Negroes. The *Enquirer* reported that Robeson had occupied most of the attention of the delegates on the convention's last day.

A week after the convention ended, a *New York Times* reporter went back to Cincinnati and reported thusly on 11/11/51:

> The self-styled National Negro Labor Council, which was organized here on Ootcber 28, has so few sympathizers here that it has been unable to form a local branch, a Negro leader said today.
>
> Joseph A. Hall, Executive Director of the Urban League of Greater Cincinnati, a unit of the Community Chest, added that the organization's influence appeared to have departed along with the convention.
>
> John J. Hurst, President of the Cincinnati Central Labor Council, AFL, said today that all indications were that the NNLC made very little impression on Cincinnati.
>
> . . . The *New York Daily Worker*, did most of the editorial promotion of the much ballyhooed meeting of the NNLC, in Cincinnati, last week. This attracted the attention of the FBI and the local police with the result that both organizations were heavily and regularly represented at the sessions. Meanwhile, the responsible Negro press, as in the case of the *Pittsburgh Courier*, stood back and regarded the affair with commendable suspicion.

Some delegates took issue with Hall's statement that the convention had no lasting influence on Cincinnati. They pointed out that although none of the hotels would permit the NNLC to hold its convention in any of them, the delegates did force integration of many of the restaurants in the downtown area, especially one hotel that did not permit even a black shoe-shine boy.

In summing up the NNLC convention, the *Daily Worker* commended the *Cincinnati Enquirer* for doing an "about face" on reporting the events of the convention. The *Worker* compared the *Enquirer's* hostile editorial comments on the convention before it convened with the straight reporting during the convention. The editor of the *Enquirer* explained their position on November 10, 1951:

> Lest anyone be beguiled into thinking that The *Enquirer* did any "about face" on the fellow-traveller-loaded meeting, perhaps we should point out that it is a conventional newspaper practice, in free countries to express editorial opinion in editorial columns and report the news, factually, in the news columns. Our "factual" reporting of the meeting was quite apart from our editorial attitude toward it. The Daily Worker, like all Communist excuses for newspapers, never disassociates editorial attitude from news. . . . There was never any attempt made to prevent the meeting. It took place without the least of interference, and despite all the promotion, was a definite flop.

The Flint (Michigan) Council was organized early in December, 1951. Forty people met at the Flint Community Center to hear NNLC President Hood: "I warn you against company-minded labor leaders, stool pigeons and potential Fascists. It is time for the black workers and their white allies to stand up and fight enemies who are running America. We will fight for greater Negro representation in the shops and for Negro representation in top councils of the union." The group chose Herod Wilson, President; and E. L. Holmes, Executive Secretary. The seventh council to be established after the Cincinnati meeting was organized in Cleveland (Ohio) on December 14, 1951. National Secretary Coleman Young represented the national body. He reported that six new chapters were in operation – Flint, Dayton, Pittsburgh, St. Louis, South Bend, and Fort Wayne. Other branches were scheduled for Toledo, Louisville, Milwaukee, Gary and Denver.

Chairman of the Cleveland group was Bert Washington of the United Electrical Workers' Union. He stressed the need to fight for jobs for Negroes. Their plans included a survey of job opportunities in the Cleveland area, with interviews of union officials regarding the integration of Negro workers in industry and in the unions. He promised to try to force the inclusion of an anti-discriminatory clause in all local contracts.

William Chester, NNLC Regional Director for Northern California, was the principal speaker at the first regional Conference for the western district of NNLC held in San Francisco on January 26 and 27, 1952. He opened with a progress report: "Here in the west, since the birth of NNLC, much has been accomplished. In Seattle, the local chapter has already opened the lumber industry to Negroes. In Oakland, the jim crow key system has been broken to the effect that Negro men are hired as bus and street car operators. In Los Angeles, a lilly-white machine shop and several other plants have been forced to hire Negroes." The delegates discussed techniques for bringing more pressure on stubborn industries and plans for securing jobs at Pacific Telephone and Telegraph Co. Dr. Carlton Goodlet, well-known bay-area physician and publisher of the *Sun Reporter,* pledged the support of his newspaper. He reminded the gathering that his readers are the bed-rock of any forward movement in this country. Ralph Cuaron, of the Mexican American National Association, was a guest speaker. He traced the history of support that Mexicans have given to the Negro's fight for civil rights from the Civil War to the present.

The first day's meeting dealt with three main topics:

1. Methods of securing California's quota of 400,000 signatures in support of a permanent FEPC.
2. Condemnation of legislation proposed by State Senator Jack Tenney and the America Plus, Inc., which proposed an amendment to the state Constitution which would bring all of the jim crow laws of the deep south and encourage discrimination in unions, jobs, housing, and public accommodation.
3. How to fight for 100,000 jobs in industries barred to Negroes.

An action program was prepared and presented at the end of the second day which:

1. Established a committee to handle problems of domestic workers.
2. Initiated a fight to end wage differentials between men and women.
3. Began the organization of domestic workers.
4. Started a campaign to open up jobs for Negro women.
5. Launched a campaign for low-cost housing.
6. Pledged to fight slander of Negroes on T.V.

William Chester gave the delegates a final word in parting: "We cannot rely on federal, state or local authorities. Any effective struggle for Negro equality must be a mass struggle."

Robeson's efforts on behalf of the western district of NNLC encountered considerable opposition from the establishment. The director of the Oakland, California municipal auditorium cancelled the permit for a NNLC concert scheduled for 5/23/52 when he learned that Robeson was scheduled to sing. By a unanimous vote, the trustees of the San Francisco War Memorial refused to permit the use of the Opera House for the Robeson concert. This action was recommended by the managing director of the War Memorial who said that he did not want to be classified ". . . as a fellow-traveller with such men as Robeson." The Opera House was rented for the concert on April 21 by the San Francisco chapter of the NNLC. Upon learning that the facility was to be used for a Robeson concert, San Francisco mayor Elmer Robinson blasted the Opera

House trustees for renting the hall. The mayor was joined by the American Legion and other groups. Following a meeting on April 28, the vote to deny Robeson use of the hall was nine to zero.

The NNLC announced on May 1, 1952 that Robeson would sing on May 22 at the Macedonia Baptist Church located on Sutter Street, San Francisco. It was announced on May 8 that Robeson would sing also in Berkeley, California at the high school community theatre on the night of May 23. Mayor Lawrence Cross of Berkeley spoke on behalf of Robeson's appearance in sharp contrast to the stance taken earlier by the mayor of San Francisco.

The NNLC was headquartered in Detroit, Michigan at 410 E. Warren Avenue. The official organ of the organization was called: *Without STRUGGLE There Is No Progress.* The first issue of *Struggle* was published early in 1952 and some of the items in that issue may be seen in the Appendix, p. 161.

President William Hood issued a call for the national council of NNLC to meet in Detroit on March 1 and 2, 1952 to discuss plans for the second annual convention of NNLC. Cleveland, Ohio was chosen as the host city for the meeting for November 24, 1952.

The two-day convention began on schedule in Cleveland's Municipal Auditorium with 1500 delegates in attendance, both black and white. They came from all states east of the Mississippi and several western states. The twelve local chapters of the 1951 convention had grown to 30. Three bus loads of black and white youth, 18-25 years of age, came to the convention from Winston-Salem, North Carolina. Mixed delegations came from such die-hard southern states as Alabama and Florida.

The Council established a Maritime Commission that was directed to call on President Eisenhower once he assumed office and demand FEPC legislation as well as revocation of the Executive Order under which Coast Guard Screening was operated. The Council took militant action on many issues affecting the rights of Negro people in America. They recommended the picketing of railroads and airlines to protest discrimination against Negro workers in these industries.

A special resolution was passed on behalf of Harry Bridges, J. R. Robertson, and Harry Schmidt, condemning the "frame-up" of the three ILWU leaders and called upon the Supreme Court to review their cases. Each delegate was given copies of a special four-page leaflet entitled "American Minorities and the Case of Harry Bridges." The publication reported that "certain agencies of the Federal Government have expressed their dislike of ILWU and its militant stand for freedom and democracy for all of its members. The government's 18-year-long attack on Harry Bridges is an expression of this dislike." Other resolutions were passed which:

1. Demanded full and fair employment for Negroes on the railroads and airlines.
2. Insisted on full and fair employment for Negro women in all branches of American industry.
3. Petitioned the Federal Government to pass a National FEPC, backed up with 1,000,000 signatures.

Convention delegates listened to addresses by Capt. Hugh Mulzac, first Negro to command a ship during World War II; Maurice Travis, and Paul Robeson. After recounting the significant successes of the organization, Robeson ended his statement with a timely warning: "The fact that you have been so successful makes the enemy more determined than ever to destroy the National Negro Labor Council. There are too many people depending on this organization for us to allow this to happen. Already, the enemy is here among us ready to do his dirty work. But, I say to you, Hold On! Hold On! Keep Your Hands on the Plow, Hold On!"

The NNLC continued to face problems. On 3/10/52, the *Militant*, a labor newspaper, reported that a conference of trade union leaders meeting at the Hotel Theresa in New York City voted to expand the Negro Labor Committee into a national organization. This Committee was founded in 1935 to operate in New York City. The new group had the support of the AFL and CIO which were represented at the Conference by James B. Carey and Lewis Hines. This move was designed to compete with NNLC for the Negro workers within the AFL and CIO. As early as 1951, The House Committee of Un-American Activities (HUAC) began to focus its investigative eyes on NNLC. A sub-committee of HUAC convened a hearing in Flint, Michigan, early in 1952 where a "witness" testified to a Mr. Tavenner that he had been directed by the Communist Party to infiltrate the NAACP, the Civil Rights Congress (CRC), and NNLC. The Annual Report of the HUAC of the second session of the 82nd Congress (page 11) provides the following information:

> The NNLC is a Communist-front organization, designed to infuse Communism into Negro life. By accusing established labor organizations of overlooking the needs of the Negro, it hopes to capture more Negroes for Communism. It deals in propaganda to put across its line. One illustration of this can be seen from the following incident:
>
> > William Hood, telephoned the Ford Motor Co. and asked for an appointment to discuss labor problems affecting Negroes. He sought the appointment as President of NNLC. He was advised that Ford Motor Co. refused to discuss any problem with NNLC. Hood then requested the appointment as Recording Secretary of Local 600 UAW-CIO, a position which he held. After the interview, Hood claimed that NNLC, had obtained certain benefits as being in the main, an agreement to hire Negroes in a bomber plant that Ford was repairing. The Communist NNLC claimed that never before had Negroes been hired in that building. This claim is false, as all Ford workers know; but in making the claim in the *Communist Worker*,

they know that Negroes in other parts of the U.S. did not. The Communists have thereby used the story to convince unsuspecting Negroes that in NNLC they find their only friend.

The NNLC held its third annual convention in Chicago, on December 4-6, 1953. Only 800 delegates and visitors were in attendance, with the railroad, automobile and packinghouse workers making up the bulk of those present. Several factors contributed to the diminished participation of trade unionists at this time. Between the second and third conventions the Council was placed on the Attorney General's list as a "subversive" organization. The officers and other representatives of the organization were harassed by the investigators of HUAC and representatives of the established unions.

Due to stresses inside and outside of the Council, the date of the convention was changed from October to December, causing confusion among some of the delegates. There were internal problems too. Some members felt that the Council duplicated the work of the NAACP and should be merged with that organization. The Council's position was that the NAACP was the best civil rights organization of the period but that there was the need for an organization to deal with the special problems of labor.

The question of dual unionism came in for considerable and heated discussion. Council spokesmen pointed out that their three-year experience had disproved the charge. They reported that literally thousands of Negro trade unionists had been motivated by the Council to work within their own unions for better conditions. Their experience with the United Electrical Workers was cited as an example: "During 1952, Local 475, of the United Electrical Workers, recruited 558 members for the Council and brought in 600 in 1953. Representatives of Local 475 stated that supporting the NNLC does not weaken their union but makes it stronger by bringing Negro and white workers closer together around a common problem and bringing workers closer to the union." For those who criticized the Council for being too narrow in its approach to the problem of the black worker, the Council offered the Louisville (Ky.) experience as an answer:

> As one of its first projects, the NNLC began a major effort to rally Negro trade unionists and the Negro community in a fight for jobs in the new General Electric plant in Louisville. In order to meet the need for vocational training, the Council pressed the Louisville Board of Education to institute vocational training programs. Several hundred black youth were trained in the school and some of them were hired at G.E., in production work. The Council was supported by the NAACP, the Urban League. some black ministers and other civic groups. The Council demanded that G.E. increase its Negro employees to 16% of the total, the Negro population percentage in the city.

An important item on the agenda of the Chicago convention was "the disgraceful situation that exists in the railroad industry." The

National office of NNLC issued a leaflet entitled, "Make Every Train A Freedom Train – End Jim Crow Hiring on the Railroads!" It began: Did you know that –

1. In 1890 there were more than 6,000 Negroes employed as firemen by the nations railroads?
2. Today there are less than 1,000 Negro firemen at work?
3. In 1908, 90% of all road service jobs were held by Negroes?
4. In 1949, less than 2% of these workers were Negro?
5. Of the 128,000 jobs held by Negroes on Class I railroads (9% of total employees), 97% of these Negro workers were confined to jobs as red caps, cooks, waiters, train attendants and janitors?
6. Of the 46,000 conductors, not one is a Negro?
7. Of the 36,000 telegraph operators, not one is a Negro?

The delegates explored many avenues of possible relief for the Negro worker in this important transportation industry. Another area of concern was the south where textile, lumber, and tobacco industries denied Negro workers equality of opportunity for employment and advancement.

As had been true in the two previous conventions, the delegates prepared a brief on behalf of the rights of Negro women workers. Many industries, such as G.E., G.M., Chrysler, and Ford were severely criticized for their practices of hiring Negro women for menial jobs only. The Convention passed a resolution to designate and celebrate Negro Woman's Day as a part of a campaign to insure equal rights for women.

In its stand for civil rights, the Council mounted a major counterattack against the false charges of Senator Joseph McCarthy, the U. S. Attorney General, and HUAC.

At the close of the meeting, the convention adopted the following action program:

1. Increased concentration on fight in basic industry for model FEPC clauses, upgrading, on-the-job training, etc.
2. That we make plans to step up our job campaign in run-away shops in the south and rural areas and at the same time give every support and encouragement to the efforts to organize the Negro and white workers of the south.
3. That we must come to stronger grips with the airlines as a related campaign to the railroad fight in the coming year.

In 1954, the HUAC prepared a special publication entitled "The American Negro and the Communist Party." On page 11 is found:

> One of the Communist-front organizations currently active in seeking to deceive American Negroes into serving the Communist cause is the NNLC, which was first cited by this Committee in 1952.
>
> . . . The NNLC, deceitfully states that its purpose is to unify "all Negro workers" in order to obtain "first-class citizenship based

> on economic, political and social equality." A study of the operation of the Council shows that rather than helping the Negro worker, it has been a deterrent to him. It had made charges of discrimination against the UAW-CIO, which has done much to advance the cause of the Negro worker. In fact, the Council has continuously attempted to discredit the efforts of non-Communist organizations. It has encouraged disunity, rather than unity and thereby, performed a distinct disservice to the cause of the Negro worker.
> The Committee believes it would be helpful, at this point to list organizations and publications which have been officially cited as Communist-fronts by the Attorney General and HUAC. (The National Negro Labor Council was listed.)

In 1956, the Attorney General petitioned the Subversive Activities Control Board for orders requiring the NNLC to register as a Communist-front organization. The petition was dismissed by the Attorney General on the grounds that the organization had ceased to exist. The NNLC was one of twenty-three organizations listed by the Attorney General as Communist-front and required to register under the terms of the Internal Security Act. None of the organizations ever registered, but only four of them survived. The NNLC, was among those of the nineteen that were destroyed by the harassment of the government and rival labor organizations.

The three-year story of the NNLC represents an important chapter in the bitter struggle of the black worker for a fair share of the products of his labors. This organization must not be confused with the Negro Labor Committee (NLC), formed in the middle 1930s to recruit black workers into the CIO. In the early 1960s, A. Philip Randolph, head of the Sleeping Car Porters union, became impatient with the slow progress of integration in the AFL-CIO. He and other black unionists formed a pressure organization, National Negro Labor Council. The name was soon changed to Negro American Labor Council (NALC).

AT DETROIT'S SOJOURNER TRUTH HOUSING PROJECT

From 1940 onward, Robeson made several trips to Detroit in the interest of the UAW's organizing drives against the automobile industries. His ultimate goal was more jobs for black workers. On some occasions his interest extended beyond jobs, as in March, 1942. Detroit, the arsenal of Democracy, attracted thousands of workers during World War II. Housing conditions for most workers were poor; for black workers housing was overcrowded, often of slum level, and severely limited by unyielding geographical boundaries. Real estate brokers, the banking industry, and neighborhood improvement associations co-operated to maintain rigid control of the boundaries of black neighborhoods. A complacent government gave more than silent approval to these oppressive practices. Under the prodding of the Detroit Housing Commission, the Federal Housing Authority built a $1,000,000 Sojourner Truth Housing project in northeast Detroit in the early 1940s. The announcement that the project was to be occupied by blacks caused violent protests by several white organizations, especially the Seven Mile Road-Fenelon Improvement Association and the National Workers League.

The Federal Housing Authority announced that the units would be ready for occupancy in February, 1942. Several black families were approved and plans were made for them to move in on February 28. Groups of white pickets began converging on the Sojourner Truth project soon after midnight on the morning of the 28th. When the first black families arrived, they were greeted by some 200 hostile protesters armed with clubs and baseball bats. Despite the presence of large numbers of policemen, the black families were repulsed in their attempts to move in. Black reinforcements joined the families, and they made a second attempt to enter the project. A fight broke out and some of the blacks were arrested. The remainder of the blacks retreated.

The black community responded by forming the Sojourner Truth Citizens Committee to maintain pressure on the city and federal governments on behalf of the eligible occupants of the housing project. Like the white groups, they sought strong friends in Washington who could force the local representatives to act on their behalf.

Paul Robeson came to Detroit a week after the violent confrontation to give a concert under the auspices of Ford Local 600 on March 7, 1942. A group, representing the Sojourner Truth Citizens Committee, visited Robeson, filled him in on the background of their struggle and asked for his help. It was agreed that Robeson would address a mass meeting at the Bethel AME Church at St. Antoine and Kirby on the following afternoon. He spoke to a standing-room-only crowd:

> . . . This war (WWII) is for freedom and particularly for the freedom of the colored races. Don't think that because the Japanese are colored they are leading the fight for freedom. A small, ruthless minority in Japan persecutes all the rest of the Japanese and all other races they can reach. Don't think that the Japanese propagandists aren't using this Sojourner Truth issue against the U. S. This is why it's important to settle this issue right.
> The Ku Klux Klan must be taught that it cannot upset the decisions of our government to have the Negro families move into the units that were built for them.
> For a long time, I thought the artist had a special place; but I was kicked back. I sang before royalty and nobility, but my problem was still there. I could have stayed in the Soviet Union, where my color makes no difference, but I could not forget my people or any people who are oppressed. I had to come back and help.
> The basic thing about this was the struggle of the 95% of the people for freedom against the 5% who want to keep what they have even if the rest of mankind starves.

The group was stimulated and a collection of several thousand dollars was raised. A portion of the money went for the defense of those blacks who had been arrested on February 28. The remainder of the money went to support the work of the Sojourner Truth Citizens Committee.

Encouraged by this demonstration of public support, the Sojourner Truth Citizens Committee demanded the recall of Representative Tonerowicz, who declared that Negro insistence on his rights was a Communist plot. Their resolution stated that the congressman acted in a manner becoming an agent of the enemy (Hitler). Black Detroiters pointed an accusing finger at Charles Edgecomb of the City Housing Commission, charging him with stalling in inplementing the federal directive for occupancy of the project. Edgecomb responded that he supported black occupancy but hoped for a "little delay so that the opposition could cool off."

Several weeks passed before black families were permitted to move into the houses. By this time the raw seeds of ill will were scattered throughout the Detroit community. They came to fruition sixteen months later during the week of June 20, 1943.

The Detroit riot was the bloodiest and most destructive domestic act of World War II. Thirty-four people were killed and 461 were injured. A million man-hours of war effort were lost. Losses due to vandals and looters were put at $2 million; and the federal government spent nearly $1 million to maintain an army of occupation in Detroit during the riot. Three housing projects similar to the Sojourner Truth could have been built for these sums.

ROBESON AND THE SONG "JOE HILL"

No story of Paul Robeson in the labor movement would be complete without reference to the song "Joe Hill." The two of them were synonymous throughout the world of labor. The song, "Joe Hill," by Earl Robinson and Alfred Hayes, has been called the national anthem of organized labor. Certainly, the song has been sung at more labor gatherings than any other during the last fifty years. "Joe Hill" was the principle musical oration at Walter Reuther's funeral.

There is no doubt that Robeson is largely responsible for the international fame of "Joe Hill." A good argument could be made that the opposite is also true. A brief look at the life of Joe Hill, the man, will show that he and Robeson had much in common. Small wonder that Robeson could sing "Joe Hill," the song, with a depth of feeling unmatched by anyone else.

Joe Hill was born Joseph Hillstrom in Sweden about 1882. He came to America in 1902. Unable to find steady work on the east coast, he drifted westward, working at such odd jobs as pipe layer, smelterer, copper digger, and dock worker. When not working, Joseph wrote about workers and their poor working conditions. His works were published, and migrant workers adopted his songs and poems. Fame followed publication and Joseph Hillstrom became Joe Hill. Like Robeson, Joe Hill could not escape the events of his time. More than sixty years ago, the Industrial Workers of the World (IWW) began to form trade unions; and Joe Hill was one of their organizers.

W. J. Henry, writing in *International Review* (October, 1972) said: "In Bingham Canyon (a copper mine) 5,000 men were employed, Greeks, Italians, Slavs, Finns, Hungarians, and a few English. Last year, 500 men were killed doing their work. These killings were so common that they excited no comment whatever; their frequency brutalized the working class along with their masters."

Many workers had attempted to improve their working conditions individually without success. Thousands joined the IWW, seeking a better way of life. The IWW encouraged the workers by sending recruits among them. Rioting broke out at one of the recruitment meetings and scabherders rushed in with pistols drawn, clubbing the recruits right and left. Panic followed and the meeting was ended forcibly, on a bitter note. The owners of industry, recognizing the threat of the IWW, were pleased when the labor leaders were picked up by the police and given stiff sentences for various infractions of the law.

It was not long after that event when Joe Hill got in trouble with the law. One night in January, 1914, a Salt Lake City (Utah) grocer was murdered. Despite the fact that the grocer's thirteen-year-old son failed to identify him, Joe Hill was charged with the crime. The arresting officers sought to strengthen their case by writing to San Pedro, California where Joe Hill had worked among transport workers. The San Pedro Chief of police answered that Joe Hill was an "undesirable citizen, an alien, an IWW agitator and the author of working-class songs." The union came to Joe Hill's rescue and hired one of the ablest lawyers in the country, Nelson Hilton. The trial lasted more than twenty-two months.

Aware of the enormous amount of money being spent for his defense Joe Hill wrote a note to "Big Bill" Haywood, Secretary of IWW: ". . . I can see where money can be used to greater advantage at present by the organization, and there is not need to be sentimental about it. We cannot afford to let the whole organization go bankrupt on account of one individual."

The Joe Hill case aroused cries from all sections of the country for his release. Millions of people signed petitions, in many languages; and they were sent to President Woodrow Wilson. Despite the widespread reaction, Joe Hill was sentenced to death. On September 18, 1915, the Board of Pardons agreed not to interfere with the death sentence. Intervention by the Swedish Government demanding a fair trial for Joe Hill failed to move the American government to action. The Secretary of State passed the ball on to the Governor of Utah to decide if a new trial should be held. He sat on his hands. President Wilson, in a last-minute move, delayed execution for sixteen days. Feverish efforts to secure a retrial failed. On a cold November morning, the guards led Joe Hill into the Utah prison yard and shot him dead. His last poem was:

MY LAST WILL

My body? Oh, if I choose,
I would to ashes it reduce
And let the merry breezes blow
My dust to where some flowers grow.

Perhaps some fading flower then,
Could come to life and bloom again.
This is my last and final will,
Good luck to all of you, Joe Hill.

Before the final shot rang out, Joe Hill left a charge for all working men everywhere: "DON'T MOURN FOR ME: ORGANIZE!"

Robeson took Joe Hill's final command seriously, at home and abroad, supporting the trade union movement wherever he went. At every concert or union meeting, the audience demanded that he sing "Joe Hill." He sang "Joe Hill" to a capacity audience on the University of Utah campus in 1947. Officials of the local copper mines were present. Seton (1958) reports that Robeson brought his considerable artistic talents to play in the presentation causing some members of the audience to feel uncomfortable. Seton believes that this event was the real beginning of Robeson's estrangement from the American Establishment. The rapid succession of the cancellations of concerts in Peoria (Ill.) and Albany (N.Y.) lends support to her position. Despite these reverses, "Joe Hill" remained one of the most popular favorites wherever Robeson sang.

JOE HILL

Words by Alfred Hayes
Music by Earl Robinson

I dreamed I saw Joe Hill last night,
Alive as you and me, says I,
But Joe you're ten years dead,
"I never died," says he. (Repeat last line)

"In Salt Lake, Joe, by God," says I
Him standing by my bed,
"They framed you on a murder charge,"
Says Joe, "But I ain't dead (Repeat last line)

"The copper bossed killed you, Joe,
"They shot you, Joe," says I
"Takes more than guns to kill a man,"
Says Joe, "I didn't die." (Repeat last line)

And standing there as big as life
And smiling with his eyes,
Joe says, "What they forgot to kill
Went on to organize." (Repeat last line)

"Joe Hill ain't dead," he says to me,
"Joe Hill ain't never died,
Where workingmen are out on strike
Joe Hill is at their side." (Repeat last line)

"From San Diego up to Maine,
In every mine and mill,
Where workers strike and organize,"
Says he, "You'll find Joe Hill" (Repeat last line)

I dreamed I saw Joe Hill last night,
Alive as you and me.
Says I, "But Joe, you're ten years dead."
"I never died," says he. (Repeat last line)

THE PEEKSKILL AFFAIR AND ITS AFTERMATH

THE AFFAIR

On two previous occasions, thousands of working-class citizens from New York City and environs had travelled forty miles to the north to hear Paul Robeson's Peekskill concert. The week-end outings drew garment workers from midtown Manhattan, furriers from the east forties, public workers from Harlem, and dock workers from the west side piers. All came to pay homage to the hero from the left-wing labor movement, Paul Robeson.

The two prior concerts had gone off without significant event. The 1949 song-fest promised to be something different. The cold war was more than two-years old, and labor unions were being polarized by its politics. Those that favored Truman's anti-Communist foreign policy were in favor while those who opposed it were suspect. For the most part, those unions identified with Robeson's Peekskill concert belonged to the suspect group. The concert attracted other groups also. These were the super-patriots who were loudly vocal in their expressions of loyalty to their country and itching to demonstrate this loyalty in deed. These two groups were on a collision course. Unless something dramatic happened, they were scheduled to collide in Peekskill, New York, on August 27, 1949.

Sponsor of the concert was the Harlem chapter of the Civil Rights Congress (CRC), a three-year-old radical organization that raised the ire of the government by championing unpopular causes. Just before the 1949 Peekskill concert, the Attorney General listed the CRC as a Communist-front organization and named Robeson as one of its chief supporters. These disclosures escalated the explosive potential of the situation.

On Tuesday, August 23, just four days before the concert, The *Peekskill Evening Star* gave an editorial warning that Robeson's appearance was sponsored by People's Artists, Inc., an organization which had been listed by the California Committee of Un-American Activities in 1948, and that funds collected from the sale of tickets would be used for the Harlem Chapter of the Civil Rights Congress which the paper noted had been cited as subversive by Attorney General Tom Clark. The newspaper's letters-to-the-editor section tended to support the paper's call for action. Local veterans groups sent protests to the state Attorney General and requested a restraining order against the concert. Meanwhile, they sent out an area-wide call for recruits to help picket the concert in the event that the restraining effort failed. The veterans were joined by the Junior Chamber of Commerce of Peekskill in their denunciation of Robeson. They called attention to Robeson's citation by the HUAC for attending a peace conference a few weeks before where he made remarks friendly toward Russia.

The voices of moderation, always present in the community, were drowned out by the call for violence. The threat grew each day. On the day of the concert, in the absence of any official action to the contrary, the threat of violence became a frightful, painful reality.

Paul Robeson, Jr., was scheduled to go to the concert, but his wife fell ill and he remained at home with her. The automobile in which he was to have travelled was attacked by rioters. The elder Robeson arrived at the Peekskill railroad station alone, unmindful of the violence in the concert area. He was met at the station by a woman and two children, ages ten and twelve. She hustled him away before he was recognized.

Concert-goers began heading toward the picnic grounds as early as 6:00 p. m. They found that the main roads leading to the grounds were blocked by rocks, trees, and overturned cars. These obstructions caused long lines of cars to back up some distance from the concert site. Several would-be-concert goers corroborated the following account of events that followed:

> As the cars lined up behind the obstruction, a man wearing a Legionnaire's cap came along inspecting all the cars. He opened the doors of some of them. "We're going to get those goddam Jews," he exclaimed.
>
> As the visitors approached the gate they saw one man being punched and mauled by two men wearing legionnaire caps. Not more than 150 visitors got inside the picnic grounds. Some 400-500 veterans and other local groups stormed into the area. At first small fights erupted between the two groups. The struggle intensified and the men of the visitor group linked arms to form a shield around their women and children. The attackers charged the circle time and time again. They hurled stones and sticks into the group, cursing as they did so. Infuriated by the strong defense of the group, the attackers set fire to the seats, the platform, music and programs. The police did not interfere. After about two hours, the cars were allowed to leave the area.

Governor Thomas Dewey, responding to widespread public criticism, sent District Attorney George Fanelli to investigate the outbreak. The *Evening Star,* quoted Mr. Fanelli on August 30: "The facts that I now have would indicate that the demonstration by the

Veterans Associations was peaceful and orderly, and that after they disbanded the pro-Robesonites provoked the violence." Many people in Peekskill were jubilant. Some carried placards on their windshields which read "WAKE UP AMERICA, PEEKSKILL DID."

Early the following week, a mass meeting was held in Harlem to review the situation and decide on a course of action. When Robeson entered the hall he was greeted with a thunderous ovation. He vowed to return to Peekskill and the crowd roared its approval and support. Various labor unions pledged their support.

Unable to rent the picnic grounds again, the People's Artists, Inc., rented the Hollow Brook Country Club, now a meadow, from Stephen Szego for Sunday, September 4. This meadow was located in Cortland, just outside of Peekskill. A day or two before the concert, six shots were fired at Szego's house from a slow-moving automobile. On the night of the concert and the following night, four separate attempts were made to set fire to Szego's house. When he presented the claim for fire damages, his insurance contract was cancelled.

Vincent Boyle, leader of the anti-Robeson forces, scheduled a public demonstration for his group at 2:00 p. m. on the same date as the concert, just opposite the site of the concert. By 2:00 p. m., nearly 25,000 people jammed the meadow.

> The program opened with the national anthem, followed by an invocation. Robeson began with a chanson and "Go Down Moses," and ended with "Ole Man River."
>
> Rank and file trade unionists formed the tight bodyguard that escorted Robeson from New York City to the concert and back home. Most of them were members of the International Fur and Leatherworkers' and Warehouse Workers' Union.
>
> During the concert, Robeson sang with his back against a tree while his flanks were protected by a phalanx of alert workers. Hundreds of other unionists patrolled the concert area, but the local police thwarted their efforts to protect the concert goers from the violence of the local mobs.
>
> Collection baskets passed among the crowd in support of the Civil Rights Congress and the concert ended about 3:30 p. m. The program went according to schedule despite the shouts and threats from the oposition as they marched outside.
>
> With his part of the concert finished, Robeson was hustled out of the area under tight security. He was not injured, but his car was damaged as his union escort ran the gauntlet of sticks and stones. Thirty cars left the concert grounds in the first group and passed along Red Mill Road. They ran a gauntlet of stone-throwing, cursing rioters. Others took Locust Avenue and were greeted in similar fashion. Many of the passengers sustained cuts and bruises in the melee. Some drivers fled their cars only to have them overturned and burned.
>
> Many trade unionists were listed among the casualties of the post-concert melee. Sid Marcus, a fur operator, suffered the loss of one eye and the injury of the other when a rock was thrown through the windshield of his car. Later, the doctors reported that he had sustained a skull fracture and a crushing injury of the nose and cheekbone.
>
> Irving Potash, an official of the Furriers' Union, and Anthony Iavezzari and Catherine Parker, of the Warehouse Workers' Union, local 65, required medical attention for their injuries.

Labor unions led the protest against the Peekskill violence. Potash, despite his injuries, scheduled street corner meetings in downtown New York City, to protest the mob violence. He was joined by officers from the United Electrical, Radio and Machine Workers Union (CIO). They called on Atty. General Howard McGrath to prosecute those who caused the Peekskill riots. The group issued the following statement: "The Cornerstone of American democracy is the right of men and women to free speech and assembly. A violent attempt was made to deny people that right in Peekskill, September 4, and when this undemocratic attempt failed, a mob, incited by veterans organizations and the press, resorted to cowardly, brutal and restrained stoning of men, women and children leaving a concert. This violence . . . is part of a pattern being used increasingly by the forces of reaction through mobs as well as police themselves."

Several drivers reported that the policemen made little effort to stop the attacks, but they gave out traffic tickets to those drivers with broken windows and windshields. Those drivers who tried to flee their attackers were ticketed for speeding.

Battle lines extended as far south as Yonkers, New York and at the height of the attacks, the riot covered an area of ten-square miles. Scores of injured were transported to nearby hospitals by ambulance. Hundreds of automobiles were damaged; some were destroyed. Freedom-loving whites of Peekskill took strong exception to the lawless mob action, and they blamed Dewey for the outrage. The conservative press blamed Robeson and his "Communist sympathizers."

Editorial comment from abroad was often pro-Robeson. The *New Statesman and Nation* of London, in its issue of 9/30/49, noted that ". . . to attack his (Robeson's) meeting is to mobilize the maximum Communist and Negro agitation . . .". The *Statesman and Nation* also reported that among the injured were members of a party returning from a respectful pilgrimage to former President Roosevelt's home.

The members of the Newspaper Guild of New York (CIO) called upon Governor Dewey to launch a full investigation of the violence and remove from public office all state and local officials responsible. The International Longshoremen's and Warehousemen's Union (ILWU) through an editorial in the *Dispatcher* raised an important question with respect to the riot: "Does all of this have anything to do with us as a union? We believe that it does. It started this way in Germany, and what happened in Germany is certainly well known to all of the members of our union, many of whom lost sons or brothers in the fight to put it down." From this point onward, trade unionists, both black and white, provided a tight security network for Robeson wherever he went. If he arrived in a town by plane they met him at the airport. If he chose the train, the guard met him at the railroad station, delivered in person by pullman porters.

Officials of the Civil Rights Congress declared, "we charge Governor Dewey with complicity in the conspiracy of the Klan and other fascist elements to commit murderous acts against peaceful citizens."

Vincent J. Boyle, head of the Associated Veterans Committee which sponsored the protest demonstration, blamed Robeson's "storm troops" for the disturbances. The American Jewish Congress called on Governor Dewey to name an independent commission to investigate anti-Communist violence in Peekskill. In Seattle, George N. Craig, newly-elected Legion National Commander, said that his organization believed in law and order but no violence.

The *Peekskill Star* published the following editorial on September 9, 1949: "It may be that more good than harm will come from the recent unpleasant Cortland Town incident. The Boston Tea Party was not in accordance with the existing law, but historians agree that the patrons who participated focused attention on a great injustice as it could not have been done in any other manner." Father O'Brien, rector of St. Peter's Protestant Episcopal Church and chairman of Peekskill's Council of Christian Clergymen said: ". . . A most frightening thing is that reasonable men also took part in the violence and they still feel proud of it. They have no feeling of shame or contrition."

A few days after the second Peekskill riot Robeson spoke to Dan Burley of The *New York Age* and gave him "MY ANSWER" to the violence of Peekskill:

> Where will the next Peekskill be? What new battleground have the reactionary police and those behind them selected? Where will they demonstrate further the "Old Southern Custom" of beating in the heads of Negroes and all those identified with the struggle to free the shackles of the greedy exploiters of his labor and his talents.
>
> To be completely free from the chains that bind him, the Negro must be part of the progressive forces which are fighting the overall battle of the little guy — the sharecropper, the drugstore clerk, the auto mechanic, the porter, the maid, the owner of the corner diner, the truck driver, the garment mill and steel worker.
>
> I am well equipped now, although I have not always been so, to make the supreme fight for my people and all the other underprivileged masses wherever they may be. Here, I speak of those bereft of uncompromising, courageous leadership that cannot be intimidated and cannot be swerved from its purpose of bringing true freedom to those who follow it.
>
> God gave me the voice that people want to hear, whether in song or in speech. I shall take my voice wherever there are those who want to hear the melody of freedom or the words that might inspire hope and courage in the face of despair and fear.
>
> I told the American Legion that I have been to Memphis, Tennessee, the stamping ground of such Negro-haters as Ed Crump and others of the cracker breed, and I have been to the lynch belt of Florida. I told the Legion I would return to Peekskill. I did! I will go North, South, East or West, Europe, Africa, South America, Asia or Australia and fight for the freedom of the people.
>
> This thing burns in me and it is not my nature or inclination to be scared off.
>
> They revile me, they scandalize, and try to holler me down on all sides. That's all right. It's okay. Let them continue. My voice topped the blare of the Legion bands and the hoots of the hired hoodlums who attempted to break up my concert appearance for

the Harlem division of the Civil Rights Congress. It will be heard above the screams of the intolerant.

My weapons are peaceful; for it is by peace that peace can be attained. The song of freedom must prevail.

THE AFTERMATH

One of Robeson's first appearances after Peekskill was in Detroit. The *Detroit News* announced the event on September 20, 1949: "Paul Robeson, Negro baritone and avowed Communist, will sing and speak at a public 'rally' here on 10/9/49, according to Coleman Young, a Progressive Party official. Robeson's last appearance was in Peekskill, N.Y., on 9/4/49, which occasioned a riot in which 54 people were hospitalized, 14 were arrested and 40 were taken into protective custody. The Detroit appearance will be sponsored by the Detroit Committee To Welcome Robeson."

This announcement added to the rising tide of anxiety that swept over many portions of the country, including Detroit. Many Detroiters feared that Robeson's presence could be the spark to ignite a conflagration. Just the week before, Albert Cobo had won a landslide victory in the city's primary race for mayor. By a 3:1 majority, the electorate approved a charter amendment, supported by Cobo, to establish a Loyalty Commission with powers to determine the truth of disloyalty charges brought against any city employee. The vote was 642:212 (see pp. 70-71 for further details).

While some delight was expressed upon the approval of the charter amendment, some Detroiters did not share this enthusiasm for the ordinance. Five voting districts of working-class blacks rejected the measure. Yale Stewart, President of the Joint Board of the United Public Workers' Union (CIO), threatened a suit to test the constitutionality of the amendment. In September, 1949, other protests against the amendment were published in the letters-to-the-editor section of the *Detroit News*.

Prior to his appearance in Detroit in October, 1949, other events were to occur that would bear upon the mood of the people relative to their acceptance of Robeson. Among these were the following:

1. Luke Miller, black candidate for mayor of Detroit and his campaign manager, filed suit for $1 million for false arrest. They reported that company police had arrested them at gun-point as they passed out campaign literature at the Ford Rouge plant.

2. The Chairman of the HUAC announced that Robeson would appear at the Foley Street court house in defense of the Communist leaders charged with subversion. George Crockett, Detroit attorney, would conduct Robeson's pre-trial examination.

3. The Detroit daily newspapers predicted that the big civil rights battle in Congress, anticipated earlier in the session, would be postponed for another year – until 1950.

4. The Congress and President Truman agreed to put off consideration of the FEPC legislation until 1950.

5. Communist China announced the establishment of a new republic (on the mainland of China), and 1278 westerners embarked on the SMS General Gordon from Shanghai.

6. Russia admitted having the atomic bomb.

7. Stanley Novak, former candidate for Detroit's City Council, was threatened with deportation. He was charged with concealing his prior membership in the Communist party.

8. Army Secretary Gordon Gray ordered company commanders to give Negro troops equality of treatment and opportunity but refused to abolish segregation as the Navy had done. Secretary of Defense Louis A. Johnson approved the Army policy; the Air Force chose to remain segregated.

Tension mounted as the date for Robeson's arrival approached, especially among city officials and conservative organizations. The Am-Vets, American Legion, Catholic War Veterans, and Veterans of Foreign Wars organizations instructed their members to stay away from the vicinity of the Forest Club at 700 E. Forest (where Robeson was scheduled to appear) and warned against any form of demonstration. Phil Cantor, spokesman for the Jewish War Veterans, was against demonstrations but left it up to the individual veteran to decide if he wanted to attend the concert. A concensus of top officials of veterans organizations issued a statement carried by the *Detroit News* of 9/25/49 that ". . . it is natural for any good American to resent Robeson and the things he stands for . . .".

William Smedler, speaking for the all-black Charles Young Post of American Legion, did not approve of Robeson's visit to Detroit, either. It was recalled that the Forest Club, located very near the Charles Young Post building, was the site from which some believe the Detroit Riot of 1943 originated. Officials of another segregated American Legion Post, The Frederick Douglass, decreed that no member of their organization could visit the concert. Clarence Jackson, made their position clear: "It is the policy of our organization to wage war on all things which are dangerous to American welfare. The Communist Party, which is apparently sponsoring Robeson's appearance, has done everything in its power to overthrow our government. I believe we can best promote democracy by ignoring his (Robeson's) visit to Detroit. Legion members will be strongly urged to stay away from the meeting. They will be asked to stay out of the vicinity of the Club House" (*Michigan Chronicle,* 10/1/49).

On 10/7/49, the *Detroit News* offered the following editorial advice: "IGNORE HIM THAT'S ALL . . . . It would be hard to discover any evidence of persecution in the past of one so widely admired and acclaimed, in other times, as Paul Robeson has been.

Veterans and other good citizens are wise to abstain from actions calculated to ad color to the great singer's current delusion."

Several departments of the city government moved swiftly to prepare for Robeson's arrival. Oliver R. Beasley, Executive Secretary of the Detroit Chapter of the Michigan Committee of Civil Rights, and George Schermer, Director of Detroit's Interracial Committee, worked in tandem to distribute an eleven-point directive to all members of their staffs. With Mayor Van Antwerpt's approval the memo was also sent to the newspapers, veterans organizations, and other civic groups and community leaders (see Appendix, pp. 161-162 for the eleven points).

The directive informed the reader that Robeson was scheduled to appear in Detroit between October 8-11, 1949. It recalled the incidents of the Peekskill riots and continued:

> It is clear that as a result of the Peekskill affair, Paul Robeson has become an extremely valuable instrument of the Communist Party. A program is afoot to arrange for Robeson to appear in the major cities throughout the northern and western parts of the country. His appearances will serve two purposes, one will be to raise funds, the second will be to build him up as a champion of the downtrodden of the minority groups and for civil rights . . . .
> There are sufficient super patriotic anit-Communists and race hate elements in Detroit to fall easy prey to this Communist challenge . . . . The only weapon that can be used effectively against Robeson and his crowd is good sense and silence. It is the opinion of the staff that the basic responsibility of keeping our city on an even keel rests with top level authority in the city government, particularly with the Police Department and with the local press, radio business, civic church and labor leadership.

As Robeson started westward from New York City, Horace White, minister of Detroit's Plymouth Congregational Church, challenged him to a public debate at Oberlin College in Ohio. White stated his position:

> What I think is wrong and must be challenged is the feeling that in order to correct our inequitable situation, Negroes must find themselves into the position of error or by design of siding with Russia.
> Mr. Robeson, has allowed himself to be placed in the vortex of international trickery; but more than that he gives the impression of trying to drag the American Negro population with him. In so doing he is trying to remove the ground from under our feet, the very ground on which we must stand if we are to really fight for civil rights in this country.

Robeson refused to accept White's challenge. "The issues are not those to be debated with another Negro," was his answer.

The two men did meet at the Phyllis Wheatly Home in Cleveland, Ohio, just before the Detroit concert. White, along with others present, asked Robeson a series of questions:

Question: "Is it true that you advocate that all Negroes follow the Communist line?"

Answer: "Leave Communism out of this. You know the things

which the Negroes suffer in this country. The Negro wants civil rights.

"The American press took my Paris speech out of context when I was quoted in this country to the effect that 15,000,000 Negroes would not go to war against Russia. What I said was Negroes would not go to war against democratic Russia for an America that denies democracy. In this connection I was talking about world peace.

"I went to Paris conference with a mandate from foreign students in England. The students wanted me to say that they wanted peace, not war."

Question: "Why have you allowed the present situation to develop in the minds of too many Americans that you are Communist inclined?"

Answer: "I don't care what 'they' think of me so long as we Negroes get all the rights of citizens right here in America.

"Revolution is silly . . . I have never advocated revolution on the part of Negroes in America . . . . I want Negro leaders to move for civil rights. We can get them now."

Reverend White, reported this exchange and concluded with this comment: "Robeson or any other Negro who hopes to really contribute to the betterment of the American Negro's lot must seek to make that contribution on the basis of the Declaration of Independence and the Constitution of the United States." ("Facts in Our Times," *Michigan Chronicle*, 10/15/46.)

Police Commissioner, Harry Toy, issued a news bulletin just before the Robeson concert. He reported that arrangements had been made for mounted police, riot squads, police commandos, and special details armed with tear gas equipment, ready to quell any disturbance that may break out at the concert. Toy said, "We want to be able to preserve law and order" (*Michigan Chronicle*, 10/8/49).

As soon as Robeson arrived in Detroit he was placed under a heavy guard of trade unionists that covered him wherever he went. They accompanied him to the Gotham Hotel, where he held a press conference: "We can never achieve any sort of freedom and civility through gradual means. If a man can be stepped on in a second, he can be treated like a man in a second." Crowds of working class citizens began gathering at the Forest Club in the early afternoon on October 9. By 7:00 p.m., the hall was packed and hundreds of people clogged the streets around the building. All vehicular traffic was forced to detour three blocks away on all sides of the Forest Club.

One thousand policemen, uniformed and in plain clothes, were on duty for the concert. Local unionists set up their own security system. Aside from the special detail that guarded Robeson, armed black unionists were scattered throughout the Forest Club, and others infiltrated the crowd outside. White unionists patrolled restaurants, bars and other businesses in the nearby white communities on Woodward and Cass Avenues. They were instructed to report any signs of trouble to a central information pool previously established.

A loud, long, standing ovation greeted Robeson when he entered the Forest Club. The audience was made up chiefly of working people, white and black. They listened to the folk songs of many lands and Negro spirituals. Between the songs and at the end of his appearance, Robeson turned his attention to the events of the day. He denounced the establishment of loyalty commissions to harass the public. He blasted the Federal Government for making a political football of the rights of blacks and other minorities. The Army and Air Force came under heavy criticism for their racist practices. He pointed an accusing finger at the government and business for unfair practices in housing, job opportunities, and public accommodations. He made unfavorable comparisons between the United States and Russia relative to racial tolerance. After his Forest Club appearance, Robeson went several blocks away to Shiloh Baptist Church. Willie B. McIntosh, a member of Shiloh Baptist Church for fifty years, recalled Robeson's visit there on the night of October 9, 1949: "Reverend S. D. Ross was our pastor. He was a compassionate man with a deep sense of justice. He believed a man should be free to express his views. He allowed Robeson to come to the church over some people's objections. People were all over the place. There were plenty of police around too. But there wasn't the slightest evidence of any violence, during the concert or afterwards. I remember that Robeson spoke about civil rights. He said that the rights of every man should be respected."

Robeson's tour carried him to many other cities. In each, he left many working class supporters who fell prey to the super-patriots of the period.

Warner Taylor, was one of the many Detroit detectives assigned to keep close serveillance over the Robeson concert on October 9. In the crowd, he recognized Thomas Coleman and made note of it in his classified report of the event. Slightly more than a year later, Thomas Coleman learned that his presence at the Robeson concert was an act of subversion.

ROBESON AT THE PEACE ARCH PARK

Dominating the western extremity of the Canadian-American border is the International Peace Arch. This unique sixty-seven foot tower, dedicated in 1921, is surrounded by fourteen acres of beautifully landscaped parkland, a showplace of the northwest. The Peace Arch commemorates the Rush-Bagot Agreement entered into by his majesty the King and President Monroe in 1817 by virtue of the provisions and the spirit of which the whole line from the Bay of Fundy to the Straits of Juan de Fuca, for more than 200 years, has been ungarrisoned and unfortified. The Peace Arch also recalls an even earlier concord established by the Treaty of Ghent signed on Christmas Eve, 1814 in which the desire of the signatories is expressed for a "firm and lasting peace." The Monument proclaims that the peace then established has never been broken.

This proclamation of peace was shattered on January 31, 1952 when a group of Canadian trade unionists declared "war" on the United States' government. At issue was freedom – Robeson's freedom to travel and sing and their freedom to hear him. This international struggle lasted for more than three years and ended in victory for the Canadians.

Harvey Murphy, President of the Mine, Mill, and Smelter Workers' Union of British Columbia, invited Robeson and Vincent Hallinan, a West Coast attorney, to come as special guests to their Vancouver Convention. Union officials knew that Robeson's passport had been cancelled two years before by the U. S. State Department. "No native-born American ever needed a passport to enter Canada before," recalled Murphy during a personal interview early in 1973.

Hallinan tried to enter Canada through an eastern portal but was stopped by immigration officials. He sent his regrets to the union officials in Vancouver.

An honor-guard of convention delegates came to the Blaine (Washington)-Douglas (British Columbia) portal, the site of the Peace Arch Park, to escort Robeson to Vancouver. This was to be a great convention. Even standing room had been sold out. Robeson had reached the border earlier. Upon their arrival, the delegation found him embroiled in a bitter verbal battle with the petty border officials armed with an executive order signed by President Truman. This Directive was tailor-made from a law passed in 1918 and used only once before. It warned Robeson that if he crossed the border, it would be at his own peril; and he would be fined $5,000.00.

The Canadians took up positions alongside Robeson. United States' immigration officials stood their ground, calling Washington at intervals for legal reassurances. Robeson summoned his dormant legal training and the contest lasted for three hours. In the end, the will of the government prevailed. Robeson retreated south to Seattle and his Canadian alies returned to Vancouver emptyhanded but filled with rage and a desire for vengence. The State Department had won round one.

The *New York Times* reported this incident on the following day, February 1, 1952. The article brought to mind that Robeson's passport had been cancelled by Secretary of State Dean Acheson in 1950 under the terms of the International Securities Act of 1950. The Secretary stated that it was in the national interest to keep Robeson from making his inflammatory speeches abroad. Now, two years later, Robeson learned that the Canadian Border was closed to him also.

The Mine, Mill and Smelter Workers' Union had been a thorn in the side of the United States' and Canadian governments for many years. The circumstances of the union's birth in an Idaho jail in 1893 should have served warning of what was to come. At first, the union was international with locals on both sides of the border. Mine and Mill Workers of Canada broke away from their southern neighbors when John L. Lewis gained control of the United Mine Workers' Union and instituted policies which displeased them. Many factions in the south were happy to see them go. They never forgave Bill Hayward and Canada's western federations for their decisive role in the election of Asbury Howard of Bessemer, Alabama, as the first black international vice-president of the Union. Such practices alienated the Ku Klux Klan in the States and drove a wedge between the two unions.

The popularity of the Canadian unionists fell to a new low in the States when they elected Harvey Murphy as their president in the 1940s. He was a tough resourceful alumnus of the Communist school of organizers. Enroute to the presidency, Murphy had worked in the coal fields of Illinois and Ohio, at International Harvester in Chicago, the Dodge and Ford plants in Detroit, the Ford plant in Windsor, and the lumber mills of Thunder Bay and Alberta.

Murphy went underground at the outbreak of World War II but was arrested and held at Hull, Quebec until the war was over. He proudly recalls his work on behalf of the Sacco-Vanzetti and other freedom causes. Thus Murphy brought wide experience and great discipline to the office of the presidency. He would need both as his organization took on the U. S. Government in their pursuit of freedom.

Mine and Mill Workers were quite aware of Robeson's pro-labor activities and looked forward to his arrival with great anticipation. Robeson, aware of the union's stand with respect to their black members and other oppressed peoples, readily accepted their invitation.

After their face-off at the border, Robeson went directly to the headquarters of the Marine Cooks' and Stewards' Union, in Seattle. Already an honorary member of the union, Robeson was welcomed with open arms. They assisted him in arranging a long-distance telephone hook-up with the convention in Vancouver. The next evening, right on schedule, Robeson sang songs of freedom to a packed throng of 2,800 angry miners. He encouraged them to continue the struggle for peace and freedom.

Robeson's words electrified the crowd. Regular union matters were swept aside as many speakers strode to the rostrum to hammer out a declaration of war against their enemy to the south.

The first union official, his anger well controlled, tried to set the pace of those to follow:

> Such a wholesale wiping up of the fundamental civil rights of a people has not been witnessed within the British Commonwealth or on this continent before . . . . I think that we have some cause to be alarmed with the state of affairs existing in the nation to the south and in our country today.
>
> I think that the incident of the stopping of Robeson and Hallinan yesterday may well serve to highpoint some of the problems that lie ahead of us. And I think that you all will agree with me that if the occasion of his (Robeson) being prevented from coming here tonight will serve the purpose of alerting all the Canadians to the extent to which Fascism is gaining in our North American continent, then I think that you would join with me in saying that it was a good thing that he was stopped, if it will result in a greater understanding of the part that Canadian people must play in order to carry the flight for the freedom not only of the Robesons and the Hallinans to cross the border and the right of trade union duties, but to lift the veil that is rapidly descending on this country and once more restore for all of the people the civil rights that so many of our predecessors died to establish for us.
>
> I think that this is the message that I will take from this meeting to the membership of my union. I am sure that my union will not join in a protest as we are doing here tonight but will from here on in be much more vigilant and much more determined and much more active on the broad front of civil rights.

Harvey Murphy, chairman of the meeting, introduced the final speaker. This spot was reserved for Nels Thiebold, District Board Member of District No. 8 of the International Union of Mine, and Smelter Workers and formerly president of Sudbury local, the largest local of all the unions in Canada. Murphy taunted him in the introduction with the remark: "With sixteen thousand members in

Sudbury digging up all that nickel that we send down to the the United States, we can't get Robeson in. Ladies and gentlemen, Nels Thiebold."

Mr. Chairman, Ladies and Gentlemen, I am sorry that I am not pleased to be here. I am sure that you are no more pleased to be here than I am. But you are here because of an indignity arising from an autocratic and highanded treatment that has been extended to you by the United States Government. You are here to protest against the position of ridicule that you have been placed in before the eyes of the world. We know that we do not like it because of the blood and bone that go into the making of the Canadian working people. To know that the world today is paying Canada for gradually becoming a subjugated colony of the United States. Yes, too many times we hear it said, sneeringly, so that everytime that the U. S. Government coughs, Canada sneezes (applause), Now, we heard Paul Robeson tonight. He sang the song "Joe Hill" which is undoubtedly much closer to the hearts of us as miners than it may be to some of you here. It is close to the hearts of all workers; because Joe Hill, in practically every respect, was what Paul Robeson is today. Joe Hill was a worker with a past. He spent his days working in mines, composing poems, traveling from one place to the other, working with people and reciting his poems. "Joe Hill" was shot by a firing squad in 1915, framed by the copper mining bosses because they feared him. They feared him and they hated him for the fear he conjured up in them. Wherever he went, workers flocked to hear his poems. Stories of the slums in America, oppression that caused misery and suffering. Yes, and in these poems too. And what created the greatest fear in the hearts of those barons was the way they must follow to free themselves from the oppression. So they shot Joe Hill. Thank God that today they dare not shoot Paul Robeson. But they do hate Paul Robeson, because they fear him.

Paul Robeson, while he does not recite poems, he does it through songs. Gifted with a golden voice and with a determination that this world should be established on the basis of equality, that there should be peace among the people that there shall be security and happiness throughout the world.

In his songs, he tells the people of the way to follow to that end. Yes, he sings of the modern day, the modern oppression, subjugated present day workers in the United States of America and the whole world. That is why Paul Robeson is not with us tonight. But things will not be like this all the time. That was Paul's reassuring message to you over his telephone conversation with Harvey Murphy. He called upon you to stay shoulder to shoulder and not give up this fight until the workers had emerged into this kind of new world. I know the propagandists try to play down people like Robeson and messages that come from men like Paul. But it is not everyone who is blinded by that propaganda. There are some people in high places who are with the fight the workers are making today against oppressive government. I want to read to you a few passages from none other than William O. Douglas, U. S. Supreme Court Justice.

> There is an ominous trend in the nation. We are developing tolerance only for the orthodox point of view in world affairs, intolerance for new or different approaches. Orthodoxy has normally stood in the path of change, the enemy of new ideas, at least new ideas that are disturbing. He who was wedded to the orthodox was isolated from the challenge of new ideas. The democratic way of life rejects standardized thought. It rejects orthodoxy. It wants the fullest and freest discussion, within peaceful

> limits of all public issues. It encourages constant search for truth at the periphery of knowledge . . . .
>
> You know how I feel and I know how you feel, I'm sure. I believe that you want to have an occasion here to rise up and express your feelings. I am sure that you want to discuss some resolutions that will go direct to the proper places on this question, on this insult to the people. Feeling sure that this is what you want I conclude my statement (applause).

Harvey Murphy took over the meeting to bring the discussion to a head.

> To you the citizen trade unionists, we've got to do something about this. We don't want to meet Paul Robeson at the border. We want him to come and feel the warmth of the people of Vancouver. You can do a lot. You can write letters, not only to the press, but also to the members of parliament. I've spoken today and requested that some of the members of Parliament appear and say what they think; they would not do it. They leave all of this protest to us. We won't drop back. Some people think that they will save their rights to cross the border by being nice and quiet. I know some trade union leaders who said, "Well Murph, you know things stink; but if I speak out I won't be able to cross that border."
>
> And now ladies and gentlemen, we have this resolution. What is your opinion? I move for the adoption of the resolution and that it be sent to the United Nations.

The resolution passed unanimously, followed by applause. The resolution pledged the union to use its full resources to avenge the insult they had suffered from the United States Government.

Robeson returned to the east to continue his large struggle against the establishment. Agents of the FBI shadowed him wherever he went. The House Committee on Un-American Activities was making life miserable for Robeson, his wife, Eslanda, and his son, Paul, Jr. His annual income that had been well over $100,000 in the early 1940s, was reported to be less than $5,000 at this time. Despite the pressure and privation, Robeson responded to the second call of Mine and Mill to return to the Peace Arch Park on May 18, 1952. Union officials sent notices to all of the affiliates in the region and they seized the opportunity to register thir protest against the U. S. Government. Cooperating Americans brought a truck within one foot of the border on the United States' side. From this platform Robeson sang and spoke to thousands of people, who seemed to fill the landscape from "horizon to horizon." The durable Harvey Murphy was in charge again:

> This Sunday, May 18, 1952, at Peace Arch Park, in the State of Washington, on the Canadian border, breaking all records for public gathering in the northwest, 30,000 men, women, and children, from British Columbia and the State of Washington, are massed in this sunlit field to hear Paul Robeson.
>
> Ladies and gentlemen, trade unionists, brothers, and sisters in the United States and from our own Canada, I welcome you here today on behalf of the International Union of Mine, Mill and Smelter Workers. We are here today to welcome an outstanding American and World Citizen (applause). I know that you came here

to hear a singer, but you also came here to demonstrate the brotherhood and fraternity of the people of the United States and Canada. But we have a common mission in this world, to march along with other people of this world for peace and security for all of us and all of our children.

We're so happy to be the means of bringing you together. But I know that Paul Robeson, that name stands for what every decent American stands for (long applause).

Robeson strode to the microphone:

> I want to thank you for being here today. I want to thank Harvey Murphy and the Mine, Mill and Smelter Workers. I can't tell you how moved I am at this moment. It seems that nothing can keep me from my beloved friends in Canada (applause).
>
> I stand here today under great stress because I dare, as do all of you, to fight for peace and a decent life for all men, women and children, wherever they may be. And especially today, I stand fighting for the rights of my people in this America in which I was born (applause). You have known me for many years. I am the same Paul, fighting a little harder; because the times call for a harder struggle.
>
> This historic occasion, today, probably means that I shall be able to sing here and there (applause). What is being done in this Peace Arch today will ring out, is already ringing out around the world. I thank you dearly.

Robeson sang folk songs from many lands and in many languages to the partisan crowd. He was their hero, for the most part. There were at least two people who were not there because of Robeson. Mrs. Isabel Murphy, the wife of Harvey Murphy, never forgot the two white women who spoke to her just before the concert got started:

> "How come so many of you Canadians are down at the border today?" asked one of the women of Mrs. Murphy.
>
> "We came to hear Paul Robeson sing" she answered.
>
> The two women looked at each other and shrugged: "Paul Robeson? Who is that," both women asked.
>
> Mrs. Murphy was incredulous. "You've never heard of Paul Robeson? Well, he is the best singer in the United States. Just wait. You'll see."
>
> Wait they did. When Robeson climbed up on the truck, the two women looked at each other speechlessly. The one to gain her voice first exclaimed, "My God, a nigger!"

Among the favorite songs that Robeson sang that afternoon were:

"No More Auction Block"
"Water Boy"
"Love Will Find A Way"
"Ole Man River"
"Joe Hill"
"Loch Lomond"

At the end of the program, Robeson again thanked them for coming and vowed to continue the fight for freedom as long as he could. He vowed to return to the Peace Arch the next year if he could not enter Canada willfully. Not only did the crowd take a heavy toll on the park, they blocked travel across the international border for several hours. Impatient travelers vented their spleen on the helpless, frustrated border officials. None of this was lost on the jubilant Canadians. Park officials spent the following week replanting annuals, azaleas, hydrangea, juniper, and rhododendron – the state flower of Washington. A report of these events was filed with the State Department for future reference.

Union officials taped the program and released an LP recording a few weeks later. The record jacket summarized the events of the international struggle and made a prediction for the future:

> . . . That meeting took place on May 18, 1952, and this is a recording of one of the most amazing concerts ever held on this continent. For some forty-five minutes, accompanied by his one friend, Laurence Brown, Robeson, sang to an audience of approximately 40,000 men, women and children, mostly Canadians. Roads were blocked for miles around and the border was closed for hours. Canadians thereby, delivered a crashing blow to the United States' State Department whose refusal to allow him (Robeson) to sing to 2,600 people in Vancouver had resulted in fifteen times that number coming many miles to see him. "I will see you again, I will be in Vancouver in a few months," was Robeson's farewell. Mine and Mill make this promise that if his forecast is not confirmed before the summer of 1953, then there shall be another Peace Arch gathering to hear Paul Robeson.

Robeson bade his friends good-bye and continued his relentless search for the elusive twins, peace and freedom.

National politics filled the air when Robeson performed his 1952, Peace Arch concert. Before the year ended, an Eisenhower-Nixon ticket was swept into the White House for eight years of Republican rule. John Foster Dulles replaced Dean Acheson as Secretary of State, but none of these changes made life any easier for Paul Robeson.

During the first half of 1953, Robeson and the members of Mine and Mill waited in vain for some evidence that Robeson's travel ban to Canada would be lifted. Instead, they saw many events that were dismaying and prophetic. A review of some of them will reflect the social and political climate that covered the nation when Robeson gave his second Peace Arch concert in August 1953.

Dr. James Conant gave his final statement as president of Harvard University on January 25, 1953. He denounced the destructive methods of investigating Communists on college campuses. Congressman Harold Velde (R-Ill.), chairman of the House Un-American Activities Committee, accused Mrs. Eugene Meyer, wife of the Board Chairman of the *New York Post,* of having written a letter praising the Soviet people. When the charge proved false, the congressman said, "It is better to wrongly accuse one person of being a Communist than allow so many to get away with such Communist acts, as those that have brought us to the brink of World War III." The New York Teacher's Union withdrew from the left-wing United Public Workers on February 15, 1953. The New York Board of Education fired 15 teachers for refusing to say whether or not they were Communists.

Despite his pre-occupation with many other things, Senator McCarthy, found the time to complete and submit a long list of books that should be taken from the shelves of federal libraries and burned. Among the authors on his list were Mrs. Eslande Robeson, the wife of Paul Robeson, and Walter White, former head of the NAACP.

During the annual conference of the NAACP, June 1953, held in St. Louis, a directive was sent to President Eisenhower demanding that he live up to his pre-election campaign promise to eliminate second class citizenship for Negroes. The call was especially for an order ending segregation in government projects, in the national guard, and in federally funded housing. Job discrimination came under fire.

The NAACP launched a ten-year fight for freedom to do away with all racial discrimination by 1963, the 100th anniversary of the Emancipation Proclamation.

The U. S. Supreme Court ruled on June 8, 1953 that District of Columbia restaurants could not legally refuse to serve Negroes. The NAACP filed a comprehensive complaint with the Interstate Commerce Commission for an order banning segregation of interstate passengers. An independent statement by Congressman Adam Clayton Powell, supported the NAACP demands. He said: "Qualified Negroes reject government jobs rather than expose their children and their families to segregation in Washington. Although I am a Congressman, I can get into only two of Washington's picture houses. Many of Washington's playgrounds, swimming pools and hotels still refuse me."

Assistant Defense Secretary John Hannah said in a UP interview that the military bases should not "jeopardize" essential operations by precipitating action to end discrimination among civilian employees. The Navy Under-Secretary said that the Navy would abolish segregation among civilians in the south if ordered to do so, but no such order had been given.

On the day of Robeson's second Peace Arch Park concert, Senator William F. Knowland (R-Calif.) said, "The day that Communist China goes into the United Nations, the United States goes out." Senator Alexander Wiley (R-Wis.), chairman of the Senate Foreign Relations Committee, issued a warning to other United Nations countries on August 18 that a move to admit Red China would be a very serious matter as far as the American public and the congress of the United States are concerned.

The Congress remained inactive on Civil Rights during 1953. Only one bill was reported out of committee and no action resulted. The House Appropriations Committee reduced funds for Howard University, Freedmen's Hospital, and the Public Housing programs. The

House Labor Committee refused to hold hearings on a Fair Employment Commission bill.

In Chicago and Cleveland, violence flared when blacks attempted to move into white neighborhoods. The Supreme Court called for re-argument of the five school cases first heard by the court in 1942. An NAACP task force of 100 lawyers, political scientists, sociologists, historians, and other experts was formed to do the necessary research.

So the prospects for freedom were dim when Robeson joined his Canadian friends at the Peace Arch for their third assault on the international border in mid-August on a hot Sunday afternoon.

The members of Mine and Mill waited until the following May before starting definitive plans for their second Peace Arch Park celebration. Secretary of State Dean Acheson instead of freeing Robeson for travel to Canada, extended his list of those who could not leave or enter the country to include some of the most illustrious names in the world. True to their word, Mine and Mill scheduled the 1953 concert for August 16, 1953. Almost as many people came as the year before. The crowd was experienced in blocking international traffic and frustrating immigration officials. They came early and stayed late to achieve their purpose – to force open the border for Robeson.

Twenty years later, Harvey Murphy described the events of the 1953 concert in amazing detail:

> Almost as many people, mostly Canadians, heard the greatest voice of our time and saw a man who future historians will rate as one of the few really great men of the age. He was the greatest living American at that time. Mr. Robeson, also spoke in fighting words, which by this time have winged to Asia, Africa and all four corners of the world where there is colonial oppression. He demanded freedom for the exploited and downtrodden of the earth, and he forecasts peace, freedom and brotherhood throughout the world, despite the efforts of American reaction.
>
> His program was varied from the one the year before, but he asceeded to the many requests as he sang such favorites as:
>
> "Oh, No John No"
> "Loch Lomond"
> "The Four Rivers"
> "Why Not Every Man"
> "Brothers of Israel"
> "Drink To Me Only With Thine Eyes"
>
> His voice was as strong and as warm as ever. As usual, Mr. Robeson made no charge for his appearance before a labor group, but during the intermission we took up a collection of $1,000 to defray the expense of the concert.

At the end of the concert, Robeson made an impromptu, extemporaneous speech that kindled the fires of resistance in the souls of friends and fomented increased hatred and oppression among his enemies. The speech, an example of Robeson's courage and prophetic insight, is given in its entirety on Appendix pp. 162-164.

Reverberations from that speech were heard in the halls of the mighty. Perhaps the immigration officials took the group lightly the year before, but more serious consideration would be given this time. Their report to Washington would describe a total paralysis of international commerce for several hours – angry travellers, delayed schedules and general chaos. Adding to the psychological pressure was a rumor of unknown parentage that rode the west wind to Washington. It was reported that other unions were planning a series of border concerts for Robeson, all the way to Nova Scotia.

The Union kept up the pressure and the tension mounted. Finally, the State Department capitulated. Harvey Murphy recalled the surrender with a tight-lipped smirk of satisfaction: "They tipped me off. I knew that we wouldn't have to have another concert at the Arch. We were responsible for bringing him in. The next convention greeted him in person." The United States Immigration Service reported that the ban against Robeson's right to travel to Canada would be lifted in July of 1955. A report from Ottawa, Canada let the world know that the final decision of Robeson's entry into Canada rested with the Canadian Government. His application would be considered on its merits. The Canadian Government did allow passage and Robeson re-entered Canada to attend a Vancouver convention in the fall of 1955 – the first break in his five-year detention in the United States.

There was jubilation throughout the Northwest Territories of Canada and elsewhere. The greatest power on earth had lost out to the unity and perseverance of ordinary people. For some, however, the victory was tinged with a bit of sadness. Mrs. Murphy expressed it forlornly, despite the passage of twenty years:

> Where we had the concert was a beautiful setting, and the weather was nice each time. I sat on a hill with my son, Bill, on my lap. Living out west, I suppose it is a different part of the country too. The people I knew in the labor movement considered the concert the biggest cultural event of the year. They would look forward to it every year. The chance to hear Paul sing so beautifully. It didn't cost anything either, you know. Then when we heard that he would not be coming back to the Peace Arch, we were glad but a little sad, too.
>
> One final thing, I'll never forget those two women as long as I live. The concert certainly gave them something to think about. I'm sure it did; because they sat there throughout the entire concert.

Diligent research of the available press files of many United States' newspapers revealed only one reference to the first concert, and none to the second. On the other hand, the Vancouver *Sun-Province* reported the first concert on May 19, 1952:

> **THREE MILE CAR JAM AT ROBESON CONCERT**
>
> A traffic jam nearly three miles long at its peak, clogged King George Highway Sunday, as thousands of British Columbians flocked to Peace Arch Park to hear an international concert by bass-baritone Paul Robeson.
>
> Many who parked their cars on side roads and walked more than a mile to the U.S.–Canadian border, heard only a part of the hour-

long program by the American Negro who has become a controversial political figure.

On August 17, 1953, the *Sun-Province* reported the second Peace Arch Concert:

> **30,000 PERSONS HEAR PAUL ROBESON AT BORDER**
> More than 30,000 persons turned out Sunday at International Peace Arch to hear Paul Robeson sing at the outdoor concert sponsored by Mine, Mill and Smelter Workers' Union.
> Harvey Murphy, regional director, said the famous bass-baritone sang 15 songs from the American side of the border.
> Mr. Robeson can't come to Canada. U. S. authorities have refused to give him a passport because of his controversial political views.

Fortunately, the resourceful Harvey Murphy taped the second Peace Arch concert. Otherwise, Robeson's last major address before an American labor group would have been lost to history.

SUMMATION

A testimonial dinner sponsored by Local 600 (Ford Motor Co.) in January, 1947 was perhaps the high-water mark of Robeson's popularity with all segments of the labor movement. Union official Percy Llewelyn, paid high tribute to their honoree's many years of support for organized labor. His remarks to Robeson ended on a hopeful note: ". . . I bring you the wish that you will carry on for many years, winning more and more recruits for the cause in which all of us have enlisted for the duration." Nineteen forty-seven was a fateful year for the country, in general and for labor, in particular. Many events conspired to make Llewelyn's wish an impossible dream.

The death of Henry Ford in April of 1947 was a turning point in the course of the Ford Motor Company and its relationship with the UAW. Soon after the death of his grandfather, Henry Ford II began a series of brilliantly conceived and well executed public relations activities that served notice on everyone that the old order was dead and buried and a new regime was in control of the empire. The following month he dropped in on Philip Murray, President of CIO, while in Washington on "other business." They met in May of 1947 just before a new round of wage talks were scheduled with UAW officials.

On June 4, the nation's news media showed Henry Ford II shaking hands with assembly-line workers in Ford's Kansas City plant, the scene of many acts of anti-union violence during the 1930's. Walter Reuther made his successful bid to capture control of the UAW at their Atlantic City convention in 1947. He rode in on an anti-Communist platform. Henry Ford II gave Reuther a timely boost from a Schenectady (N.Y.) press conference: "I heartily approve Reuther's stand to rid the UAW of Communists. We are as much opposed to Communists as Walter Reuther, and there is every reason to believe that he can handle the situation one hundred percent."

A few weeks later on December 4, 1947, Henry Ford II and Detroit's City Council President, George Edwards, visited Reuther in his UAW office. Although the agenda of that meeting is not available, their post-meeting statements suggested bilateral congeniality. Reuther said:

"The conversation was a friendly, down-to-earth meeting. Ford's ideas and beliefs on human engineering are a whole lot closer to the union's than most people believe." Henry Ford II returned the compliment: "I think Reuther is on the right track; and he has some good, sound ideas." Soon after this meeting, Henry Ford II left for Hapeville, Georgia, a suburb of Atlanta, to participate in the formal opening of a new Ford assembly plant.

Less than one year after his grandfather died, Henry Ford II's good deeds had earned him citations from the New York Writers' Association, the National Management Advancement Society, the National Conference of Christians and Jews, and the Thomas A. Edison Centennial Award Committee, to name a few such organizations. The sentiments of many groups toward Henry Ford II were expressed by Henry W. Johnson as he presented the Thomas A. Edison Award: "Henry Ford has provided leadership in developing true human relations in industry that makes collective bargaining more than an idle phrase; and he showed both management and labor the road to a sound relationship which will benefit everyone."

Henry Ford II did not exhaust all of his magnetic charisma on the high and mighty. Many rank and file workers fell under the charm of this new, young ruler of the realm. One, who wishes to remain nameless, was heard to exclaim, "Thank God for young Henry! About all he got from the old man was his name."

Thus, it became obvious in both word and deed that Henry Ford II was motivated by something higher than the corporate call of duty. These, and his other diverse humanitarian acts, presented Robeson's brand of militant unionism with an elusive target against which to mount an attack.

Additional events in 1947 had a profound effect on Robeson's relation with many other unions across the country. In March, the Truman Doctrine became operative, establishing a comprehensive loyalty program for government employees. From this evolved an anti-Communist foreign policy that was reinforced by the Smith Act, the Mundt-Nixon Bill, the Internal Security Act, the Taft-Hartley Act, and many other measures of doubtful constitutional validity passed in the name of national security.

Senator Joseph R. McCarthy (R-Wisconsin) was waiting in the wings, testing the strength of the anti-Communist line with which he would soon strangle a nation. The House Un-American Activities Committee sought and got almost unlimited power and funds to set a dragnet that would snare all non-conformists in its anti-Communist sweeps.

The prosecution of the Cold War demanded compliance from all segments of the community, especially labor unions, "the haven of leftists, Socialists, and Communists." Cold War politics influenced the UAW's Atlantic City convention. When Reuther captured the control of the UAW, he ousted many of his former friends whose militant unionism had planned and executed the Ford organizing drive. There was no longer any room in the UAW for radicals, including Robeson.

Two events occurred in February, 1948 that had an adverse effect on Robeson's future as a labor activist. (1). The Supreme Court upheld the constitutional authority of the House Un-American Activities Committee to gather facts of "the utmost intensive public concern" and "that power is not diminished by the unchallenged rights of individuals to speak their minds." Justice William O. Douglas, Frank Murphy, and Wiley Rutledge dissented. The case involved Leon J. Josephson, a Trenton (N.J.) attorney, who had been fined $1,000 and sentenced to one year in prison for refusing to give the HUAC information that was requested. (2). Attorney General Tom Clark ordered the FBI and immigration agents to arrest Ferdinand C. Smith as he left home for work on February 28. A native West Indian, Smith was charged with being a Communist alien and in this country illegally. It was also asserted that Smith had failed to produce a valid immigration visa when he last entered the country on March 6, 1946, two years before! Smith was taken to Ellis Island, held without bail, and deportation proceedings were begun.

Smith had been identified as a radical trade unionist since the middle 1930s when he led a large group of black seamen out of the International Seamen's Union (AFL) to help form the new National Maritime Union (NMU)-CIO. His first fight for the rights of black workers brought him to the attention of union officials. By the time of his arrest he had become one of the best known and most highly respected black labor leaders in the country. Smith and Robeson had been friends for many years. He had helped to mobilize Robeson's support for NMU and he approved Robeson's candidacy for honorary membership in NMU. Smith and Robeson had fought together for black American workers in the National Negro Congress and for black Africans in the Council of African Affairs. They shared the same philosophy—labor unions should be instruments for social change. Both opposed conformity of the trade union movement to the demands of the cold war and supported peaceful co-existence with world communism.

For the first decade of the NMU, Smith and Joseph Curran, NMU president, worked hand-in-glove against all of the enemies of labor. Smith rose through the ranks to become second-in-command of the union. His arrest brought to the surface internal strife that had begun many months before over union policy. Curran's comments, after Smith's arrest, made his position clear: "No member or officer of this union should receive any sympathy or support who deliberately violates and continues to violate the constitution of our union. I shall resist any move to have the union participate, financially, in Smith's deportation fight."

Michael Quill, president of both the Transport Workers' Union and the greater New York CIO Council, had not yet been won over to the side of the cold-war conformists. He called the Smith proceedings outrageous and charged that the power of deportation was being used to "disrupt unionism and intimidate all those who did not agree with the present (Truman) administration." Despite such public pronouncements, public hearings and public demonstrations, Smith's harassment continued for many months; and he was finally deported. With the defeat and routing of the Smith faction, the welcome mat was no longer out for Robeson at the NMU.

The politics of the cold war permeated the highest levels of the trade union movement, causing internecine warfare between the National Council of the CIO, which favored support of the Truman Anti-Communist foreign policy, and the International Council of CIO, which opposed it.

Latent hostilities flared into open warfare during the preparations for the Transport Workers' convention in December of 1948. Robeson, an honorary member of TWU for ten years, was invited to appear, again, as guest artist during the convention. Joseph Germano, president of the Illinois State CIO, and Michael Mann, Secretary of the Chicago Council and CIO Regional Director, objected to Robeson's appearance and stated that they would not appear on the same program with Robeson. Michael Quill, now a Truman man, sent special telegrams to Germano and Mann reassuring them that Robeson's appearance would be blocked and, furthermore, that the influence of the International Council was no longer a factor in their Union's affairs. There was an immediate response from Douglas MacMahon, the Union's international secretary-treasurer and leader of the anti-Quill faction. He saw no reason why Robeson should be denied the chance to appear since he had been welcomed to all of their previous conventions. He accused Quill of "pulling a power-play to gain control of the union and put his men in the top positions." Quill, still smarting over the recent loss of New York State to the Republicans, which he blamed on Robeson and the Progressive Party, held sway and another door was closed to Robeson.

Pro-administration forces were in control of most of organized labor in the United States by the early part of 1950, the eve of the Korean War. Philip Murray, acting for the Executive Board of the CIO, gave an eight-page summary of his organization's economic policy for the Korean Emergency to Stuart Symington, Chairman of the National Security Resources Board. Murray stated that the document was their position paper with respect to the war. Placing military needs first, he explained that expansion of production would lay the groundwork for the largest possible military program. He concluded that "labor is willing to do all in its power to increase production through the establishment of labor-management committees or other means."

Murray did not speak for all of the CIO unions when he made his presentation to Symington. At least eleven affiliates defied the CIO's efforts to force them to conform to President Truman's anti-Communist position. They refused to sign non-Communist affidavits and resisted attempts to purge their organizations of radicals. The list of rebel unions included ILWU; International Mine, Mill and Smelter Workers; the Fishermen's Union; Marine, Cooks and Stewards' Union; the Food, Tobacco and Agriculture Workers; the Fur and Leather Workers; the United Public and Agriculture Workers; the Fur and Leather Workers; the United Public Workers; and the United Electrical, Radio and Machine Workers' Union. Robeson could and did appear before some of these rebel unions during the late 1940s and as long as they survived during the 1950s. An honorary member of the UPW, Robeson addressed their convention in May, 1948 and denounced "the Forrestals, Dulleses, and Hoovers," and accused them of trying to establish Fascism in this country.

Such outbursts did not endear Robeson to the government or the vested interests in the country. Particularly embarrassing to the CIO and the government were the UPW campaigns in the Panama Canal Zone and against the Engraving Division of the Treasury Department on behalf of black workers. Despite extreme pressures from the CIO, the UPW refused to abandon its members and finally won its case. Within a year, the CIO had expelled the UPW, the president of the union was under attack by the HUAC, and the union was moribund.

The destruction of the UPW was a particularly sad blow to Robeson. While he did not appear to play favorites, the UPW seemed to attract him more than any other union. Proportionately, there were more black workers in the UPW than in most other major unions. The militant policies of the UPW gave strong support to the cause of black workers both inside the union and out. Aside from Ferdinand Smith, the highest ranking black union official in the country at that time was Ewart Guinier, international secretary-treasurer of UPW. Eventually, the CIO expelled all of the dissent unions and most of them were destroyed. The oppression to which they were subjected alarmed even President Truman. He warned the CIO officials against their practices of discrimination in the pursuit of security.

Militant unionism was all but dead when a group of rebel trade unionists met in Cincinnati to organize the National Negro Labor Council in 1951. Robeson was a major force in launching the organization and he supported it during the few years that it survived. At the very first meeting, Robeson picked up where he left off with a a severe attack on the U. S. foreign policy. He demanded that NNLC members do everything possible to force a change in that foreign policy. The Attorney General lost no time in listing the NNLC as a Communist-front organization. HUAC brought its investigative team into Detroit in 1952 to enquire into the loyalty of two national officers of NNLC, William Hood and Coleman Young. The government and organized labor continued to harass the officers of NNLC even after the organization had been destroyed.

Early in 1952, Robeson tried to enter Canada to address the Mine, Mill and Smelter Workers of British Columbia. U. S. immigration officials, under direct orders from Washington, halted him at the border. Three months later, in 1952 and again in 1953, Robeson returned to the border to sing and speak to nearly 30,000 workers. The 1953 speech was one of his finest orations, a fitting climax to nearly fourteen years of relentless struggle for the rights of the working man. His closing remarks left no doubt that, despite six years of constant pressure from all sides, his spirit was unbroken, his courage intact (see pp. 163-164).

The system's propensity for overkill had silenced nearly all of the voices of protest against the government by the middle 1950s. Some were deported, some detained, and others destroyed. Robeson's treatment was something special. Under constant surveillance by the FBI, he was not allowed to enter any radio or T.V. station. Recording contracts were cancelled and his records were banned from the air waves. Nevertheless, Robeson continued his unpopular crusade from the church pulpits of a few brave, black ministers who suffered severe economic and political reprisals as a result. In Detroit, the minister was Rev. Charles A. Hill, pastor of the Hartford Avenue Baptist Church. Rev. Hill's fearless fights for the working man and his long-time friendship with and support of Robeson brought down the wrath of the government, federal and local, upon him and his children.

Robeson's high hopes that labor would help to reform society so that it would serve the common man, as well as the privileged few, was all but gone. He fought well and left indelible footprints on the sands of time, but his later speeches reflected disappointment. Just as waves of despair threatened to wash away all hope for the future, the Supreme Court handed down a momentous decision — SEGREGATION IN PUBLIC SCHOOLS IS UNCONSTITUTIONAL.

Another glimmer of light appeared at the end of the dark tunnel and flared, briefly, into the civil rights movement. This quest for freedom produced a new brood of young, courageous leaders who, in due time, gave Robeson credit for charting their course and blazing their trail.

Of the several rebel labor unions to survive the purges of the

McCarthy period, the International Longshoremen's and Warehousemen's Union was one of the few with the audacity to invite Robeson to appear before them in the late 1950s. His final address to an American labor union, insofar as my research ascertained, occurred on February 7, 1958. Members of ILWU's Local 6 invited Robeson to Oakland, California to give their Negro History Week oration that became his valedictory.

Nineteen years earlier, Robeson had opened his campaign on the American labor front in support of the common man. A few of his words had changed over the years; but the goals, peace and freedom, remained the same. Like Pablo Neruda in Chile and Alexander Solzhenitsyn in Russia, Robeson cared enough to criticize the repression and hypocrisy of the system. The system, here too, rose up to discredit and destroy this threat to the status quo. This premonitory voice-in-the-wilderness refused to be silenced. He defied them, would not compromise, and refused to die.

So, bloody but unbowed, here stands this prophet-without-honor in his own land thrusting a final desperate note into his last bottle and flinging it into an uncaring sea:

> This is the eve of the birthday of Frederick Douglas. The history of the American history, one of the gradual fulfillments of human history, stretching from far back, centuries and centuries, forward into future generations. . . . It is not a history in a vacuum; it is a history lived side by side with the Irish, Welsh, Scotch, English, German, Canadian, Czech, Russian, Finnish, and Jewish. . . . And this Union took them all in. These men, women, and youth of labor have helped to build this great land of ours.
> And the American Negro, unlike the Irish, Scotch and English indentured servants, were dragged here, literally in chains, not from a savage Africa but from an Africa of ancient civilizations. . . . And in less than one hundred years, from 1863 to 1958, what a glorious example of human courage, endeavor, determination, achievement. The Children of Little Rock are but one manifestation of that mighty flow of endeavor. So is true of Montgomery, so brave. All of this is not only a part of American Negro history but of American history as well. There can be no nation half slave and half free, no not in 1863, nor in 1958.
> Here, too, as in all of American life, we must constantly and urgently strive and work for full equality, equality of opportunity, the recognition of potentials, recognition of ability, recognition of the right to join, to advance, to move by virtue of honest labor, forward and upward to evential seniority, not restrained by ancient and worn out codes of prejudice and unscientific attitudes. There are no inferior peoples. We are one. And America cannot stand true to her democratic ideals while 1/10 of her colored sons and daughters, or 1/3 of the ill-housed and ill-fed of her laboring folk, bear the burden of the heat of the day.
> All in the trade union movement must stand side by side today . . . . Bridges, in answering Reuther's profit-sharing plan, laid down a simple guiding chart – "What is in the interest of the worker?" Start from there. Not for profit alone. Profit, at some point, always means taking it out of the hides of the workers. One must always look at production for the good of all, for well being, health of millions and millions of workers, not production for the profit of the mighty few. So start from the worker, out and up. Start from

basic interest of the rank and file and we'll be on the right road. A note to the Negro trade unionists on this their history week. You have a weighty responsibility in the liberation struggle of your people. Explain it to your fellow worker, of every color and every group. They will understand . . . . Only by understanding and fulfilling these responsibilities can we move ahead to the final, human integration that will make American Negro History Week, Human History Week.

And, finally, peace must come. We must live in peace. We must have trade and cultural exchanges with the people of Ghana, with the people of the Soviet Republics, the Japanese and the Africans. Free the peoples of the Americas and the south. Free them from all foreign domination, occupational and financial.

A glorious future awaits us! Let us struggle militantly and unceasingly to achieve it.

EPILOGUE

Robeson returned from his Oakland, California engagement to the New York arena to resume his battle with the courts for his passport. His prospects appeared very dim at that time. Yet international forces were at work to bring relief to this beleagured warrior. The "Let Robeson Sing" movement had millions of supporters in the British Isles. Some of them were in high government positions and could convey their displeasures directly to the U. S. embassy in London.

It was on April 8, 1958 that Nehru created a diplomatic crisis between India and the U. S. by criticizing the State Department, ". . . He (Robeson) suffers for a cause which should be dear to all of us, for human dignity." On April 22, 1958, the Council of Methodist Episcopal Bishops reported that the State Department's denial of Robeson's passport was causing anti-Americanism among Africans.

Robeson's direct appeal for validation of his passport was denied by the Supreme Court. The break came in mid-June of 1958. In a 5-4 ruling, Supreme Court Justice William O. Douglas issued a landmark decision, *Kent vs Dulles*: "The Congress had not authorized the State Department to withhold passports because of alleged Communist's beliefs or associations of the applicants." The State Department notified Robeson, on 6/25/58 that his passport would be returned; it was delivered to him the following day. A collective sigh of relief escaped from much of the world's press. While hundreds of other people regained their passports under the broad application of the *Kent vs Dulles* decision, Robeson's case attracted the widest acclaim. Many writers hailed him as a hero for his uncompromising, eight-year stand that his constitutional rights had been violated by the State Department.

Robeson departed for London on July 10, 1958 to fill overdue engagements on the concert stage, radio, television, and at Stratford-at-Avon. He retained his interest in the working classes in England and Europe. It seemed, at first, that he would be able to pick up his career and carry on as before. Such was not to be. It soon became apparent that his American ordeal had taken a terrible toll on his health. His concert appearances gradually diminished, and he was forced to seek medical assistance. He was unable to come home for his brother Benjamin's funeral in early December of 1963. He did return just before Christmas thus ending a five-year and five-month voluntary exile. Today, he is in retirement under the loving care and watchful eye of his sister, Marian.

While Robeson no longer makes the scene in person, his presence remains with us evermore.

BIBLIOGRAPHY CITED

Cruse, Harold. 1967. *The Crisis of the Negro Intellectual* (Wm. Morrow & Co.: N.Y.).

Hoyt, Edwin P. 1967. *Paul Robeson, The American Othello* (World Publishing Co.: Cleveland).

Kuykendall, Ralph S. 1967. *The Hawaiian Kingdom. III. 1874-1893, The Kalakaua Dynesty* (University Press of Hawaii).

Robeson, Paul. 1971. *Here I Stand* (Beacon Press: Boston).

Seton, Marie. 1958. *Paul Robeson* (Dobson: London).

Still, William. 1968. *Underground Railroad* (Arno Press: N.Y.).

Taruc, Luis. 1953. *Born of the People* (Peoples' Publishing House, Ltd.: Bombay, India).

Wesley, Charles H. 1967. *Negro Labor in the United States 1850-1925* (Russell & Russell: N.Y.).

APPENDIX

The Hardin Report

It is necessary that I begin with the Ford Drive. Due to this drive being the first major crisis ever confronted by our union in dealing with the Negro issue, I was transferred into the Ford Drive from Chicago. Reaching Detroit Saturday, March 29, I reported to Michael Widman, Jr., on Monday, March 31. At the time of my arrival, sharp clashes were going on inside the shop. A greater amount of violence was going on between two factions of Negroes, one faction supporting the AFL and the other supporting the UAW-CIO.

On Tuesday April 1, violence broke out on a larger scale and extended from the plant into the following communities – North Detroit, West Side Deroit, Ecorse, River Rouge, and Inkster, Michigan. CIO men faced immediate attack in the above mentioned communities, should their identities become known. At this point, we were forced to admit that the AFL had the better end, due to having proceeded to utilize the service department of the Ford Motor Company. Service men had the authority to release Negroes, on Company time, to leave their jobs not merely to carry on organizational activity in behalf of the AFL but to go out in the communities and carry on full-time agitation for the AFL. All persons willing to engage in such activities were free to do so. They were required only to ring their card once a day.

Another section of this work consisted in organizing goon squads, with orders to do a job on the head of every CIO man that he came in contact with. Only a few hours of this violence existed before the strike. The first day of the strike saw the first service and goon squads in full swing. Several people were injured at the gates, both AFL and CIO. Some 5,000 Negroes were held in the plant under the pretext of doing guard duty.

The rapid rise of racial hostilities created the problem beyond the control of our then existent organizational machinery, which consisted, at that time, of Emil Mazey, Director of Negro Activities, and the following International Representatives: Leon Bates (Local 1212), John Conyers, Sr. (Local 7), Veal Clough (Local 600), William Bowman (Local 668), Joseph Billups (Local 600), James Allen and Johnson Buchanan (Local 599).

The work of the Negro staff, at that time, consisted primarily of the organization of Negro Ford workers on the basis of building within the Ford Company and in the homes of Ford workers. This method of organizational activity was constructive and practical, under ordinary conditions, but not under the impact of the crisis, of what we may say developed overnight, affecting approximately 14,000 Negroes in the Ford Rouge plant. It was necessary to revamp the Negro organizational staff.

At this point I was placed in charge as Director of Negro Organizational Activities and Emil Mazey was made Coordinator, thereby broadening the basis of the staff.

The following Negroes were immediately called to our staff – Oscar Noble (Local 653), Leonard Newman (Local 212), and Miriam

Lee. This brought our staff to ten full-time Negro organizers. Added to this number was a volunteer staff of some twenty people. Immediately, two offices were opened, at 4743 Millford (West side with John Conyers in charge) and 3462 Hastings. Sound cars were assigned to full-time duty. Noble, Buchanan, and Billups were assigned to churches.

A full-time publicity staff was also assigned. This staff consisted of Christopher Alston, editor of Negro *Ford Facts,* assisted by Cecil Whittaker, employee of the publicity department. Fifty thousand copies of *Ford Facts* were distributed the first week. This distribution was made at the Rouge gates and the Negro communities.

Emerson Brown was added to the staff and given charge of publicity and transportation. He had 25,000 copies of CIO literature, along with 50,000 copies of *Ford Facts* per week for distribution. Such distribution was made possible through the whole-hearted support of the Women's Auxillary No. 233, headed by Sister Enid Botts. This coupled with the special conference of Negro leaders, was responsible for getting active church leaders and ministers to take a position.

The first break occurred when Father Malcolm Dade permitted a meeting to be conducted in his church, sponsored by the Progressive Pastors and chaired by William Bowman, of our staff.

Preceeding this was a banquet, comprising some eighty religious, civic, and political leaders, resulting in the NAACP taking its first stand with labor.

Further luncheons were also conducted. Mrs. Lee, under special assignment, succeeded in building up a banquet attended by Michael Widman and Judge Lila Neuenfelt, with approximately 85 women representing the greater number of women's organizations. Widman placed the principles and policies of the UAW-CIO before this broad representative group of active women. This affair struck at the very root of community hostility. The last of these luncheons was conducted by the entire staff, to pay respect and appreciation to the Negro press for the splendid way in which it had handled the whole Ford situation.

. . . The staff further launched a series of meetings in the schools of the east and west sides of Detroit, together with a well-attended meeting sponsored by the Ford organizing staff and conducted under the auspices of the Democratic committee of the 15th congressional district.

All in all, we can attribute our success in averting one of the greatest racial hostilities that ever existed in American industries, to the whole-hearted support given by the many progressive organziations throughout the city, coupled with a 24-hour service of our own research, education, and publicity departments.

The Miles Report

NEGRO WORKERS JOIN CIO: MARSHALL PRESSURE FAILS

By REV. JOHN N. MILES
Chairman, Negro Division,
Ford Organizing Committee

I have been interested in the problems of the Ford workers for the past fifteen years. In 1925, I came to Detroit as a member of a Yale University research group. We were to work in the Ford plant as students and to gather material first hand from the workers and the management on the problems of labor and industry.

Our group had not been at Ford's very long until we learned

that honest independent research into the problems of Ford workers was impossible. No investigation of any kind can be conducted unless the investigator has absolute freedom of action. We soon found out that at Ford's there could be no freedom.

We had to do our work in an atmosphere of fear, distrust and oppression. It was like trying to take a Gallop Poll of public opinion in present day Nazi Germany.

The Ford workers would not talk to us. They feared anything they might say might be the cause of losing their jobs. They gave us no information except what they had been instructed to use as stock answers to questions.

Little Change

The Ford plant has changed very little since 1925. Their labor policies still belong to the days of the Tin Lizzie. They still depend on fear, oppression and insecurity to keep the Ford workers from making any change for the better in wages, working conditions and status as free citizens of a free country.

However, there is one difference. Ford knows it cannot halt the steady advance of the UAW-CIO in its palnts. They know they cannot stop the thousands of Ford workers who have already joined the union from exercising their rights. The best they can hope for is delay.

In their frantic attempts to halt the steady influx of the Ford workers into the UAW-CIO, the officials of the Ford Motor Company are driven to do many desperate and stupid things.

The other evening, an official of the Ford Motor Company made a move which back-fired. The Negro Division of the Ford Organizing Committee sponsored a debate in one of Detroit's Negro churches. The subject of the debate was: Resolved, that the Negro should affiliate with the UAW-CIO. We had two speakers, one to take each side, and there was to be a question period at the close of the meeting.

Pressure Fails

However, shortly after the meeting had been announced, the pastor of the Hartford Avenue Church, where the meeting was to be held, received a message from Mr. Donald Marshall, personnel man at the Ford Plant and recently defeated candidate for Congress. The message from the Ford man advised the pastor of this church against allowing the meeting to be held there.

I do not need to elaborate on the fact that this kind of threat has been much too successful in the past in keeping free discussions of the unions out of many of our churches. Through the same Mr. Marshall, the Ford Motor Company has been able to build up a patronage system through which jobs are made available to church members with the provision that such workers surrender their American rights to join the Union.

Despite the threat of Mr. Marshall, the meeting was held on schedule. The speakers presented the preliminary arguments and we came to the question period. It soon became evident that the Ford Motor Company had attempted another way of breaking up the meeting. Individual hecklers, obviously sent by Mr. Marshall, began to harass the speaker for the UAW-CIO. They were at a loss, however, when our speaker was able to take each one of their loaded questions and answer it completely and tactfully, without disrupting the meeting.

Mr. Marshall's threat to fire every Negro in the vicinity who worked at Ford's if the debate was held only served to strengthen the determination of those Negro workers who had joined the UAW-CIO. They resolved to work even harder to rid the Ford

Motor Company of the kind of influence which Mr. Marshall represents in our community.

Negroes Joining CIO

These are the same sort of methods that representatives of the Ford Motor Company have been using during the past fifteen years or more. The difference is that the general public and the Ford workers have kept up with the times. We are becoming more and more conscious of democracy – of freedom and of our rights as citizens.

The blackout for democracy in such a great part of the world had the effect of making us all zealous guardians of democracy at home. For this reason, these old policies of the Ford Motor Company stand out like sore thumbs. And they put the Ford Motor Company into even worse repute with the workers who are Ford employees, the public who are Ford customers, and the government of the United States which is still bigger than any company.

It is a source of great satisfaction to see the response which the Ford drive is finding among the Negro workers of Detroit. It is a source of great satisfaction to see that so many Negro folks feel the responsibility which they share with their fellow workers. They feel that it is up to them to do their honest share of the hard work. They feel that they must do their part now if they expect to come in for their rightful share of the benefits which will come to them later on.

They also feel that unless they do their share of the hard work now, they can hold no claim to places of leadership when the organization becomes established.

They have seen Negro workers take their places of leadership in various local union of the UAW-CIO in Detroit. And they realize that these positions of responsibility and leadership come to them the democratic way. They are elected on the basis of the work they perform – the capabilities they show, and the experience they have to offer. Only if our folks have these things to offer their organization in the beginning, can they hope to enjoy the benefits, privileges and the responsibilities on an equal basis.

Our folks have come to learn that their deliverance from insecurity, poverty and oppression, can only be accomplished through their own efforts. One has to earn his freedom through hard work and diligence or he is not really free. I have found that the answer to the problems of the Ford workers is the same answer which the sharecroppers in Tennessee found and the workers on the Chickawago Dam, and in the cotton fields of the deep south.

In the union there is strength.

I want to invite all Ford workers who have not already done so to come to our headquarters at 9016 Michigan Avenue. I spend most of my free evenings there or at nearby meetings. Come and see us. Bring your friends and fellow workers with you. Bring your problems with you and see if you do not believe that we of the UAW-CIO have the answer.

Ford Facts Editorial

The editorial in this issue was an all out effort to win the black worker to the side of labor:

This editorial of *Ford Facts* has been especially written to explain to the Negro community the program and policy of the UAW-CIO in regards to the present organizing drive. At the Ford Motor Company plants, we particularly wish to answer the slanderous propaganda that has recently been circulated to the Negro Ford workers and present to you the real facts.

The Negro worker needs organization more than any other workers.

Negro workers are the most oppressed and exploited in America today. Negro workers are generally given the dirtiest and most menial tasks and the lowest possible wages. Negro workers have been denied employment in many industries which created serious unemployment problems for Negro workers.

These conditions cannot be corrected by Negro workers on a racial basis. The problem can only be solved through the unity and cooperation of all workers, regardless of race, color and religion. Negro workers must realize that discrimination and segregation of Negro workers is not the fault of the white workers. Discrimination and segregation have been imposed on the Negro worker by employers who have divided the workers in order to exploit them on a large scale. Both Negro and white workers have been exploited and oppressed.

Paid agents of the Ford Motor Company have attempted to place the burden of responsibility for the ill-treatment of the Negro in American industry, on the organized labor movement. These agents of the company know that the enemies of labor have been responsible for the oppression of the Negro worker. They also know that the Union is the only force that has fought discrimination and segregation and oppression of Negro workers in industry.

The CIO has played a progressive role in correcting these abuses imposed on Negroes in shops that are organized. The Union has given the Negro worker a voice in determining the conditions of employment.

The Union has established equal pay for equal work in organized shops. The Union has established a greater degree of security for Negro workers through the establishment of seniority rules.

The Union has given the Negro worker higher standards of living by establishing higher wages and vacations with pay. The Union has not been content to rest on its laurels. We know that our tasks will not be complete until every worker in America is given the opportunity of earning a livelihood and a decent standard of living."

A telegram from State Senator Charles C. Diggs was published in its entirety:

Ford's program of rugged individualism and being a law unto himself has come to a climax. He has run head-on into the question of whether we will have a democracy or a dictatorship. Some innocent and ill-advised Negroes have been sought in the Ford fiasco which, in my opinion, is a blot on American history, and if it continues on the basis that Ford desires, will destroy American democarcy. I have issued a statement as I did in the Chrysler strike to the effect that the Negroe's place is definitely on the side of labor. To this plea, hundreds of Negro workers have responded favorably. There are, nevertheless a small minority of ruffians, employed by Ford and assigned to his Service Department for the express purpose of strike-breaking, that are not responding to the appeal.

The excuses for the attitude taken by these strike-breakers are as follows:

1. Ford had given them better jobs in his plants than other automobile companies.
2. The attitudes taken by the AFL toward Negroes in the past.
3. The propaganda used by Don Marshall, one of the Ford Personnel Directors, that if the CIO organizes Ford the Negro will lose out.

Assure you that I am with the movement to organize Ford and that he will be organized not withstanding the old Communist bugaboo. In Michigan, we are all good loyal Americans.

For These Things We Fight:

. . . The NNLC is our symbol, the medium of expressing our aims and aspiration. It is the expression of our desire and determination to bring to bear our full weight to help win first-class citizenship for black men, women and children in America.

. . . And we may say that those white who call the NNLC "Subversive" have an ulterior motive. We know them for what they are, the common enemy of both people, Negro and white. We charge that their false cry of "Subversive" is calculated to maintain and extend the condition of common oppression. We say to those whites "You have never seen your mothers, sisters, and daughters turned away from thousands of factory gates, from airlines, the offices, stores and other places of desirable employment, insulted and driven into the streets, many times, when they tried to eat in public places, simply because of their color.

You have never been terrorized by the mob, shot in cold blood by police. You have never had your house burned when you move out of the ghetto into another neighborhood, simply because you were black. You are not denied the franchise. You are not denied credit in banks, denied insurance, jobs and upgrading, because of the pigmentation of your skin. You are not denied union membership and upgrading, you do not die ten years before everybody else because of the many denials of basic rights.

Therefore, you who call the NNLC "Subversive" cannot understand the burning anger of Negro people, our desire to share the good things our labor has produced for America.

. . . The NNLC is dedicated to the proposition that these evils shall end and end soon. The world must understand that we intend to forge a stronger band of unity between black and white workers everywhere to strengthen American democracy for all. If this is subversion MAKE THE MOST OF IT!

Resolution No. 1 — Fifteen million Negroes do not have job opportunities equal to that of Whites. The average income of American Negroes is 55% below the general average and is only 40% of the income estimated for minimum health and decency.

While big business and its stooges in government claim on the one hand, that it stands for freedom and democracy, on the other hand a new tide of attacks are launched against Negroes.

The struggle on economic issues and for a job is basic to the struggle for Negro rights. It is this struggle that is the weakest in the fight for Negro liberation.

Resolution No. 2 — We launch a nation-wide fight for a minimum of 100,000 new jobs in those industries which now deny equal job opportunities to Negroes. The three goals are to increase job opportunities for Negro women, cracking lily-white shops and a general upgrading of jobs for Negro workers throughout the industry.

Resolution No. 3 — We open a drive to secure 1,000,000 signatures for a National FEPC.

Resolution No. 4 — The major fight will be for full freedom for Negro people in America. This will involve a campaign against poll-tax, anti-lynch legislation, abolition of jim crow in public places, official Council activity in case of police brutality and the right to integrated housing.

The following were chosen as permanent officers for the next year:

President: William Hood (UAW-CIO Local 600, Detroit)

Exec. Sec'y: Coleman Young (Wayne County Council CIO, Detroit)

Dir. of Organ: Ernest Thompson (Nat'l Sec'y (FEPC) United Electrical Workers)

Treasurer: Octavia Hawkins (Local 451, UAW-CIO, Chicago)

Vice-Presidents-at-large:

Asbury Howard (Alabama Regional Director IUMMSW)
Cleveland Robinson (Vice-Pres. DPOWA, New York)
James Husbands (Local 208, AFL Tobacco Workers, Durham)
Maurice Travis (Sec'y-Treas., IUMMSW)
Mrs. Vicki Garvin (Sec'y of New York Negro Labor Council)
Miss Marie Bowden (Los Angeles)
Mr. Phillips (The Railroad Unions)

Regional Vice-Presidents elected were:

Ewart Guinier (Sec'y-Treas., UPW, New York)
Miss Viola Brown (Local 22, DPOWA, Winston-Salem, N.C.)
Sam Parks (United Packinghouse Workers, CIO, Chicago, Ill.)
William Chester (ILWU, San Francisco, Calif.)

STATEMENT OF PRINCIPLES

CONSTITUTION

Preamble

We, the members of the Negro Labor Councils, believe that the struggle of the Negro people for first-class citizenship based on economic, political and social equality is in vain unless we as Negro workers, along with our white allies, are united to protect our people (Negro) against those forces who continue to deny us full citizenship.

Realizing that the old forms of organizations which were dedicated to the fight for first-class citizenship for Negro people have been unable to bring full economic opportunity for the Negro worker in the factory, the mine, the mill, the office, in government; to stop wanton police killings of Negroes throughout the land; to stop mob violence against us; to bring the franchise to our brothers and sisters, in the South, and gain our full say in the poiltical life of our country with proper representation in government on all levels; to buy and rent homes everywhere unrestricted; to use public facilities, restaurants, hotels, and the recreation facilities in town and country, we form the National Negro Labor Council (NNLC), an organization which unites Negro workers with other suffering minorities and our allies among the white workers, and base ourselves on rank and file control regardless of age, sex, creed, political beliefs, or union affiliation, and pursue at all times a policy of militant struggle to improve our conditions.

We pledge ourselves to labor unitedly for the principles herein set forth, to perpetuate our councils and work concertedly with other organizations that seek improvement for Negro and other oppressed minorities.

We further pledge ourselves to work unitedly with the trade unions to bring about greater cooperation between all sections of the Negro people and the trade union movement; to bring the principles of trade unionism to the Negro workers everywhere; to aid the trade unions in the great unfinished task of organizing the South on the basis of fraternity, equality and unity; and to further unity between black and white workers everywhere.

Some News Items from the first issue of NNLC's *Struggle*

Bill Chester, West Coast Regional Director of NNLC reported that 90 Negro workers had been hired by Key Systems Railroad. Sears Roebuck had hired 14 Negro Salesladies. William Hood and Coleman Young, of Detroit, reported that an agreement had been reached with Manton Cummings, Ford Motor Company's Director of Labor Relations, to hire stenographers, typists and comptometer operators without discrimination as to race.

Gerald Boyd, Executive Secretary of the Greater Detroit Council, announced that Max Shaye, Vice-President of Big Bear Supermarkets agreed to hire and integrate Negro men and women into their chain of stores.

Sam Parks, President of the Chicago Council, reported that several weeks of picketing the Drexel National Bank had resulted in the hiring of Harry B. Deas, as Assistant Service Manager. The bank officials were warned that the Council would be watching to insure complete elimination of the un-American practice of racial discrimination. The Flint Council threw a picket line around the Zerka and Bassey Supermarket, when one of the co-owners told the Council delegation: "I will hire anyone I want to and when I see fit."

Octavia Hawkins, National Secretary-Treasurer of NNLC issued a call for a parley on Negro Women's problems, to convene in Chicago on March 16, 1952. She called attention to the special plight of Negro Women in a jim crow male-supremist society.

The Eleven-Point Directive of Beasley and Schermer

Following is a course of action which we wish to submit to the Committee, to the Mayor and to the Police Department:

1. That the Mayor issue a confidential statement to a carefully selected group of community leaders, perhaps embodying some of the material incorporated in this memorandum, explaining the danger and asking cooperation for a course of action.
2. That perhaps there should be one or a series of small meetings with community leaders to assure agreement on a course of action to gain cooperation.
3. That the metropolitan press, the radio stations, the Negro and labor press and that part of the neighborhood press which can be trusted, be requested to give Robeson as little publicity as possible. This does not mean that the news must be suppressed but that announcement of his appearance be treated in a most undramatic and factual manner. There should be as little dramatic reference as possible in the local press for a period prior to his appearance regarding his national activities of the Peekskill affair.
4. Care should be taken that Robeson is not denied an opportunity to make a public appearance. It is not yet known what plans are afoot as to the location of his appearances. There needs to be some discussion as to the conditions under which he may be requested. Most likely there will be a plan afoot to raise funds, therefore it is more likely that the group will arrange for his appearances to be in a church or other non-public buildings. It is equally important that all efforts to demonstrate against Mr. Robeson be prevented. Robeson should not be given an

opportunity to claim that he is being persecuted or denied his civil rights.

5. Editorial writers, commentators and public officials should be warned against giving implied approval to groups seeking to start trouble by indulging in such comments as follows. "We deplore the activities of the hoodlums who attack Robeson and his supporters, but he has it coming to him." Over-Zealous workers for political candidates should not be given the opportunity to use Robeson's presence as a springboard for gaining notoriety and public attention.
6. It is assumed that the police will show no favoritism toward any group seeking to create a disturbance, whether they are pro or anti-Communist.
7. Contact should be made with the top leadership of all veterans' organizations asking them to cooperate. It is believed that the best approach would be for them to set up listening posts to detect any indication of planning for demonstrations and, if such plans are afoot, to reach responsible leadership to squelch the movement.
8. Newspaper editors should be requested to have their staffs listen for rumors of demonstrations and to provide for an orderly clearance of such rumors with the Police Department.
9. The Police Department might assign a team of officers to screen all rumors and to determine, if possible, whether there is any bonafide planning for demonstrations. Where it appears that such plans are afoot the responsible leadership can probably be reached and firm warnings issued.
10. The Interracial Committee can arrange for similar listening posts to be set up through the more reliable minority, civil rights, labor, church groups so as to properly channel information and to gain the cooperation of trusted leadership.
11. Procedures can possibly be set up for collecting information on and recording the actions of individuals and groups so that if any untoward incident does occur the responsibility can readily be fixed.

It is recognized that this is in part a question of race relations, in part of police problem and in part a question of political ideology and public policy. It is essential, therefore, that all of these groups work cooperatively together and that it not be characterized as simply a police problem or an interracial problem.

It is important to recognize that the role of the martyr, the role of being the militant defender of civil rights and the role of being a super pariot are always adopted by the extremists of both the right and the left. Both types of groups are beyond the usual appeals for moderation and civic responsibility. Each group gains notoriety and prestige by fighting the other. It is in the public interest that both types of groups be given as little dramatic attention as possible.

Robeson's Peace Arch Speech

Thank you again for your very great kindness in coming here today. It means much to the Americans struggling for peace in the northwest. Some of the finest people in the world are under pressure today, facing jail, facing hostile courts for the simple fact that they are struggling for peace, struggling for a decent America, where all of us that have helped build this land can live in decency and good will.

As for myself, as I said last year, I remain the same Paul that you have known throughout all these years. The same Paul, but time has made it so that everyone, I included must fight harder to preserve the basic liberties guaranteed to us Americans by our constitution. If it were not so, if this were not so, I would be

with you in Vancouver. I would be travelling all over the Canada that I cherish so deeply. And it ought to interest you to know that just the other day the Actors Association in Great Britain, the British Equity Association, invited me to London. I remember years ago, I was in London when this group was formed. We had an Actors Equity here in America, a very progressive and a very militant one. I had been playing in the Workers' Theatre, the Unity Theatre which I helped to establish in London. There was quite an argument among the actors. Some were not sure that they were workers or whether they should have a union or not. As a visiting artist, one who was very close to them, I told them that we who labor in the arts, we who are singers, we who are actors, we who are artists must remember that we come from the people, our strentgh comes from the people, and we must serve the people and be a part of them.
And in America, today, it is very difficult to play in a theatre or to sing. Whenever I go into a city like St. Louis, or to many other cities, the wrath of all the powers that be descends on one single, poor minister who wants to give me his church, or descends on the one who rents the hall. They are told by all the forces in America, the strongest business forces, that the banks will no longer honor their mortgages. Everything, just to keep just one person from appearing in a concert in this church or this hall.
I know what it means. They don't want to hear people speak for peace. Many of the bravest working class leaders are, today, in prison. And, today, we fight in America on the eve of this truce. As this truce is reported in Korea, we fight for the amnesty and the freedom of those leaders to come back and lead their people. The British Actors group sent me a contract to come and play Othello in London as soon as I could get there. They went to the British Actors Equity Association to see if I could get a labor permit. They said that there was no question of the status of Mr. Robeson, that he could come here and play Othello. But beyond that, "we would like to see him play the role that he played so well in 1930. We will welcome him to England to play Othello." And at the same time, I received an invitation that could not mean more to me. It came to me from Wales. Wales is that part of England where I first understood the struggles of whites and Negroes together. When I went down into the mines in the Rhondda Valley, I learned about the miners and lived among them. Later, I made a picture there called Proud Valley. And I came so close to them, that in Wales, today, as I feel here, they feel me a part of that land. And I've just received an invitation to appear at their Eisteddfod in October given by the miners and workers of Wales. I hope to be able to get there.

So it is very important that we are gathered here today, that our governments can understand that artists, not only myself, so many of us, so many scientists, like Dr. Dubois, one of the greatest Americans who ever lived, proudly a son of a Negro people, but one who has contributed to the advance of all mankind. And the idea that Dr. Dubois cannot leave this country to attend peace meetings, to attend scientific gatherings, all over the earth. And that goes for many outstanding American scientists, intellectuals, workers and trade union leaders. This gathering here will mean a great deal; many of us may be able to travel in the future.

Why do they take my passport away? Thy have said so in a case. They put it in a brief. They said that no matter what my political beliefs, no matter what my standing among the Negro people of my own land in America, they would have to take my passport away, anyhow, because out of my own lips they have learned of support for the freedom of the colonial peoples of Africa and that is meddling in the foreign affairs of the American Government (laughter). Now, that is just too bad; for I'm going to have to meddle.

But I stand, as I say to you, as you come here from your land in this American continent, I am proud of this America in which I was born. My father was a slave who was reared in North Carolina. I have many friends all over this earth and rightly so. Other Americans can choose their Francoes if they want to. Other Americans can choose the refuse of Nazi Fascism. They can wander around the earth picking those who would keep mankind in perpetual slavery. I choose to stretch out my hand across the ocean to brave people of many lands, of Asia. And I stretch out my hands to the people of the New China, as they build a new life for five-hundred million people (long applause). I may as an American, as Jefferson in his time, stretched his hands across to meet the great heroes of the French Revolution of 1789. I stretch my hand across the continent to shake the hand of the brave Soviet people and of the new people's democracies. That is my right as an American.

I would have liked to sing a song, today, "Peace Will Conquer War" by Shostakovich, the great Russian composer. But, I speak as one whose roots are deep in the soil of my land. But, I speak as one whose fathers and mothers toiled in cotton, toiled in indigo, tobacco and helped to create the primary wealth of this land upon which the great land of the United States was built. The great primary wealth of this land came from the blood and suffering of my forefathers. And I say, as I have said many times, that I have the right to speak out on their blood, on what they have contributed to that land and what I have contributed, also, as best I can. But, I say right here that because of their struggle, I will go around the world, but I'm telling you now that a good piece of that American earth belongs to me (shouts of approval). And it belongs to my children and to my grandchildren. I've got two of them, you know, two grandchildren, a boy and a girl. They're sharp. So there is a lot of America that belongs to me and to my people, and we have struggled too long, ever to give it up.

My people are determined, in America, to be not second-class citizens, but to be full citizens, to be first-class citizens. That is the rock upon which I stand. From that rock I reach out, as I say, across the world to my forefather in Africa, to Canada, all around the world; because I know there is one humanity that there is no basic difference of race or color, no basic difference of culture but, that all human beings can live in friendship and in peace. I know it from experience. I have seen the people. I have learned their languages. I sing their songs.

And I go about America, wherever I may go, thinking of simple things. It seems so simple that all people should live in full human dignity and in friendship. But, somewhere, the enemy has always been around to try to put back the great masses of the people, in every land. We know that. Well, I said long ago that I was going to give up my life to spend my day to day struggle in down among the masses of the people, not as any great artist up there on top, somewhere, but right here in this park, in many of the picket lines, wherever I could be to help the struggles of the people. And I will never apologize for that.

I shall continue to fight as I see the truth. And I tell you here, I hope to see you next year. No matter where I am in the world I'll come back (shouts of approval). I want you to know that I will continue this year fighting for peace, no matter how difficult it may be, and I want everybody in the range of my voice to hear, official and otherwise, that there is no force on earth that will make me go backward one-thousandth part of one little inch! (Applause.)

INDEX

D

E

F

G

H

ABOUT THE AUTHOR

Charles H. Wright, M.D., is a practicing obstetrician/gynecologist; a Robeson scholar; and a man with wide civic, community, and world-wide interests. He is a native of Dothan, Alabama and a graduate of Alabama State College. In 1943, he received the M. D. degree from Meharry Medical College, and for the next 20 years devoted his efforts almost solely to his very successful medical career. In 1963 his interests turned to literary endeavors. He wrote the musical drama "Were You There?" . . . a modern version of the crucifixion. This work was performed on stage in 1963, 1964, and 1966, and on Detroit television in 1972, 1973, 1974, and 1975. His most recent work along these lines is a modern look at the Christmas story entitled "The Caracas Gang." He is currently at work on a documentary for the Bicentennial and continues to serve as Chairman of the Board of Trustees of the Afro-American Museum of Detroit and carries on his active medical practice.